*The Social Reality of Scientific Myth*

# THE SOCIAL REALITY

AMERICAN UNIVERSITIES FIELD STAFF, INC.
535 Fifth Avenue   New York, N.Y. 10017

# )F SCIENTIFIC MYTH

## *Science and Social Change*

*Edited by*  KALMAN  H.  SILVERT

*Contributors*  E. A.  BAYNE

NICHOLAS  DE WITT

CHARLES  F.  GALLAGHER

CARL  H.  HAMBURG

F.  ROY  LOCKHEIMER

LOUIS  MORTON

C. H.  GEOFFREY  OLDHAM

JAMES  W.  ROWE

Sources of the quotations appearing on the parts division pages are:

POSTULATIONS: *Social Origins of Dictatorship and Democracy: Lord and Peasant in the Making of the Modern World* by Barrington Moore, Jr., Boston: Beacon Press, 1966, p. 508.

CASE STUDIES: *The Edge of Objectivity: An Essay in the History of Scientific Ideas* by Charles Coulston Gillispie, Princeton: Princeton University Press, 1960, pp. 8–9.

CONCLUSIONS: *The Shaping of Modern Thought* by Crane Brinton, Englewood Cliffs, N.J.: Prentice-Hall, Inc., 1963, p. 83.

Design by Hugh O'Neill

Printed in the United States of America

# *Contents*

# Acknowledgments

The American Universities Field Staff wishes to thank the Alfred P. Sloan Foundation for having made it possible for the Conference on Science and Social Change to take place in Pasadena, California, on October 19 and 20, 1967, and for having helped to defray the costs of this publication.

Our gratitude also goes to the California Institute of Technology for sponsoring the conference jointly with the Field Staff and for the care taken with the housekeeping details of the meeting. Individual thanks should go to Hallett D. Smith, chairman of the Division of Humanities and Social Sciences, and Edwin S. Munger, professor of geography, for their contributions. More general but equally warm sentiments should be directed to the many members of the Caltech administration and faculty who for so long have made Field Staff Associates feel at home on that campus.

The eight contributors of chapters to this book have been generous in bringing their knowledge and insight to bear on a theme of some importance, and in his concluding synthesis, Kalman H. Silvert, the editor, suggests new ways of studying the relationships among science, technology, and society.

TEG C. GRONDAHL

*The Social Reality of Scientific Myth*

# *Foreword*

The logic, methods, and mythology of science impregnate the effect of the modern world on the traditional. As is so often the case, however, there is nothing neat and fixed and definite about what modern societies think about and do with science. The reactions of developing countries to science and its establishments, procedures, and emotional baggage are also disparate and frequently infused with unreality. As often as not, science does not bring with it a revolution of rising expectations, but rather a bedazzlement effect, a confusion of product with the method of its production. This confounding of technology with science is conducive not only to a misunderstanding of the relation between the two, but also to a reification of both. So it is that science becomes mystery, kin to religion, for the persons who would use scientific precept in the search for ultimate truth. Conversely, science becomes lowly mechanics for those who would denigrate the "material" in a search for the "spiritual" as the only truly significant element in human life.

Whatever hopes or fears are attached to science, we should not forget that the doing of science involves institutionalized procedures. Scientific endeavor requires not only laboratories and equipment, but ways of recruiting and training scientists, of building the environments in which they work, and of decisions concerning the application of their doings. Call this complex of activities a scientific estate, or a scientific establishment, or a scientific élite, its effectively acting presence involves political and educational decisions of increasing importance, especially as the procedures and processes of development spread throughout the third world. The ideas of science and the institutions of science need to be studied together if we are to discover the social meaning of science in developing countries. It is for that reason that we have entitled this book *The Social Reality of Scientific Myth,* a

I

way of saying that we are not reexamining the logic or the ethics of science universally writ, but rather the ways in which specific cultures imbue science with mystique, and give science and its social mythology concrete form in institutional structures.

This coupling of attitudes and institutions is the hallmark of American Universities Field Staff studies of developing societies. For the seventeen years that the Field Staff has devoted itself to the problems of the emergent nations, we have attempted to be faithful to the cultural particularities of the settings in which we work, and yet sensitive also to the similarities of stimuli and reactions we see playing themselves out. In attempting to discipline ourselves in the weighing of the particular and the general, we have come to address ourselves periodically to themes that engage some of the attention of all interested Field Staff Associates. When we feel that the quality of these common endeavors warrants it, we prepare a compendium of papers such as this one. But it should be emphasized that these multi-author studies are not casually collected articles. Theoretical statements have been prepared for each theme before writing begins, and the authors have been invited to disagree as well as agree with the hypotheses advanced. The substantive editing is by only one person, and some individual contributions may have been reworked as many as three and four times. Not all articles written on any given subject are included in these collections. The inevitable differences in levels of generalization that appear in the chapters are allowed because of the judgment that differing countries and points of emphasis have validity in themselves as well as for the general subject under discussion. While we hope that each chapter will have intrinsic and autonomous worth, we also design each book so that the chapters are mutually reinforcing and so that they suggest the many differing accommodations to the same problem areas made within the sets of uniqueness that are the world's cultures.

While we strive for coherence in each volume, we also are attempting to follow a line in the series. The first to appear was *Expectant Peoples: Nationalism and Development*, published in 1963. The next, in 1964, was *Discussion at Bellagio: The Political Alternatives of Development*, a conference report on nationalism and its possible relations to governments of force or of voluntaristic and consensual participation. The third was entitled *Churches and States: The Religious Institution and Modernization*, published in 1967. The appearance of this volume emboldens us to make plain our strategic design, without, however, committing subsequent editors to adhere to it. Our approach is institutional in the sense that every study concerns culturally specific, historically bound clusters of behavior. But our approach is valorative, too, in the sense that we seek to isolate the attitudes and values with which given cultures understand their institutionalized behavior patterns. Our techniques are those of history and the case study, but we do not eschew quantification because we are opposed to "behavioralism." It is rather that quantitative analysis would demand a greater commonality of theory than either our diverse countries of specialization or the nature of the Field Staff or the degree of advance of social science thought permit us. Our interest is in behavior in the fullest sense—what man thinks as well as what he does. Our techniques are determined by what it is we are best able to do, governed always by the desire to be competent and to suggest fertile fields of study to other scholars of whatever disciplinary or methodological persuasions.

In following an institutional approach, we have treated politics as the core, the constant against which we range other institutions. It was for that reason that the first two studies concerned the state and the nature of national community. The third addressed itself to issues of religion and the state, while the present volume turns to science and such politically related issues as war, education, academic freedom, and civil liberties. This orientation is not to be understood as meaning that we assume politics to be the single determinant of modernization. But we do assume that as societies become more complex, the political institution tends to emerge as the "chiefest of the chief," the social structure whose specialized function is that of integration, of producing the higher levels of social synthesis demanded by the increasing complexity and specialization that are major earmarks of modernization. Thus, politics in modern societies touches all else in more decisive and more daily and intimate fashion than any other institution. Although this statement is not necessarily valid for societies that are not nation-states, the criterion of the social effect of politics remains a good one for comparative purposes when one attempts to think simultaneously of the developed and the developing.

We have also hoped to make a contribution to social science theory by following a comparative institutional tack. Some twenty years ago this way of studying societies fell into disrepute in the American academic community because it tended to decay into arid analyses of legal as opposed to social functioning, or else into a narrow historical reductionism in which the uniqueness of events blinded students to the possibilities of comparison. In reaction, the functionalist school developed, its principal argument being that all societies must discharge similar functions—reproduction, socialization of infants, the adjudication of dispute, the distribution of products, explanation of natural and human phenomena, and so forth. It is paradoxical that the debility of this school of thought also lies in a weakness in comparison, for to discover universals is not automatically to know how to break those universals

3

into meaningful families of events. The Field Staff approach has been based on the presumption that adequate comparison demands a study of clusters of uniqueness (learned from similar families of institutional occurrences and belief systems) guided by an understanding of those functions all peoples must perform if they are to survive and, conceivably, begin consciously to control the conditions of their survival. Although it is not in the nature of the AUFS to advance a single, coherent, and necessarily quasi-polemical social science theory, we hope that this informal series will provide a stimulus for others in the university community to be encouraged to such a task.

The Field Staff is a specialized overseas research arm of an affiliated group of American universities. As might be expected in an organization only loosely tied to its member and governing institutions, AUFS-campus relations have gone through various phases of experimentation. This series reflects the growing intricacy of scholarly identification, for whereas *Expectant Peoples* was written entirely by Field Staff Associates, the succeeding volumes have mingled member university faculty with AUFS men. As a direct result of this collaboration, the yearly planning conferences, originally designed to coordinate activities, have now become also substantive conferences, meetings of minds as well as of representatives.

This book well exemplifies the intimacy of collaboration being achieved. The first three chapters are in the nature of theoretical overviews. In the past an AUFS editor contributed the overarching theoretical statement. Now, an examination of the several meanings of science, and its possible relations to social change, is provided by Dr. Carl H. Hamburg, of the Department of Philosophy at Tulane University. He argues for the importance of seeing scientific endeavor as only one way among many in which men enrich themselves by creating perceptions that can lead to the broader diffusion and re-creation of new symbols, the way in which each person can share in the lives of many others across both time and distance. Dr. Louis Morton, professor of History at Dartmouth College, then continues with a study of the relation between military technology and social change that clearly establishes the necessity for thinking of technological innovation as different from organized, scientific endeavor. The last chapter in this generalizing section is contributed by Charles F. Gallagher, of the Field Staff, who takes us comparatively through a number of languages to test their receptivity to the introduction of new concepts—an obviously critical part of bringing scientific concepts, as distinct from mere mimetic technological practice, into the culture systems of developing societies.

The succeeding chapters emphasize the problems of specific coun-

4

tries, but do not neglect the exploration of facets of the matters touched upon in the first section. Nicholas DeWitt of Indiana University speaks of science education in Africa and its deficiencies, as well as the doing of science in the Soviet Union and the problems faced by scientists in an ambience of political totalitarianism. C. H. Geoffrey Oldham, the only participant attached neither to the AUFS nor to a member university, but to Sussex University, adroitly compares science development in Great Britain to that in contemporary mainland China, again revealing the importance of social class, values, and politics in the development of the scientific estate. Messrs. Bayne, Lockheimer, and Rowe, all of the Field Staff, devote themselves respectively to Iran, Japan, and Brazil, covering topics ranging from The Bomb to university organization, but all on the basic theme of political development, ideology, education, and science.

We hope that our pride in helping to further this kind of interaction will be pardoned. We strongly feel the importance of more intimate knowledge of the societies with whom we share the earth, and of finding more significant ways to understand that knowledge. When the field specialist and the academic practitioner can work together so comfortably, we know that at least we are being useful to each other. If we could also be useful to other segments of American life that deal with foreign affairs and policy, our sense of gratification on the home scene would be complete. The only detail left would be to find ways of being of equal service abroad. As Utopian as is that vision, let us not mock it, for sensible men can make of reasonable dreams the stuff of daily motivation. That urge to creative discovery fuels not only many scientists, but many good citizens as well.

KALMAN H. SILVERT

*Norwich, Vermont*
*August, 1968*

# I  *Postulations*

Whether the ancient Western dream of a free and rational society will always remain a chimera, no one can know for sure. But if the men of the future are ever to break the chains of the present, they will have to understand the forces that forged them.

Barrington Moore, Jr.

Quotation from *Social Origins of Dictatorship and Democracy: Lord and Peasant in the Making of the Modern World*, Boston: Beacon Press, p. 508.

# 1.

## SCIENCE AND INSTITUTIONAL CHANGE

## BY CARL H. HAMBURG

*Tulane University*

Let me start with an unceremonious statement of the theme. (1) A certain amount of effort is being expended in having us write about "Science and Social Change." Look at the connective "and" between the two nouns. It is intellectually lazy, all-inclusive, and suggests nothing. "And" neither asserts *which* relation obtains between sciences and change, *nor* does it imply that there *is* any relation. Even contradictories, such as "Life, Death"; "To be, Not to be" are connectable with "and." All of which should remind us that science may or may not be causally related to change, that they may be interdependent, if not independent, and even that one may *include* the other, as science, for example, *itself being one of the social institutions,* is capable of affecting other institutions.

(2) Suppressing at this point the philosophical inclination to speculate about "change," we merely note that change is both axiologically "neutral" and also descriptive only of structures persistent through some intervals of time. That neutrality, happily, leaves out the problem of progress as well as preoccupation with duration-less point-events, herewith happily turned back to the physicist.

(3) We therefore note that "sciencing," as a time-bound enterprise, is itself a mode of change. As an enterprise, featuring its own stratification of functions and practitioners, it also is a "social institution"; i.e., it involves learned, culturally selective behavior, and is bound to affect,

9

as well as to be affected by, other social institutions. The "and" connective is likely to denote a correlative rather than a one-way causal, or even a merely teleological relation.

(4) How about the term "science"? All sorts of theses can be envisoned, co-variant with which of its meanings is entertained. The following are perhaps worth distinguishing: (a) Science: the total body of true propositions, known to some members of a society; (b) science—a particular science, such as physics, biology, economics, etc., which, as the master-science, tacitly or overtly, serves as the model for the description, explanation, and even the justification of social change; (c) *science:* its method which, held to be universally applicable, yields the normative preference-rules (consistency, tolerance, testability, etc.) exemplary for all conduct (if conduct can be defined as "rational").

These distinctions are made, in brief, to avoid confusion between Science, sciences, and scientific method. If not distinguished, Science is in danger of begetting scientism, reductionism, or rationalism, all three of which have aroused enough enthusiasm (to construct or kill) and hostility (to do the same) as to be sufficiently important for an understanding of social or political change.

(5) All this can be expressed as the "minimum-thesis," namely, that all social change: (a) is not arbitrary; (b) that, if (a) is so, then it is described and explained by Science, sciences, or scientific methods; and furthermore, (c) that the explanation of (a) requires and is given justification by models, derived from what is distinguished under (b).

(6) The strategy of the above expression [5 (a), (b), (c)] is to bring into focus the large diversity of "theories" about both science and change, by suggesting that this diversity is due to respectively different problems and answers to the relevance of "science" (in its three meanings) for the description, explanation, and justification of political change.

(7) If we assume, therefore, that political (like normative) issues are type-wise different (ranging all the way from psychoanalytical to sociological, this- and other-worldly, inner- or outer-oriented, intuitive, empirical, or rigorous), our proposal is that this bewildering magnitude can be both distinguished and explained if mapped over the characteristically different conceptions of science, as indicated.

(8) One further point: if the employment of a single scientific method can be assumed to be invariant with regard to otherwise different procedures in different fields, and if, furthermore, science (either single, plural, or all together) can be assumed to yield a "scientific basis" for the proper understanding of both science and changes in other social institutions, if—I repeat—all this be assumed, only three alternatives remain:

(a) inquiries into political (social) change must have their base in either Science, sciences, or scientific method;

(b) such inquiries must ultimately be based on a trans-scientific base (theological, mystical, or metaphysical); or

(c) such inquiries remain in principle unintelligible to the limitations of science and its method.

(9) Since 8 (b) and (c) essentially distinguish between a trans- and a non-scientific base and since 8 (a) allows for a base in either *one* or *more than one* science, paragraph (8) can be rephrased as follows: Explanations of political change either have:

(a) an *intra*-scientific base (single-factor theories; e.g., Marx);

(b) an *inter*-scientific base (combination of plural, or any of the sciences; e.g., Weber, Lasswell, etc.);

(c) a *meta*- or nonscientific base (e.g., Toynbee, Spengler, Bergson, Voegelin).

(10) Failure to allow for this division accounts for *Scientism*, which would collapse (c) into (a) and (b), as well as for *Reductionism*, which would eliminate (b) and (c) for the greater glory of (a). Mysticism would be the pseudo-normative alternative, characterized by telescoping (a) and (b) into (c).

(11) I must now make explicit the existential bases to which intra-, inter-, and meta- (or trans-) scientific explanations and justifications make reference. Paraphrasing a paradigm once set up by Edel,[1] we distinguish the following:

(A) *a world-view*, with attendant conceptions of its constituents, processes, mechanisms, and structures.

(B) a particular conception of the *nature of man* (along with his characteristic behaviors, aims, and self-conceptions of birth, maturation, reproduction, aging, and death), his faculties and images.

(C) a particular conception, origin, and evaluation of his *community*, its nature and extent.

(D) a particular conception of the degree of *knowability* of the world, human life, community—and their processes, patternings, dangers, and moral as well as social, control-possibilities.

I pause to consider what we know if we know (A) $\longrightarrow$ (D). We know that different views concerning political change co-vary with correspondingly different conceptions of bases [A-D]. I shall not be concerned with commenting on the rather widely shared insight that science, the sciences, and the technologies incumbent upon them do, as a matter of fact, affect both the ends and the efficacy of our control of the means to promoting change. This story, however

[1] Abraham Edel, *Science and the Structure of Ethics,* Chicago: University of Chicago Press, 1961, p. 13.

important, I take to have been told often enough. In any case, it is not the philosopher who is expected to tell it well enough to maintain his professional standing. In what follows I shall dramatize what I am about by calling attention to what I think I can make out as several distinct conceptions or images of science, and to indicate briefly for each of them the conceptions implied for political change.

## THE PLATONIC IMAGE

This image is at once one of the oldest and most optimistic of all; it envisions a state of affairs in which, by deduction from first principles, a select group of knowers shall (1) know the truth, and (2) knowing it, restructure the actual "world-in-a-mess" of transitory human beings in accordance with their natures, and (3) by an eventual and gradual replacement of myth or outright error (in religion, poetry, or social customs) by rational institutions initiated by philosopher-kings.

If, as Whitehead has said, all subsequent Western philosophy is but a series of footnotes to Plato, this supreme image of science in society is not merely academic and esoteric. It is a recurrent theme, still seriously entertained, and not merely by philosophers. It is bound to suffer resurrections whenever more underdeveloped "nations" begin to attempt consciously controlled change.

But, with the population increase of experimental-minded scientists, and with the advance of at least partially successful democratic institutions, a growing number of political scientists have taken as dim a view of Plato's trust in a science-guided ruler-élite as of his system of knowledge, in which all propositions are to hang ultimately together in one closed, final, and apodictic system of mutual implications.

Briefly, the trouble with Plato's "science" is not that, if correct, it would not indeed make his model state as ruled without consent of the ruled by the possessors of scientific knowledge possible as well as desirable. (Communists, if I am not mistaken, are making this sort of claim right now.) However, two thousand years have elapsed since the inception of Platonic "science," and the gap between it and actual reality does not seem to have narrowed. The history of science is a path, marked by blasted illusions: pure mathematics, after all, is not about this world and, even if joined with physical knowledge, turns out to be only one member in the family of sciences. Apodictic knowledge may not be the only kind worth having, and knowledge, however defined, may not be so divinely important as all that.

# THE ICONOCLASTIC IMAGE

This image of science is an occasionally popular but philosophically less respectable one than the Platonic, according to which it is the prime instrument for alienating man both from God and his moral vocation. We are now at the opposite pole from Plato. Science, we are told, is as evil as Adam's grab for the apple. The mechanistically ordered universe of science, as that of Eden, cannot accommodate the Judeo-Christian value scheme along with its props: souls, deity, free will, heaven or hell.

The "value-smashing" image of mechanics started with rather puny investigations into matters which seemed innocent enough, if not outright dull. By the nineteenth century, however, the various practical and partial investigations of nature had converged to a new mechanical conception of the universe whose validity was assured by its progressive confirmation, as well as by its potency in affecting technological, social, and political changes in society. Today, opposed to this image of science, there is the "Academic Man" of the nineteenth century. He did not mind much living on the profits of industry as long as he did not have to become too closely associated with it. Science, at any rate, was viewed as intellectually inferior because the scientist's chief concern was with a world of moving bodies, liquids, or gases whose properties were said to be conceived by a "mind" which clearly did not itself possess any denotable aggregate state. Though tolerant of the humanities, science so conceived offered no rational grounds for any dedication to values or virtues which, so it was thought, were the only true ends for whose facilitation science could at best hope to make its practical contribution. Academic man of the twentieth century is still found arguing in terms of this image of science, though with this difference: contempt for the scientifically trained, but otherwise "uncultured," souls is usually replaced by more ambiguous and guilt-charged attitudes. Science, the refugee from Eden, has come a long way from its crudely mechanistic exile and, like many of our political refugees, it has become an immigrant, ready to take out citizenship papers in the new world, losing all hankering for the good old world of paradise lost, yet full of expectation for building a genuinely worthwhile alternative.

Now, as to the limitations of the Iconoclastic Image, it is true that, wherever and whenever science got started, it did have to declare its independence from the knowledge-claims of religion or any other controlling institution. The continuing career of science appears to make it clear, though, that its "destructive" effects are neither universal nor necessary. Religion has also been opposed by nonscientists—and scientists, such as Giordano Bruno, Newton, Leconte du Noüy, or Teilhard de Chardin have shown that science is not only compatible with religion and moral and political changes for "the better," but that it actually can reinforce such endeavors. If there is always the danger that science may function as a religion itself, there is also always the corresponding danger of engaging in foolish attempts to have religion take over the proper task of science. In this view of science, all important change is nonpolitical, having to do with the career of salvation-seeking souls toward heaven and away from hell, if not earth itself. As a result, we encounter in the Church, for example, a type of institution which, while sublimely knowledgeable in the world of power and politics, is also disinterested in earthly changes except insofar as they pertain to the ushering in of optimal conditions for the prospering business of redemption.

## THE PATHOLOGY IMAGE

I am thinking here of such Catholic philosophers as Maritain, for example, who has spoken of science as a "deadly disease." Not that either man or science are inherently objectionable, but it so happens that in our time the rising power of science carries in its wake a loss of confidence in "absolute truths" and "eternal values." Briefly, this science image depends for its plausibility upon a less than sophisticated reading of modern science. For example, relativity-physics is not "relativism" but a step toward equations that are held to be invariant for different frames of physical description. As time goes on, even our social scientists, in their eager search for impartially describable alternatives to our own state, are not really opening the floodgates to value indifference and cultural relativity. On the contrary, to recognize that the great variety of social value and power schemes is relative to different geographic, economic, social, and political factors and conditions may turn out to be a necessary condition for discovering such "universal"—i.e., "trans-culturally invariant" relations—as might explain and eventually overcome the great diversity of value and societal changes as it has pleased the Lord (if there is one) both to create and tolerate.

Further, history abounds in examples of societies which, when they did believe in eternal verities, also believed and abounded in a full catalogue of horrors inflicted by man upon man. And finally, if science some day should come out with the declaration that "absolutes" do have a way of changing from place to place, as well as from time to time, so much the worse, I would say, for so-called "absolutes."

What is to be feared by contrast is not "Science," but its perversion at the hands of nonscientists. Even scientists are wont to contemplate their current dilemma: if they develop weaponry, they fabricate violent changes; if they do not, they become traitors. But the horns of the dilemma are rubbery. The scientist, after all, does not create experimental or political changes; he only discovers or infers them. Nor does he use them, their use being determined by others with no science but probably a "morality" of their own. In this defense, the scientist looks somewhat like the sorcerer's apprentice who, though not responsible for the mess created by his formulae, is nevertheless unable to terminate it. Science, we are told in these post-Hiroshima days, is not evil. Of course not. Nor are scientists. It is not that man is good and science bad, but rather that science, though ethically neutral, is and can be used by men who are not. The advocates of this pathology image thus declare for a temporary moratorium on science. The time to resume, we are told, is when man's moral, social, and political developments will have caught up with his theoretic precocity in physics.

I limit myself to three brief rejoinders. First, the scientific intercourse with nature may not be the sort of thing one can stop at will. If man advances to knowledge, there is also a way in which knowledge advances toward him, triggering off cognitive advances, whether we are otherwise ready for them or not. Second, if we call a halt, will the Russians or, more recently, the Chinese? And, if they don't, are we not merely replacing a problematic doom with a certain one? Finally, the cure for bad or badly used science is probably not less but more—and better—use of scientific findings. And is not the proper use of the technological results of some sciences itself a problem whose successful solution becomes the task of some other science?

## THE NONESSENTIAL ABSTRACTION IMAGE

I make mention of this image in passing and only in the spirit of classificatory completeness. I have reference to the rich proliferation of *Existenz* philosophies, *Lebensphilosophen*, etc. This group, along with its Zen and psychedelic-chemist variety is, when not speechless, engaged in occasional references to science as offering merely "illusions" of objectivity. Science, we are told, must be recognized for what it is: a series of artificial, nonessential, and existence-falsifying abstractions.

The most I can make of this image of science is that it is probably partially, yet importantly, true in its insistence that whatever else

"Reality" may be, it could have neither future nor past unless it occurred in the present, the here and now. Recollected, the present becomes past; the future can only be anticipated in a present now. Science as well as religion and history, business, TV, and common sense perpetually either worry or excite us about what was or what may or will be. In the end, most of us are entrapped in this back- and fore-looking and we have few, if any, occasions to attend to the present, the only time at which anything can exist at all.

But, since science is not really in competition with the flower children and since, in the end, it may well be our best hope for securing and expanding the horizon of leisure and contemplation, the indignant stance against science seems pointless. Hence the peculiar gap in the *Existenz* crowd between their mania for change on one hand, and their peculiar impotence in grasping the language and practice of power, without which all hope for change remains a mere singsong.

In view of a notable lack of intelligible support for this science image at this time, and in language known to me, I will simply close with the observation that a case against science on grounds of objections to abstractions, concepts, or logical "formalities" must either itself be abstract, conceptual, and sensitive to logic, or else it condemns its advocates to a silence that must be honored by counter-silence.

## THE MODEL IMAGE

Under this heading one could group most of the more interesting attempts to envision science as the unity of what can be discovered by scientific method, and thus as a model for the successful approach to areas other than natural science as such. Proposals for changing the scheme of things in the image of science occur in various ways. By way of illustration, I shall merely mention the political model as used by the late John Dewey and by J. S. Mill before him. As seen by Schumpeter, for example, they both clearly depend for their grounding of democratic procedures on an analogy between the hypothetical and self-corrective method of science on one hand, and the similarly undogmatic approach to law-making in a democracy on the other. Starting from the assumption that the "Common Good" is just as unknown as the so-called "secrets of nature," both scientists and legislators look upon law-making (whether scientific or political or jurisprudential) as occurring in a hypothetical mood. Just as hypotheses and presumed laws of nature must be confirmed or else given up, just so for party programs and legislative proposals in a democratic order.

But this solution to the problem of the direction of societal change has become problematic again. In science, hypotheses can be junked or abandoned for better ones. Is the same true of the "hypothetical" search for the common good via democratic procedures? The answer is: probably not! Whether in public or in private life, some decisions, once taken, entail consequent decisions and narrow the scope of future behavior possibilities, whether we will it or not. There is also the disturbing spectacle of alternative and mutually exclusive political structures, even though both of them give equal credence and support to scientists and institutions of scientific learning.

The following four propositions are perhaps sufficient to describe the essential views of the radical science addict:

(1) reduce the nonscientific to the non-important;

(2) erect a dualism: either one talks non-sense or else employs the technical language of quantification;

(3) only mathematical and nuclear models are cognitively respectable;

(4) methodological omnipotence: nothing, in principle, is impossible for science.

However, there is no scientific evidence for any of these contentions. The reduction of all meanings to cognitive meanings, of cognitive meanings to scientific meanings, and of all scientific meanings to those expressible in mathematical language is itself not demonstrable as a result and instance of scientific knowledge so defined.


## THE SYMBOLIC FORM IMAGE

I have now come full circle from probably untenable conceptions of science (and their bearing upon change) to what I would hold to be the one of greatest sophistication. In this conception of science (as proposed by Cassirer, for example), it is taken as one human activity among others. Much has been made of that "Open Sesame," that powerful key to all the secrets of the universe, called "scientific method." Yet, whatever it is, it probably is not altogether different from what human thinking has been, or is now even outside of science. Nor does it hold a monopoly on truth or precision or comprehensiveness. Is science more precise than any other human endeavor? Nothing could be more precise than philology or watchmaking. Is science more concerned with truth? Nobody could be more concerned with truth than a good biographer, or the income-tax investigator, for that matter. Does the scientist look especially carefully at nature? But so does the painter! And what could offer more comprehensive systems than myth, religion, philosophy, or logic pure and simple?

Since man's habits are subsequent to different interests and abstractions as well as to different insights and methods, the comparability of all human creations as symbolic transformations of this selfsame world of data is also productive of an apparently unavoidable division of labor and skills which requires the limitation of the specialist in all cultures, whether he be an atomic physicist, linguist, or a violin virtuoso.

"If the contention that reality is perceived and experienced essentially as institutional language-habits classify it expresses one important corollary of the 'symbolic-form' thesis, its second one concerns the widening of its range beyond ordinary ('natural') languages. It bids us to conceive of all the various arts and sciences (of myth as well as of religion and philosophy itself) as of so many different 'languages' or symbol-systems by which man accounts, in different ways and for different purposes, for the manifold data of his experience." [2] Thus, the sciences not only employ symbols in order to carry on or communicate their activities and findings, but their very theories have neither being nor meaning in isolation from the contexts of their symbolic production.

Three important consequences follow. First, the Nature of physical reality becomes a function of what different stages of physical science take it to mean. "Nature" with a capital "N" thus splits into the variety of the "nature-concepts" of Aristotle, the Stoics, Spinoza, Newton, Einstein, etc., to mention only some Western varieties. Second, the Nature of social reality also does not refer to something nonsymbolic called "society." Instead, it means ordering relations and roles which derive whatever meaning they have from definitions of typical situations, problems, and precepts for normative behavior which, like a set of recipes, define what is "appropriate" action within a group. Only by the acquisition of such symbolic meanings concerning "status" and "role" can we become social as well as natural beings. And third, from these conclusions, some philosophers (notably Cassirer and Dewey) have drawn the inevitable consequence for a redefinition of the "nature of man."

Since to define man as a "social animal" would put him in the same class as creatures with whose way of life he would not always want to be identified, and since his identification as a "rational animal" may set up a class too small to accommodate all instances of humanity, it has been suggested (by Ortega y Gasset, for instance) that perhaps man has no nature at all, but only a history. Yet, if it is characteristic of man's "nature" that it is revealed in "history" (i.e., through historical change in his characteristic works) then, if man is what he does, and if

[2] Carl H. Hamburg, "Symbolic Forms: Cassirer and Santayana," *Tulane Studies in Philosophy*, New Orleans: Tulane University, 1963, Vol. XII, pp. 76–83.

what he collectively does is called his "culture," man can be identified as the culture-building animal. However, since "culture" itself is but a symbol for man's various religious, artistic, scientific, and social constructions, generated by his various modes of symbolization, we end with a definition of man as the "symbolic animal" which, for better or worse, interposes between stimuli and responses a network of symbolic meanings through which he perceives, interprets, and responds to a world whose essential features are made out in human history; i.e., as temporal developments of the various symbolic media in which "his" world is felt, understood, and acted upon.

## CHANGE: EXPLANATIONS AND APPRAISALS

There is no disagreement among philosophers of science that science does not issue in apodictic truths, but that it rather pronounces in a hypothetico-fallible mood and also that it is self-corrective in a process of change all its own. The "science and institutional change" issue should therefore be rebaptized as a correlation between scientific and nonscientific social changes. Disagreement and variant interpretations of this "correlation" have to do with what to do with it. Clearly, there are at least two alternatives. We can ask how such change comes about. And also, how it can be justified. Historians, economists, sociologists, political scientists (mostly without justification) do not address themselves to the justification issue. That, it appears, is the unsponsored hunting-ground of the philosopher. I shall start, therefore, with the growing volume of books, monographs, and symposia dedicated to the complex but quite intelligible task of describing, explaining and, perhaps, predicting the effect of scientific change—via technological change—on social change. Surely, if the application of science to technology is mostly a matter of design, the action of technological on institutional change is falling into the class of phenomena called by most sociologists "unanticipated consequences." These results have been traced in countless area studies, contemporary and historical. To give a particularly well-argued example: [3]

> How did feudalism expire? It gave way to capitalism as part of a subversive process of historic change in which a newly emerging attribute of daily life proved to be as irresistibly attractive to the privileged orders of feudalism as it was to be ultimately destructive of them. This subversive influence was the gradual infiltration of commercial relationships and cash exchanges into the everyday round of feudal life, each act of marketing binding men more fully

[3] Robert Heilbroner, "The Future of Capitalism," *Commentary*, April 1966.

into the cash-nexus and weakening by degree the traditional . . . relationships on which feudalism was based. . . . Could there be in our day an equivalent of that powerfully disintegrative and yet constitutive force—a force sufficiently overwhelming to render impotent the citadel of capitalism, and yet as irresistably attractive to it as the earlier current of change was to feudalism? . . . This revolutionary power is the veritable explosion of organized knowledge, and its applied counterpart, scientific technology.

This argument makes a strong case, I think, both for the interaction of technological and social change during the period described and for a program to proceed along similar lines for other, if not all, periods of history. It also argues for the feasibility of predicting social change, so long as we remember the cognitive gap between the "feasible" and the "certain." For a touch of the "uncertain" in these matters, I quote the cautious words of E. G. Mesthene: [4]

The Enlightenment held science and democracy to be inseparable partners in the progress of man. Yet science sometimes appears to prosper in nondemocratic societies, and we occasionally fear that it might increase the pace of social change beyond the point at which democratic institutions can contain it without threat of social revolution. So much technical content has accrued to vital questions of public policy that the electorate feels left out of its traditional partnership in the decision-making process.

After all is said and sometimes done, there still remains another issue: are we to remain mute in the face of any change, no matter how well explained or predicted? If the effects of science are met in technologies, and if technologies increase the scope of material possibilities, and if new material possibilities require appropriate social changes to cope with them, the only control left to us would merely be the discovery of means for the attainment of ends which are both inevitable and unanticipated. Throughout all the familiar rhetoric expended on this problem, one discerns the clarion call of ethics: remember the obligation not just to describe and explain the changing configurations of institutions, but also to appraise and control them in ways prescribed by gods, God, conscience, Reason, reasons, the superego or the changing panorama of value schemes!

As was shown, there is a philosophical tradition, as time-honored as apparently time-less, to the effect that science, and its sorcerer-apprentice technology, are not automatically programmed to initiate the changes that ought to be brought about. This, however important,

[4] Emmanuel G. Mesthene, *An Experiment in Understanding, The Harvard Program Two Years After*, Cambridge: Harvard University, Program on Technology and Society, No. 2, p. 489.

is not the problem of the present discussion. Yet this much can be said: if science can lead to intellectual changes which, under certain conditions, can be conducive of technological changes, then these can, in turn, provide new options for social change which, in their turn, can make for changes in value schemes which themselves may either condone or condemn the very institutions which made those value schemes possible. This is really not as paradoxical as it may sound or read. To value (positively or negatively) one or several social institutions is, after all, either arbitrary or not and, if not, one's evaluations must be justifiable as well as factually describable or explainable. Without entering into a full-fledged argument of the ethical issue involved here, I shall conclude with statements of such generality that they are not likely to be too controversial: if social changes correlate with technological changes, and if technological changes make for changes in social institutions, then such institutional change not only affects moral change but it can itself be affected and changed by the ethical quest for justification. There are no insuperable difficulties here if it can be shown that the criteria for moral justification as well as the theories for explaining social and technological change must both be traced back to science as to that body of reliable and self-corrective knowledge which alone can provide intelligible grounds for what we take to be the nature of man, as well as of nature and society.

# 2.

## WAR, SCIENCE, AND
## SOCIAL CHANGE
### BY LOUIS MORTON
*Dartmouth College*

The connection between science and military affairs and their effect on social change hardly need to be demonstrated to a generation that since 1945 has lived under the threat of weapons of unprecedented destructiveness conceived and created by scientists. But this relationship between technological invention and war is nothing new; it has existed throughout history, although it has not always been as direct and apparent as it was during and immediately after World War II. We know that the ancients used combustible mixtures in war and surrounded their cities with high walls to keep out invaders. The engineers and artisans of antiquity were especially ingenious in designing instruments of war, both for offense and defense. Leonardo da Vinci was a practicing military engineer who conceived new and terrible weapons—giant ballista, steam guns, bombs, tanks, and underwater craft. Galileo displayed a strong interest in military matters, taught fortifications, and stressed to the Doge of Venice the military advantages to be gained from a telescope he had built. "Perceiving of what great utility such an instrument would prove in naval and military operations," he presented it to the Doge as a gift and received in return one thousand ducats and a life professorship. Governments and princes have always encouraged scientific interest in weapons. As A. R. Hall wrote, "the power and skill of the state in making war depend (among other things) upon its technological development, and this in turn depends upon the application of science."[1] This observation about the seventeenth century is equally applicable to the mid-twentieth century. There is not much difference in principle between the encouragement of scientific experiment on gun carriages by Louis XIV through the Académie Royale des Sciences, and a research grant from the U.S. government for work on guided missile systems to a university laboratory.

Any attempt to explore the history of the relationship between science and war must first dispose of a semantic difficulty. Contemporary usage makes a sharp distinction between pure or basic science and applied science or technology. Not only are different types of activities and goals implied in this distinction, but so too are the values and prestige of those involved. Pure science—the term itself connotes loftier aims than those related to the development of mere contrivances and machines—is concerned only with the search for an understanding of the basic principles governing nature, with no thought of the utilitarian purposes to which the discovery of such principles may be put.

This concept of science is probably little more than a century old. Before that time, the distinction between pure and applied science, between the work of the skilled craftsmen and the "scientist," was vague at best. There is little evidence that the Greeks, who excelled in mathematics, viewed matters in this way, and the Romans were even less inclined to do so. Plato, it is true, believed that science was an end in itself and that the scientist should devote himself to contemplation rather than to practical or utilitarian matters. But he made an exception for the military, which he called "the noblest of the useful aspects of science." "It is obvious," he writes in *The Republic*, "that all that part of it [war] which bears upon strategy does concern us. For in encamping . . . deploying troops, and in executing all the other maneuvers of an Army in the field of battle on the march, it will make every difference to a military [man] whether he is a good geometrician or not."[2]

As late as the seventeenth century, when modern science may be said to have its beginnings, no distinction was made between pure or applied science generally, although such men as Sir Francis Bacon were well aware of the difference. The men of the seventeenth century did not draw a sharp line either, as we do today, between the various branches of science—between mathematics, physics, astronomy, and chemistry. For the great figures of that century—Newton, Leibniz, and Boyle—knowledge of all these fields lay within their grasp and

[1] Alfred R. Hall, *Ballistics in the Seventeenth Century*, New York: Cambridge University Press, 1952, p. 5.
[2] As quoted in John D. Bernal, *Social Function of Science*, New York: Macmillan Company, 1939, p. 12.

they speculated about all of them. Nor did they limit their activities to the search for truth. They were men of affairs as well as of the intellect, interested and active in many fields, including the military. They were not unaware of the practical aspects of their theories, and felt no hesitation in drawing on the experience of craftsmen to further their own work. As Robert Boyle wrote: [3]

> The phenomena afforded us by these [mechanical] arts ought to be looked upon as really belonging to the history of nature in its full and due extent. And therefore as they fall under the cognizance of the naturalist and challenge his speculation, so it may well be supposed that being thoroughly understood they cannot but much contribute to the advancement of his knowledge. . . .

It is evident, then, that if we limited ourselves in this discussion to science in the modern sense, we would have to begin with the late eighteenth or early nineteenth centuries. To do so would be absurd, for we would thereby exclude the work of the artisans and craftsmen of antiquity, the builders of war chariots, body armor, hand weapons, and the ingenious contrivances of siege warfare. We would also exclude the metal workers of the Middle Ages, the engineers, the "intuitive" inventors, and the beginners of modern science. It is they who have been responsible throughout most of recorded history for the instruments with which men fought, and sometimes even for the way they fought. They performed their work, it is true, without any real "scientific" understanding, relying on tradition, experience, and trial and error. For a thousand years and more, skilled craftsmen worked metals without knowing why beating hardened the metal, and gunpowder was known and used for almost five centuries before the reasons for the action of this particular combination of ingredients were fully understood. To omit these and a long list of other developments from a study of the relationship between science and warfare and their effect on society would serve only to inhibit our understanding of this complex subject.

Much more work needs to be done on the links between war and science, but it is a difficult subject, lying outside the realm of any single discipline or profession. The historian generally knows little of science and less of military matters. And those who know one do not usually know the other. The scientist, lacking historical training or perspective, is equally disadvantaged. And the military man is ill-suited for the task either by training or the values of his profession, which place a low premium on the pursuit of scholarship.

An understanding of science in any consideration of its effect on

[3] Quoted in A. R. Hall, *op. cit.*, p. 3.

warfare is self-evident; not so clear is the importance of a knowledge of the military art. But without an understanding of the way military forces are organized and employed, or why, the contributions of science may have little meaning. The art of war in any age depends as much on organization, tactics, and generalship as on weapons and supplies. The pike is nothing but a thrusting spear, not much different from the sharp stick of primitive man. Yet in the hands of the Greeks it was powerful enough to turn back the great armies of the Persian empire. The reason lay in the formation they created to use the pike—the phalanx. The Romans used the same basic weapons as the Greeks, a pike and a sword, but employed them differently. The result was the Roman Legion, the most successful and remarkable formation devised by any society until modern times, Other weapons—the bow, the musket, the rifle, and the machine gun—have proved of little value until man learned how to organize them, singly and in combination, for their most effective use. It was through such formations that the English archers were able to win a victory over the French at Crécy in 1346, that the Swiss infantry, armed with pike and halberd, overthrew the armored knight to make way for a new social system in Europe, and that Napoleon with his artillery became master of the entire European continent, with all the political and social implications this mastery implied.

The nature of the relationship between war and science is more complex than appears on the surface. It is often assumed, for example, that war or the threat of war stimulates the growth of science. Actually, the proposition can and has been argued both ways. Military requirements, many assert, have been largely responsible for most significant technical advances throughout history as well as for many of the benefits of mankind. The urgencies of war place a premium on innovation and provide financial support for efforts that would be totally impossible in peacetime. The classical example of modern times, of course, is the atom bomb, developed in three years and involving sums greater than had been spent on science since the beginning of time. "As a scientific and industrial enterprise," writes J. D. Bernal, "this development represents the most concentrated and, in absolute figures, the greatest scientific technical effort in the whole of human history." [4] But it can be argued also that war slows down basic research, that the scientific principles that made possible the chain reaction were known long before the war, and that no new principles came out of the enormous scientific effort of World War II.

The connection between war and science does not necessarily imply, as is so often assumed, a relationship that is either direct or inevitable.

[4] John D. Bernal, *Science in History*, London: Watts and Company, 1954, p. 577.

Nor is it necessary to accept the claim that this relationship has been responsible for many important social and economic benefits in such fields as transportation, communication, and medicine. A strong case can be made for this proposition, but John U. Nef argues the opposite strongly and persuasively in his *War and Human Progress*. A. R. Hall, one of the closest students of the subject, asserts that manufacturing and the economic basis of society were hardly affected by science until the nineteenth century, and Sir Solly Zuckerman is by no means persuaded that scientists of an early age were moved by military needs or that their work had any effect on the conduct of war.[5]

It is often assumed that the impact of science on war has been principally if not exclusively in the development of weapons. Actually, weapons development represents only one aspect and perhaps not the most important of the contributions of science to warfare and social change. War has many needs and employs many skills, most of which have their counterpart in civilian life. Soldiers need to be transported, fed, supplied, and healed when sick or wounded. From these and other requirements have come a large number of technological advances. For example, many of the more important technological developments of the eighteenth and nineteenth centuries were due to the search for more efficient weapons, and many of the devices developed to meet military needs, such as the bulldozer, the jeep, radar, jet air travel, and surgical techniques, have found wide use in civilian life. Similarly, new machines and methods developed initially for civilian use—the railroad, for example—have had a profound effect on warfare.

Science and technology have been responsible also for the introduction of specialized troops into military formations—for example, artillery and engineers—and this fact has had significant social and political results. For one thing, it opened the military profession, formerly limited to the nobility, to the bourgeoisie, who were the only ones competent in those areas where technical expertise was required. And as armies became more and more complex as a result of technological change, the importance of business and management skills provided opportunities for the bourgeoisie in the administration of military affairs. Technical education became an essential part of the training of officers and was responsible for the establishment of the first scientific schools of modern times. When rulers realized that the support of science could pay military dividends, they established scientific societies as a means of furthering military knowledge and improving existing weapons. Both the Royal Society of London and the Académie Royale des

[5] Alfred R. Hall, *Ballistics in the Seventeenth Century;* Sir Solly Zuckerman, *Scientists and War: The Impact of Science on Military and Civil Affairs,* New York: Harper & Row, 1967.

Sciences, established in the 1660s, performed work of value to the military.[6]

The attitude of scientists toward war has been ambivalent. In principle they have often opposed war and refused to lend their knowledge and talent to the search for more efficient mean of destruction. Yet, under the threat of enemy invasion or for other reasons, they have usually succumbed to the pressures of society and contributed to the military effort. When the Romans besieged Syracuse in the third century B.C., Archimedes placed his knowledge at the service of his country, designing huge engines of war to repulse the invader. Leonardo da Vinci kept his design for an underwater craft secret "on account of the evil nature of men," but offered his services as military engineer to the Duke of Milan in a letter that is a classic example of the connection between the scientist and war.[7] Niccoló Tartaglia, who laid the foundation of the science of ballistics, after working for years destroyed his manuscript, "ashamed and full of remorse" for the time spent on it. But when Italy was invaded by the Turks, he changed his mind "in the sight of the ferocious wolf preparing to set on our flock, and of our pastors united for the common defense."[8] Other examples certainly would not be difficult to find in more recent times.

It has also been a common delusion of scientists that their dicovery of new ways to make war more destructive would have the effect of ending war altogether, since men would recognize the folly of destroying each other. Witnessing the flight of the first balloon in 1783, Benjamin Franklin wrote that war had become too terrible to contemplate. For the cost of five warships, he noted, it would be possible to build five thousand balloons to rain destruction on any city. "And where is the Prince," he wrote, "who can afford so to cover his Country with Troops for its defense, as that ten thousand men descending from the clouds might not in many places do an infinite deal of mischief before a force could be brought together to repel them."[9]

Like some scientists after World War II who believed the atomic bomb would ultimately make war obsolete, Franklin failed to appreciate the full extent of man's folly. J. P. Joule, the discoverer of the mechanical equivalent of heat, had few illusions on that score. "I know there are those," he wrote, "who think that these improvements [in weapons] will tend to put an end to war by making it more destructive

---

[6] Henry Guerlac, "Vauban: The Impact of Science on War," in Edward Mead Earle, ed., *Makers of Modern Strategy*, Princeton: Princeton University Press, 1941, p. 32.
[7] Quoted in J. D. Bernal, *Social Function of Science, op. cit.*, p. 167.
[8] *Ibid.*, p. 169.
[9] Quoted in Ignatius F. Clarke, *Voices Prophesying War, 1763–1984*, London: Oxford University Press, 1966, p. 73.

but be carried on with greater ferocity. . . . And thus by applying it-self to an improper object science may eventually fall by its own hand." [10] But like Tartaglia, he was willing to compromise his convic-tions if the "integrity and liberties" of Great Britain were threatened.

Scientists were not the only ones who believed that the increased de-structiveness of war would provide the ultimate deterrent. In 1864, Victor Hugo wrote that aircraft—he had the balloon in mind—would lead to the abolition of warfare, that science would lead the way to peace. As he saw it, the balloon would bring about "the immediate, ab-solute, instantaneous, universal and perpetual abolition of frontiers. Armies would vanish and with them the whole business of war, exploi-tation and subjugation. It would be an immense peaceful revolution. It would mean the liberation of mankind." [11]

It was a firm article of faith in the Victorian period that science was an unmixed blessing. Whatever it produced was good, including "new arms to the warrior." To the Victorian, the engineer was a demigod, the maker of modern civilization. The benefits of the new technology were limitless, and among them were the weapons of war. Erasmus Darwin, celebrating the new steam engine in verse, wrote of a flying chariot, powered by steam and filled with "warrior-bands," to drive off the armies on the ground, beneath its shadowy cloud." [12] The first balloon ascents in 1783 led to imaginary battles conducted high in the air by "aerostatic" machines armed with several decks of cannon. The outcome of such a war would be quickly decided, and the terrors of war consequently reduced. Many believed that Robert Fulton's subma-rine and torpedo would have the same effect. Admiral St. Vincent is supposed to have remarked that Fulton was laying the foundation for doing away with the British Navy altogether, a result the admiral viewed with extreme misgivings. Robert Southey believed that "the chemist and the merchant will succeed where moralists and divines have failed," [13] and the German militarist Baron Colmar von der Goltz wrote in 1883: [14]

> The fact that each new invention and each mechanical improve-ment seems somehow, in these days, to find its way into military service need not, therefore, alarm us. . . . By these means, on the contrary, the battle is only the more rapidly decided and the war brought to an end sooner than in the days of old.

[10] J. D. Bernal, *Social Function of Science, op. cit.*, p. 171.
[11] I. F. Clarke, *op. cit.*, p. 3.
[12] I. F. Clarke, *op. cit.*, p. 74.
[13] *Ibid.*, p. 76.
[14] *Ibid.*, p. 78.

Thus, by the middle of the nineteenth century, there were two con-
tradictory views about the effect of science on war—both apparently
held simultaneously. The first was that science held out the possibility
of doing away altogether with war by making it too terrible to fight;
the second, that weapons had become so effective that wars would be
extremely brief and therefore more humane.

## THE BASIC WEAPONS OF WAR

In the panorama of human experience, there are few periods when man
was not busily engaged in fighting—for goods, for land, for women,
for a cause, and even for the sake of fighting. War is the oldest of social institutions. Some have even argued that organized society and
social structure, as well as most economic and social progress, are the
result of military necessity; that war has been the most important influence in the growth and decline of civilization. It is not necessary to
accept such extravagant claims to recognize the persistence of war in
history, or the prominent role it has played, for good and evil, in shaping social organization. It has affected almost every aspect of human
activity, political, social, economic, and cultural, and in turn has been
affected by them. In no area has man shown greater ingenuity than in
devising means for killing and maiming his fellow man, employing
each advance in his understanding and control of the world about him
to serve the cause of war.

The earliest primitive societies made no distinction between economic and military activity. The tools of the hunt were the weapons
of war. The hunter was the warrior, and the skills that brought down
the game were the skills that won victory over the enemy. Society was
organized on a military basis; the leaders of the tribe were the best
warriors, and the spoils of war went to him who was the strongest and
most powerful.

The first and perhaps most important technological advance in the
history of warfare came with the introduction of metal, first bronze
and then iron. Bronze is a soft metal, but craftsmen of antiquity
learned after centuries to harden it for knife-edge weapons by beating.
We do not know who first discovered the secret of iron, but it was
already in use about 2500 B.C. Thereafter, for a thousand years, the
techniques of iron-making were improved and disseminated throughout the Near East, and instruments of iron came into general use. Possession of iron weapons gave an enormous advantage to the user, and
Toynbee tells us that the Minoans, who used bronze, were overcome
by the culturally inferior but technologically advanced Dorians with

29

their iron swords.[15] Advances in metallurgy, many of them stimulated by military need, continued to affect warfare in fundamental ways, not only by increasing the lethality and durability of weapons but also by making possible the development of armor to protect the head and other vital parts of the body. The plate and chain mail armor of the Middle Ages was the product of long experience, passed down from master armorer to apprentice, and modern artillery, tanks, and aircraft were made possible in part by the discovery of alloy steel, aluminum, and new techniques in metallurgy.

About midway through the second millennium B.C., at the time the process for hardening iron by carbonization was discovered, the Asiatic people of the steppes brought about a revolution in warfare by hitching a horse to a light wagon or cart to produce the war chariot so characteristic of the early empires of the Near East. Development of a chariot sturdy enough to carry one or two men into battle and light enough to move easily over rough ground was undoubtedly the work of many centuries; it must have taken many more to breed and train the horse, a naturally skittish animal, and to discover how to control and guide it. The war chariot altered the nature of warfare by giving to the armies of the ancient world a new mobility and speed, and the charioteers, usually members of the nobility, became the élite corps of all ancient armies. But infantry remained the principal arm, and the foot soldier with spear, axe, sword, and shield, wearing protective clothing of leather and metal, constituted the most important element in war throughout antiquity.

From the war chariot of Egypt and Assyria to the mounted warrior seems but a short step, yet it took many centuries and the development of a secure seat for the rider and a means of guiding and controlling the horse before the transition could be made. Like the war chariot, cavalry was developed in the steppe-lands of Asia and from there passed on by wandering tribes westward to Eastern Europe and eastward to China. The typical horseman of this early era, from about 500 B.C. onward, was mounted on a small fast horse and used as weapons a throwing spear or javelin and a bow and arrow. He had a saddle, actually a horse blanket rather than the padded saddle of a later day, but not stirrup, that device dating, as best as can be determined, anywhere from the first to the fifth century A.D. It was the stirrup that gave the rider a firm enough seat to use a thrusting rather than a throwing

[15] Arnold Toynbee, *A Study of History*, New York: Oxford University Press, 1950, Vol. III, p. 160. Toynbee's point here is that war is responsible for the breakdown of civilizations, for the dominance of a superior by an inferior civilization. But the resultant civilization of the Greeks hardly bears out this proposition.

weapon, and with the curb-bit, horseshoe and spur, all of which were developed in the West, made possible the heavy cavalry of Byzantium and medieval Europe.

Weapons may be said to be of two types: shock and missile. The former is held in the hand and used at close quarters, deriving its effect largely from the muscle of man. Examples are the thrusting spear or pike, axe, sword, or war club. A missile weapon is thrown at the enemy; there is no hand-to-hand, or body contact. The first missile was probably a stone, but as primitive man became more adept at shaping weapons, he learned to hurl other instruments—spear, axe, and even a stick that returned to the thrower. Other ancient missile weapons were the sling, which David used against Goliath, and the bow, perhaps the oldest weapon in continuous use. The first bows, developed in Asia around 2000 B.C., were composite bows, about four feet long and made of layers of horn and wood. The technique of shooting with these bows required constant practice, and they became the weapons of professionals who specialized in their use and hired out as mercenaries. The light horse-archers of the Asiatic steppes also used the hornbow to good effect and became as expert at it as the American Indian on the western plains with his bow. A variant was the crossbow, used in China about 200 B.C. and then forgotten until it was reintroduced into Western Europe more than one thousand years later.

The weapons of siege warfare round out the armament of the ancient world. Walled cities and fortified places are as old as mankind, and even by modern standards, the fortifications of antiquity are impressive indeed. The design and construction of defensive positions were well understood at a very early period. The Mesopotamians surrounded their cities with high walls, broken by regular series of massive towers. Nineveh, in 2000 B.C., had stone walls 50 miles long, 120 feet high, and 30 feet thick, and the Great Wall of China, built in 200 B.C., extended for 1400 miles. Ancient engineers understood the basic principles of fortification, and constructed positions that were well-nigh impregnable. Troy held out under siege for ten years and Nebuchadnezzar gave up the siege of Tyre after thirteen.

The weapons for reducing fortified positions, aside from treachery, surprise, and starvation, were varied and ingenious. There were battering rams and huge spears mounted on wheels, catapults to shoot arrows and stones, and movable towers. Incendiary materials, blazing arrows, pots of boiling oil, and naphtha were also used, and at the siege of Delium in 424 B.C. the Greeks employed gas in the form of sulphur fumes.

## THE ANCIENT WORLD

The ancient kingdoms of the Near East—Egypt, Chaldea, Assyria, and Babylonia—were military states ruled by a military (and priestly) hierarchy. The dominant class in these societies was comprised of the warrior, whose possession of and ability to use the instruments of war constituted his chief claim to superiority. Most of the weapons in the arsenal of war were already in use in one form or another. The Assyrians, the most warlike people of antiquity, were armed with spears, axes, swords, shields, and bows. They wore scale armor, small metal plates sewn to a leather garment, and constructed walls about their cities and the siege weapons to destroy them. The war chariot had already been introduced, and none excelled the Assyrian in its use.

The conquest of the Minoans brought the Greeks into the Eastern Mediterranean, where by the sixth century B.C. they had gained control of the Greek peninsula and established a city-state form of government and a culture that lies at the root of Western civilization. As in so many other aspects of life, the Greeks showed the way by producing a military system that provided a model for later ages. Military service in Greece was a privilege reserved for the citizen, who provided his own arms; others could serve, but not in the line of the phalanx. There were slaves to carry equipment and men to serve as auxiliaries, but only the free citizen could be a warrior. It was this fact that made the phalanx so effective. The Greek citizen formed a solid line of infantry, eight to twenty men deep, protected by helmet and armor of bronze, armed with a nine-foot, iron-tipped spear and a short iron sword. Flanked by lightly armed, missile-throwing infantry composed of non-citizens, the highly trained, self-disciplined formation of Greek citizens of the phalanx was able to move forward inexorably, shoulder to shoulder, warding off arrows and javelins with shields, to close with the foe. When phalanx met phalanx head on, a test of weight and stamina ensued; there was no room for maneuver or generalship.

Perhaps the most striking example of a society based on a military system in which technological superiority was a necessity is Sparta. At an early date, the Spartans discovered how to shape their weapons to a steel-like hardness, and achieved an enviable reputation on the battlefield. As a result, when Sparta began to feel the pinch of population pressure, she responded not as the other city-states by the conquest of new lands overseas, occupied by technologically inferior peoples, but by conquest of the neighboring Messenians in two terrible wars. The occupation of this territory, in which the numerous Messenians con-

tinued to live, shaped the whole of Spartan existence. To keep the conquered people subdued it was necessary for the Spartans to remain ever
on a war footing. Their institutions, their way of life, marriage customs,
child-rearing, education, values, and ethical system—all were designed
to produce and maintain a military superiority that would keep the
Messenians in check. The conqueror had become the conquered.[16]
Here perhaps is an example of social immobility rather than change induced by military necessity.

The army of Alexander the Great contained all the elements of ancient warfare in their most developed form. Unlike the Greeks and
most of the peoples of Europe at that time, the Macedonians made
wide use of the horse in war. Under Philip, Alexander's father, a body
of about two thousand horsemen called the King's Companions was organized. Drawn from the land-owning aristocracy for obvious economic reasons, the Companions constituted an élite body of heavy
cavalry, armed with sword and thrusting spear and wearing heavy
body armor. In addition, Alexander's army included light horse-
archers of the Asiatic type, but the Companions, led by Alexander
himself, was the striking force. The phalanx, in its classic Greek form a
solid and unmaneuverable body of infantry, became under Philip and
Alexander a more versatile instrument—deeper but less densely packed
to make it more maneuverable and to give the men greater individual
freedom of movement. Its major weapon was still the pike, but one
lengthened to eighteen feet or more. There was also a corps of light infantry to back up the phalangists, and a host of lightly armed missile
men, usually mercenaries, equipped with javelins, slings, and bows.
Finally, there were military engineers to bridge the unfordable rivers
and besiege the fortified places. By all accounts, this was the most versatile and formidable army yet assembled, but its enormous success was
due less to numbers or sheer strength than to the skill and intelligence
with which its various elements—infantry, cavalry, and artillery—
were used.

The Greeks made their greatest contribution to Alexander's conquests and to the creation of his empire in the invention and construction of siege machines. Although they were not preeminent in engineering like the Romans, the Greeks laid the basis for the science of
military engineering. It was a Greek, Harpalus, who in 481 B.C. designed the bridge that enabled the Persian army to invade Greece by
way of Hellespont—a task to give pause even to a modern engineer.
The bridge consisted of two rows of galleys, 314 in one and 360 in the
other, linked by cables of flax and papyrus and covered to provide two

[16] Arnold Toynbee, *War and Civilization*, New York: Oxford University Press,
1950, Chap. III.

floating roadways. Greek engineers applied the principle of the bow to construct a huge crossbow, increasing the tension by mechanical means. This device, called the ballista, was used by the tyrant Dionysius about 400 B.C. against Carthage. Greek engineers also built catapults on the tension principle, unlike those of the Romans which were powered by torsion, capable of hurling a projectile several hundred yards. The onager, meaning wild ass because its end kicked up when fired, may be described as a mechanical stick-sling, and could be used to throw incendiary materials as well as stones and arrows. In the description of the siege of Rhodes in 305 B.C., we find mention of flame throwers, probably onagers, hurling pots containing inflammable material much like the Greek fire of later times.

Perhaps the greatest achievement of any scientist of antiquity in the military field, certainly one of the most publicized, were the machines constructed by Archimedes. These instruments discharged against the Romans all kinds of arrows and stones "with an incredible noise and violence." Some threw iron hooks or claws into the wooden ships of the Romans, and by means of counterbalances lifted them up and tossed them into the sea or dashed them against the rocks. The Romans had constructed a vast siege machine on a raft formed of eight ships. Against this Archimedes hurled huge stones, breaking up the raft and "tearing asunder" the ships.

Although no one was able to duplicate Archimedes' feat, instruments similar to those he employed were in common use by the armies of the period. They constituted the artillery of ancient times, and, in principle, remained virtually unchanged down to the invention of gunpowder. Accounts of the sieges of antiquity are filled with descriptions of these machines and other ingenious devices. Alexander, whose engineer was the Thessalian Diades, used them, as did the Romans, who improved upon them but added no new principles.

It is tempting to follow the course of Alexander's conquests, but that is not our purpose here. Alexander's army was the product of a fusion of Greek and Macedonian institutions, utilizing the Greek genius for creative intellectual achievement and the technology of the time. And his conquests came at a time when Greece was facing economic depression. Greek exports were competing unfavorably with those of Carthage and other countries, and population in the mountainous peninsula was pressing on the meager food supply. In these circumstances, the appeal to Greek superiority and the right to take over the areas governed by barbarians made a strong impression and provided an ideological basis for Alexander's bid for Empire. These circumstances also forced many Greeks to seek their fortune elsewhere. Many hired themselves out as mercenaries; the ten thousand of Anabasis fame had taken service with Cyrus the Younger in 401 B.C., and there were large numbers of Greek troops in foreign service elsewhere. Alexander therefore had little difficulty recruiting men for his army.

Alexander's success was due in large part to the weakness of the far-flung Persian Empire, whose integrity depended upon an army composed of many nationalities and languages. Its central core was the cavalry, composed of the Persian land-owning aristocracy, but there was no Persian infantry and no class from which it could come. The remainder of the army was made up of mercenaries and men from conquered provinces and tributary states, lacking the discipline and spirit that motivated the Greek soldier.

Although Alexander's Empire did not survive, it brought Greek culture, science, and technology to all parts of the Mediterranean world. In Egypt, with an ancient culture of its own and great wealth, the Museum at Alexandria became a center of scientific research that had no equal until modern times. The rulers of Egypt lavished their resources on it and in return were rewarded with a large number of important theoretical discoveries and new machines, many of which could be used for military purposes.

Like the Empire, Alexander's army fell apart after his death. In the hands of his successors, it declined in quality and was finally bested by a new infantry formation, the Roman Legion. Based on the original Greek phalanx, the early legion reflected the society from which it came and was composed of the citizen in arms, the arms consisting of a thrusting spear, short Greek sword, breast plate, helmet, and shield. By Caesar's time, the legion had changed greatly. It was composed largely of long-term professionals, armed with the pilium or throwing spear, and a large two-edged sword for close-in fighting. Each legionnaire carried a rectangular, semicylindrical shield and wore armor of chain or small plate sewed to a leather garment. Organized into cohorts in checkerboard fashion, the legion constituted a remarkable tactical formation, wide and deep but extremely flexible and capable of being shifted rapidly. Numbering about six thousand men, with its small cavalry detachment drawn from Celt and German tribes and auxiliary troops, archers and slingers, drawn from Crete and the Balearic Islands, the legion was virtually invincible at the height of Rome's greatness.

The decline of Rome coincided with a decline in the quality of the Roman army. As more and more foreign mercenaries were introduced into the army, its character changed. The traditional reliance on the highly disciplined heavy infantry gave way to dependence on formations and weapons preferred by the mercenaries from the conquered provinces who composed the Roman army by the fourth century. Infantry was more lightly armed and armored; archers were made a part of the regular formation rather than auxiliaries; weapons were changed; and the light Celtic cavalry, descendant of the horse-archers of the steppes, became more numerous. It was not until the Battle of Adrianople in 378, when the heavy cavalry of the Goths inflicted an overwhelming defeat on the Roman Legion, that the Romans turned increasingly to heavy cavalry. By the fifth century it was the dominant arm of the Roman army, and after the fall of the empire in the West became the mainstay of the eastern empire at Constantinople.

The cavalry of Byzantium (the cataphract) had its origins in the aristocratic landowners of Parthia who covered themselves and their horses with armor from head to foot and carried, in addition to the terrible composite bow, a long spear or lance. To bear this large weight, the Parthians bred a horse larger and stronger than any yet known. Because they had no stirrups they used the lance in an overhand thrust with limited effect, relying on the grip of knees and thighs for support.

The Romans discovered no new scientific principles and contributed little to scientific knowledge. But they applied the knowledge of the Greeks and other ancients to excellent effect. They built a system of roads that tied all parts of the empire together and enabled the legions to move swiftly to any threatened portion of the border. They constructed buildings that have stood the test of two thousand years— aqueducts, lighthouses, pumps, and even fire-control systems. They were especially adept in the military arts, modifying and improving the large siege machines, first developed by the Greeks. They built larger and better catapults, ballistae, and onagers. Their movable towers were as high as twenty levels of floors, weighed as much as one hundred tons, and were equipped with drawbridges, battering rams, and a variety of missile weapons. In Roman hands, the simple battering ram became a machine, the long, heavy iron-tipped beam sliding on rollers or suspended by ropes in a frame built on wheels. So numerous were these engines in the Roman army that they exceeded the ratio of artillery to men in Napoleon's army.

The Roman army played a central role in the life of the empire. It made and unmade emperors, policed the long borders, maintained peace in the provinces, and carried Graeco-Roman culture to all parts of the empire. Its support constituted the main burden of the government, and its camps became the site of many of the large cities of Europe. Once the servant of the government, it ultimately became the master. "Be united, enrich the soldiers, and scorn the rest," Septimus Severus told his sons.[17] By the fourth century the empire had become

[17] Quoted in Richard A. Preston, S. F. Wise, and H. O. Werner, *Men and Arms*, New York: Frederick A. Praeger, 1956, p. 46.

a military dictatorship, ruled by a soldier and a military aristocracy. The central government was administered by military men and the governors of the provinces were invariably generals. Although the ancient traditions of Rome were paid lip service, the population was entirely at the mercy of a military machine that was increasingly barbarian in composition. By the time the empire in the West collapsed, the military traditions and system that had made Roman power supreme had disappeared completely. The decline of the army was not responsible for the fall of Rome; it was a symptom of the internal decay that had affected all parts of Roman life and left it exposed and helpless against the onslaughts of the barbarians.

## THE MIDDLE AGES, 400–1400

The fall of Rome ushered in a period of anarchy and barbarism in the West, a period in which the achievements and technology of Rome were largely forgotten. The Roman art of war was forgotten, too, and with it the techniques for building and taking fortified places. Warfare reverted to its simplest form, with tribal chiefs leading their personal followers. Weapons and equipment were rudimentary—spear, sword, and axe. The horse and the bow disappeared in the West where the Franks, a German tribe that fought on foot, ultimately succeeded to the Roman imperium.

Though it appeared that with the rise of the Franks infantry would once again rule the battlefield, it was the cavalry that finally won out. The reasons lay partly in the nature of the invaders who descended upon Europe during the Dark Ages, and partly in a technological innovation that altered radically the method of fighting on horseback. Among the invaders were light horse-archers from the East, the Byzantine cataphract who defeated the Franks at Casilinum in 554, and the Saracens who invaded southern France in the eighth century. Against these horsemen the Frankish hordes with their battle-axe, the francisca, were largely helpless. They had to learn to fight on horseback or risk destruction.

The second factor in the victory of cavalry was the introduction of the stirrup into Western Europe in the eighth century. The origin of the stirrup is not clear, but it was apparently known in India and China at least several centuries before it came into Europe. The Byzantines were apparently using it by 600, but whether it was introduced by them into Europe, or by the Northmen, or by some other route is not known. What is remarkable is the length of time it took to reach the West, and, even more remarkably, the profound effect it had on the structure of medieval society. For the stirrup made possible the heavily armored knight, the most formidable heavy cavalry yet devised, and the system of warfare as well as land tenure that prevailed in Europe for at least five centuries. It helped work this change by giving to the mounted warrior so firm a seat that he could withstand both the weight of his armor and the shock of contact with the enemy horseman. The lance, his main weapon, he could carry couched under his arm and deliver his blow with the combined force of his own strength and the weight of his mount. Similarly, he could wield his long sword, a pointed, doubled-edged four-foot-long weapon, with some assurance that he would not fall helpless after the first swing or thrust. The stirrup, in Lynn White's words, "effectively welded horse and rider into a single fighting unit capable of violence without precedent." [18] By adding animal to human power, it increased greatly the knight's capacity to damage his enemy. Cavalry, for the first time, became truly a shock weapon, the shock weapon *par excellence*.

The introduction of the stirrup altered, in a fundamental way, the tactics of mounted warfare and enhanced enormously the importance of the cavalry, for no infantry of the time could withstand a cavalry charge. It also limited the military profession to a small number of well-to-do, for only those with considerable means could afford the horse, the expensive and increasingly heavy armor, weapons, and other necessities for this kind of warfare. In the eighth century, military equipment for one knight cost the equivalent of twenty oxen. And horses had to be fed, cared for, and replaced when they grew old or were killed in battle. Swords and lances were broken and the work of the skilled armorer came very high. Moreover, the knight needed to be physically fit and practice the use of his arms; these were his entire excuse for being. He was, in effect, a skilled professional and he spent all his time on his profession. To learn to fight like a knight, according to a Frankish proverb, one had to start at puberty. In these and other ways the stirrup introduced a revolution in medieval life and had a profound effect on medieval social structure. The type of warfare it made possible, "found expression in a new form of Western European society dominated by an aristocracy endowed with land so that they might fight in a new and highly specialized way." [19]

The necessity for providing a system that would assure the level of economic wealth and leisure needed to maintain a force of armored knights in a society that was disorganized and whose economy was based on a subsistence agriculture ultimately produced the system of

[18] Lynn T. White, *Medieval Technology and Social Change*, Toronto: Oxford University Press, 1962, p. 2.
[19] L. T. White, *op. cit.*, p. 38.

land tenure and political fealty known as feudalism. The first step in this development came in the reign of Charles Martel, early in the eighth century, with the seizure of church properties and their distribution to his followers in return for military service. At about the same time, other such grants specified that this service must consist of mounted men. By these means the ruling monarch secured a body of mounted warriors, who, in return for the lands that enabled them to maintain the necessary horses and equipment, took an oath of military service to the ruler. Possession of the land carried with it military obligation. By Charlemagne's time, the system seems to have been firmly established and under him it was greatly expanded, in part by eliminating the individual obligation of the small landholder for military service in return for collective support of a single knight. At the same time, Charlemagne took every possible measure to increase the quality of his cavalry, defining precisely the equipment each mounted soldier would carry and forbidding the export of armor. The effect of these measures was to limit even further the social base of the Frankish military force.

The social structure of feudalism received its final form in the ninth and tenth centuries as a result of the invasions of the Magyars from the east and the Vikings from the north. Horsemen of the Asiatic type, the Magyars struck quickly, seizing whatever they could, and then rode off. The Vikings came by sea but seized horses whenever they could to strike more deeply and swiftly before making off with their booty. Neither invader could be turned back by untrained infantry, and it was the success of the local feudal knights in meeting the threat that set the seal on the system. Small landholders granted tracts of land to a few men in return for military service, and larger landholders in turn received oaths of fealty from lesser knights in return for military support. From top to bottom, medieval society became a system of contractual relationship based on military service.

The mailed knight was only one aspect of medieval warfare; the other was the castle, the domain of the lord and the stronghold to which he and his followers retired in the event of danger. The art of fortification had been lost during the Dark Ages, and it was not until the invasion of the Northmen in the tenth century that fortified places began to appear again. But castles built as late as the eleventh and twelfth centuries were constructed of earthwork and timber. The more elaborate castles, familiarly identified with feudalism, many of which still stand, were the product of a later period and of knowledge acquired by the Crusaders in the Middle East. In the twelfth and thirteenth centuries, castles became more elaborate and more impervious to attack with the weapons of the time. The building of these structures became a specialized art, carried to its highest perfection by the French. Ultimately, many of these castles were combined with the towns that grew up around them and were included in their defense.

While the art of defense became more scientific, the knowledge of siege warfare, brought to so high a state by the Romans, lagged behind. Against the towers, walls, moats, and inner and outer rings of defense, the battering ram and scaling towers were of little use. The miners who in early times had dug their way up to the walls of the fort were helpless against the complex system of battlements manned by watchful soldiers. The missile weapons of the period were scarcely any different from those used by Alexander. Catapults hurling large stones or incendiaries proved of limited value against the massive stone castles. The only new siege weapon developed during the medieval period was the trebuchet, which utilized the principle of counterweights rather than torsion or tension to throw a heavy object a considerable distance. But this weapon had no decisive effect, either; Europe would have to wait for the introduction of gunpowder before it acquired a weapon powerful enough to reduce the castle.

The medieval knight was the most heavily protected soldier in history. This protection depended on the skill of the metal worker who fashioned not only the armor worn by the soldier and his mount, but his weapons as well. Much has been written about the armor of the Middle Ages, and there is little need to trace the development from the chain mail tunic to the full suit of armor, made of plate, cunningly fashioned at the joints, beautiful in design and finish, and sometimes inlaid with precious metal.

The weight of the armor worn by both men and horses was enormous, and only specially bred horses could have carried it. Sometimes it was too much even for them, and there is evidence that the knight himself on occasion found the weight of his armor too great. And the heavier the armor became, the slower and more unwieldy became the mounted knight, until he had lost virtually all mobility and speed and became, in effect, a lumbering tank. Unhorsed, he was as helpless as a turtle on his back.

The steady increase in the armor of the knight after the tenth century was not a whim or fashion, but a military necessity in response to the appearance on the medieval battlefield of an ancient weapon, the hand crossbow. An adaptation of the Greek ballista, the crossbow was first made of horn and wood, later of steel. It employed the tension principle, mechanically applied, to release a short arrow capable of piercing any but the stoutest mail. The Italians became most adept in its use, employing it on horse and shipboard. So lethal a weapon did it become, so dangerous to the knight's monopoly of warfare, that it was outlawed, without effect, by the Pope, and survived even after the introduction of gunpowder.

The manufacture of the crossbow, like armor, called for the utmost skill of the artisan and metal workers. Working without knowledge of the principles of mechanics, the craftsmen devised a variety of contrivances to bend the steel bow and lock it into position until the archer was ready to fire. These contrivances included a goat's-foot lever, windlass, or cranequin, and involved the use of pulleys and gears. The same mechanical ingenuity and skill displayed in working with metals was evident in the construction of other instruments of war. By the fourteenth century, European craftsmen had learned the techniques of iron-casting and knew how to make wrought iron and crucible steel, relying for power on the water mill. No scientists or theoreticians, they nevertheless invented the crank, the hinged rudder, and the mariner's compass.

The most spectacular weapon of the Middle Ages was the "Greek fire" of Byzantium. Fire had been used as a weapon of war since ancient times, the flaming arrow representing perhaps the first use of such a weapon. At an early date, the peoples of the Middle East had discovered oil seepages that provided a combustible substance, and apparently were familiar with the combustible properties of saltpeter, sulphur, bitumen, resin, and tar. Collectively, these were known as naphtha, but there was no knowledge of the chemical properties of these substances or the process by which they were ignited. Fire pots were used as early as 500 B.C., and Procopius tells us: [20]

> The Persians were the inventors of this: having filled vessels with sulphur and that drug which the Medes call *naphtha* and the Greeks "oil of Medea" and lighted them, they hurl them against the frame-work of battering rams, and soon set them ablaze. . . .

Greek fire was apparently an improved version of the older fire pot. It was first used by the Byzantines during the Mohammedan attack on Constantinople in 673 and was responsible for the survival of the empire on this and other occasions. Used aboard a galley and squirted through tubes, the pasty mixture ignited on contact with sea water, defying all efforts to extinguish it. Its composition was kept a closely guarded secret for many centuries but was later acquired by the Muslims, who used it against the Christians during the Crusades, flinging their fire pots against the wooden castles of the French.

Like Western Europe, the Byzantine empire relied on heavy cavalry, but its political and social system bore no resemblance to feudalism.

[20] Quoted in Charles J. Singer *et al., A History of Technology,* 4 vols., Oxford: Oxford University Press, 1956, Vol. II, p. 375.

Heir to the tradition of Rome and occupying the strategic and wealthy region between East and West, the Byzantines developed a highly efficient military system that survived a thousand years. The empire was never subject to the anarchy of the West; its strong, centralized, autocratic government had little difficulty maintaining internal peace. But under the pressure of attack from outside, it created a powerful army and navy, a system of fortifications, and a military system that enabled it to turn back all invaders, and even for a time to regain part of the old empire. For local protection the land was divided into a number of military districts called themes, each with its own army corps and a local militia to meet an attack. Political institutions were gradually militarized, the provincial civil administration falling into the hands of the theme commanders. Massive defensive works were constructed to guard the frontier, and when necessary the central government sent in its regular forces to back up the themes.

A feudal array and a Byzantine army drawn up for combat offer a striking contrast and a vivid illustration of the close interrelationship between political and social institutions and the conduct of war. Both relied on heavy cavalry, the feudal knight, and the cataphract, but there the similarity ends. The feudal army consisted of small independent units of irregular size, each led by a powerful lord. There was little discipline and command was based on social status. Rarely was there a single commander powerful enough to bring order to the chaos and confusion of divided command. A single attack by some minor lord could precipitate a general engagement at a most inopportune moment. There was little in the way of tactics and no strategy, the attack consisting of a frontal assault by the main body of knights. Infantry armed with pike and bow played a subsidiary and generally despised role. The Byzantine Army, on the other hand, was a well-disciplined, well-led force. Battles were avoided unless victory was assured, and every effort was made to discover the weakness of the enemy and utilize any advantage the ground might offer. Rarely did the Byzantine assault head on; the aim was always to envelop the enemy's line by flank attack. The infantry played a subsidiary role, as in the West, but it was not despised and was used as a reserve force and to take fortified positions or difficult ground. Yet one should not underestimate the effectiveness of the feudal army, and in the contest with the East during the Crusades the ironclad cavalry of Western Europe proved to be extremely effective.

The decline of the feudal order and the rise of the nation-state were the result of many factors, among which the reappearance of infantry and the introduction of gunpowder—both based on technological innovations—were of first if not decisive importance. Contrary to the popular view, it was not gunpowder that unhorsed the armored knight, opening the way for revolutionary change in the social order, but two ancient weapons in new form—the bow and the pike. The first, the longbow, appeared in England early in the thirteenth century and by the end of the century had virtually become the national weapon, encouraged by the monarch and given an important role in battle.

Constructed first of elm and later of yew imported from Italy and Spain, the longbow was six feet long and shot a three-foot arrow. It had an effective range of 200 yards and a maximum range of 400, with a rate of fire of 10 to 12 arrows a minute, much greater than the crossbow. Fired in volley, the feathered arrows made a disconcerting humming sound that added to their effect. The arrow could penetrate mail, but not plate armor, yet its effectiveness on the battlefield in concert with the dismounted knight was sufficient to overcome the cream of the French cavalry. But though the longbow was a better weapon than the crossbow or the first handguns, it was never adopted elsewhere because it was difficult to use and required a lifetime of training.

The demonstration by the English that infantry properly armed and deployed could defeat cavalry was confirmed by the Swiss in the fourteenth century. Free peasants, patriotic, individualistic, and accustomed to the hardships of the rugged land in which they lived, the Swiss in 1291 revolted against the feudal domination of the Hapsburgs. Favored by the nature of the terrain and their effective use of the triple-threat halberd, an eight-foot spear with an axe-blade and a hook, the Swiss proved successful on their own ground. On more level terrain, they would have to face the charge of heavy cavalry. The solution they hit upon was the Greek phalanx and the Macedonian pike, an eighteen-foot spear with a three-foot iron shank. The solid mass of infantry, disciplined and motivated, armed with long pikes, constituted a hedgerow of sharp metal spikes held firmly in place and impenetrable to any charge. On the rim of the phalanx were missile-throwing infantry and inside were the halberdiers for close-in work.

Against the heavily armored knight of the fourteenth century, by now capable of little more than charging straight forward and completely helpless when unhorsed, the Swiss phalanx proved extremely effective. Not only could it stand on the defense against cavalry, but it was capable of taking the offense. The Swiss infantry, unencumbered by heavy armor or equipment, moved swiftly, marching in unison to the sound of music in battle formation. Unhesitatingly, it attacked cavalry, and so fierce was the assault and so terrible were the Swiss in combat, that invariably the cavalry fled the field. Imitated widely and in great demand as mercenaries, the Swiss remained masters of the battlefield until the advent of gunpowder.

# THE AGE OF GUNPOWDER

The English and the Swiss had virtually driven the mounted knight from the field, but infantry was helpless against the inner defense of feudalism, the castle. It was gunpowder that furnished the means for breaching the last citadel of knightly power and destroying the feudal system. The same technology that produced church bells could be used for casting gun barrels, and since it was easier to build a large cannon than a small efficient gun, the first effects of gunpowder were felt in siege warfare. Handguns were clumsy affairs and it would be many years, actually not until the middle of the seventeenth century, before firearms would be sufficiently improved to become the predominant weapon on the battlefield.

The first cannon or bombards, as they were called, were in use in the fourteenth century and by 1450 were being regularly used to reduce fortified positions. By this time they had grown in size, and some were so large as to be virtually immovable. At Constantinople in 1453, the Turks used giant bombards hurling 600-pound stone balls, and no castle or town was safe once the heavy cannons were brought up. No longer could the medieval knight defy his overlord from the safety of his castle. And with this protection gone, the feudal structure on which it was based disintegrated.

The introduction of gunpowder into Europe early in the fourteenth century precipitated a revolution in warfare that had an enormous impact on political institutions, technology, and the beginnings of modern science. The radical effects of this discovery, which substituted the explosive power of a crude mixture of sulphur, saltpeter, and charcoal for the muscle of man, has not been generally appreciated, for the first firearms were inaccurate, short of range, slow to fire, heavy and cumbersome, and sometimes dangerous to the user. Moreover, the full effects of the introduction of gunpowder were not apparent for several centuries; in this sense, it was not a revolution at all. But in its own way, gunpowder had as profound an effect on society as the atomic bomb or the first iron weapons.

The political effects of gunpowder were apparent almost immediately, for it appeared at a time when the feudal monarchs were beginning to assert their authority over their powerful vassals. We have already noted how the early cannon contributed to the destruction of the feudal system. It contributed also to the creation of the new political organism, the nation-state, that arose on the ruins of feudalism in England, France, Spain, and Portugal, and to the importance of the new class of merchants and artisans that was appearing in the towns. The new gunpowder weapons were vastly more expensive than the older siege weapons and required resources of metal ores, a class of artisans skilled in the manufacture of guns, and the capital for supporting this new industry. Only the rising monarchs of the emerging national states in alliance with the new middle class could afford gunpowder weapons. Their costliness therefore contributed indirectly to the rise of centralized national monarchies. "The triumph of gunpowder was the triumph of the national State and the beginning of the end of the feudal order." [21]

The decisive effect of the new weapons, as well as the superiority of the nation-state as a political instrument, was strikingly demonstrated in the French invasion of Italy at the end of the fifteenth century. Divided into numerous city-states and defended by mercenary troops armed with old iron cannon, the Italians suffered a crushing defeat at the hands of the French. The improved cannon with which the French were supplied was only one factor in their success. Perhaps equally important was the effectiveness of the centralized state and the embryonic national army created by Charles VIII. The new national state that had succeeded the feudal system placed in the hands of the monarch the fluid capital of the rising middle class as well as the wealth of the old feudal landowners. The growth of the great banking houses of Europe made available large funds to finance the armies of the monarch, and men with financial experience to serve the royal treasuries and devise new means of raising money for the king. The monarch and his financial advisers were aware also of the dependence of the state on a technology capable of building bigger and better weapons and a commerce and agriculture to pay for them, a recognition that found expresssion in the prevailing economic ideas of the time.

The introduction of gunpowder created many military problems that were resolved only after several centuries of trial and by the gradual improvement of the basic gunpowder weapons. The development of the flintlock musket and the invention of the bayonet in the seventeenth century solved many tactical problems and increased the importance of infantry. Similar improvements in siege warfare also emphasized infantry, for cavalry was of little use in such operations. With the predominance of infantry came an expansion in the size of armies, changes in their composition, and a tactical formation that required strict discipline, constant drilling, and long-term professionals. War in the seventeenth century became more technical and expensive, creating a need for greater skills and increased taxes, thus emphasizing anew the importance of the commercial and manufacturing classes. A pro-

[21] J. D. Bernal, *Science in History, op. cit.,* p. 238.

fessional officer corps was born, and troops, because of the need for year-round training, were retained on a permanent basis. Mercenary armies disappeared and the standing army, involving additional expenses for the monarch, became standard in almost every country. And once armies became permanent institutions, barracks had to be established, administration centralized, uniforms and equipment standardized. These occurrences led ultimately to production, standardization, and interchangeability of parts—the basis of modern industry. Moreover, the methods and practices developed to administer the increasingly complex military arm of the nation-state were found to be so efficient that they were adopted for civilian agencies of the government as well.

These developments were carried further during the next century. As the size of armies and the cost of weapons increased, the expense of maintaining standing armies became enormously high, draining the treasuries of Europe. Prussia spent approximately 90 per cent of its revenue for military purposes in 1752; France, two-thirds of its income for the army alone in 1784. And because of the need for goods and taxes, the authorities discouraged artisans, farmers, and merchants from enlisting. Wars were fought in such a way as to keep costs down and interfere as little as possible with normal civilian pursuits. There was no foraging; armies carried their own supplies. Effective discipline as well as economic considerations required large commissariats, state magazines, and fortified bases well supplied in advance for armies on the march.

The effect of gunpowder on science and technology was as profound as its effect on political and military institutions. Modern industry is based on coal and iron, and both became military necessities after the introduction of gunpowder and the development of cannon and small arms. The output of iron in parts of Europe increased greatly during the sixteenth century in response to military needs, and iron foundries were established for the manufacture of cannon. England quickly assumed a dominant position in the iron industry and its iron-foundries gained an envied reputation for their skill and ingenuity.

They also enjoyed the support of the monarch, for their talents represented a national asset. Elizabeth interested herself in mining and metallurgy, and Charles I maintained an ordnance research workshop at Vauxhall to encourage experiment in military hardware. Technical developments in South Germany and Northern Italy, both centers of the iron industry in the fifteenth century, were the results largely of the demand for cannon, and the leading technical writers of the period devoted considerable attention to the military aspects of their work.

Not only did gunpowder stimulate mining and metallurgy but it also led indirectly to the development of the steam engine. The early iron-foundries required coal in fairly large quantities for their coke-ovens, and this coal was mined in open pits that were often flooded. The search for an efficient means to drain the mines led to a workable fire-driven pump designed by Captain T. Savery of the Royal Engineers, then to the Newcomen engine, and finally to Watt's steam engine. Also, the machinery developed for boring cannon was used to build the cylinders for the early steam engines. "Link by link," says Waldemar Kaempffert, "the chain of inventions that joins gunpowder with iron cannon, iron cannon with coal, coal with steam pumps and steam engines is forged." [22]

Gunpowder presented problems whose solution led to some of the most important developments in science. These problems had to do with the making of the gunpowder, the nature of the explosion, the expulsion of the ball from the cannon, and the flight of the projectile. What caused these phenomena and how could they be improved and controlled? These problems led to a search for the causes of these phenomena and ultimately to important discoveries in chemistry and physics. Gunpowder, one writer has said, blew apart medieval ideas almost as effectively as it did the walls of medieval castles.[23]

Medieval science had, in fact, no explanation for the explosion of gunpowder. It was possible to improve the powder and increase the explosive charge by trial and error, but until the chemical action of the substances involved was understood no real progress could be made. The central problem was combustion, and the search for an understanding of this phenomenon promoted the development of chemistry. Biringuccio's *De la pirotechnia*, the authoritative handbook of its time on the preparation of gunpowder and the metallurgy of the cannon, is now recognized as a classic in the history of chemistry.

The early artillerists did not confine themselves to the chemical composition of gunpowder. They wanted to find out also what happened at the moment of fire. This involved a knowledge of the properties of gas as well as of the nature of metals. The fundamental problem was to explain the rapid expansion of gases.

Hooke and Robert Boyle of the Royal Society conducted experiments on this problem, as did several French scientists at the Académie des Sciences. But a true understanding of the properties of gas did not

[22] Waldemar Kaempffert, "Science, Technology and War," in Jerome G. Kerwin, ed., *Civil-Military Relationships in American Life*, Chicago: University of Chicago Press, 1948, p. 5.
[23] J. D. Bernal, *Science in History, op. cit.*, p. 238.

come until later. It is no coincidence, certainly, that Lavoisier, the father of modern chemistry, was head of the "Regie des Poudres" at the French arsenal.

Gunpowder made its most important contribution to the development of modern science in the field of mechanics. The movement of the projectile posed problems in exterior ballistics (i.e., the study of the flight of the cannon ball) that led ultimately to a new study of dynamics. The problem was to explain the behavior of bodies in violent motion. At the time cannon first appeared, the Aristotelian idea that a body moved only if pushed or was falling was already being challenged. The cannon made possible further study of the problems of motion by artillerymen, and by scientists who were interested in the gun as an engine of projection. Tartaglia's work on Aristotle's dynamics was the result of his investigation of the angle of fire and range of a projectile, and Galileo's study of the trajectory of a projectile was the basis for his statement of the theory of dynamics. It may be said with some justification, therefore, that the effort to solve the problems of ballistics led to the beginnings of Newtonian physics.

The effort to measure the force of gunpowder also attracted the scientists of the period. It was not until the eighteenth century, however, that the problem was solved by Benjamin Robins. The velocity of projectiles was an equally intriguing problem. Robert Hooke worked on it, as did others of the Royal Society, but without success. The experiments on recoil conducted by the Royal Society were more successful and demonstrated that action and reaction were equal. Thus, the sixteenth and seventeenth centuries witnessed enormous progress in the science of dynamics, spurred on by the problems of exterior ballistics. Scientists from Galileo to Newton used ballistics as a vehicle to study inertia and acceleration, the motion of a projectile—problems as old as Aristotle. By the opening of the eighteenth century, the usefulness of ballistics for science came to an end, and it became an aspect of applied physics and mathematics.

Mathematics was the basis of much of the work done on military matters in the seventeenth century, providing the means for doing more exactly and precisely those things that had been done only approximately before. The art of gunnery was in part a science depending on the use of mathematics, as Tartaglia pointed out. Manuals on gunnery emphasized the importance of mathematics. About 1670 Samuel Sturmy wrote that the gunner "ought to have skill in arithmetic . . . to be perfect in the art of decimal arithmetic and to be skillful in geometry . . . to measure heights, depths, breadths and lengths and to draw the plot of any piece of ground." [24]

[24] Quoted in A. R. Hall, *op. cit.,* p. 35.

The construction (and destruction) of fortifications also involved the use of mathematics and a number of early scientists took an active interest in the subject. Michelangelo was once engineer in chief of the fortifications of Florence, and da Vinci, it will be recalled, served the Duke of Milan as military engineer for many years. Seeking employment with the Duke, he wrote in 1481:[25]

> I have a process for the construction of very light bridges . . . and of others more solid, which will resist both fire and sword.
>
> In case of the investment of a place, I know how to drain moats and construct scaling ladders and other such apparatus.
>
> Also, if . . . it is impossible in the siege to make use of bombardment, I have means of destroying every fortress or other fortification if it be not built of stone.
>
> Also, I have means by tunnels and secret and tortuous passage . . . to reach a certain designated point, even under rivers.

Tartaglia also dealt with fortifications in his work on mathematics and Galileo taught the subject at Padua and wrote two treatises on it for his students. Ultimately, Dutch and then French engineers replaced the Italians. By the end of the seventeenth century, fortifications had become virtually a separate corps whose officers were required to have training in mathematics and mechanics.

The art and science of fortification reached its height in the work of Marshal Vauban, Louis XIV's military engineer. Vauban's genius lay not in any theoretical contribution or invention or even in his skill as an engineer, but rather on his technical knowledge, his ability in mathematics, and his understanding of how to utilize science for siege warfare. By extending mathematical techniques and quantitative methods into new fields, he became a pioneer in the field of statistics and, with Robert Hooke, of systematic meteorology. He concerned himself with all aspects of warfare, with the improvement of artillery, infantry weapons, and even naval matters, but his greatness lay, says Henry Guerlac, in the way he reflected the spirit of the age, the *esprit géometrique*.[26]

The utilization of mathematics in various branches of the military art ultimately led to the establishment of schools for the technical education of officers—the first schools of this kind to be established. In France, Henry IV and Richelieu proposed schemes for systematic military education, including the rudiments of science, and in Italy Galileo outlined a program of mathematical and physical studies for the mili-

---

[25] Quoted in J. D. Bernal, *Social Function of Science, op. cit.*, p. 167.
[26] H. Guerlac, *op. cit.*, Chapter II, pp. 26–48.

tary officer. By the end of the seventeenth century, technical education had become an essential part of the training of officers for particular assignments, especially in France. Geometry was taught in French
naval schools as an essential introduction to navigation and fortification, and in the schools of artillery as the basis for an understanding of
ballistics. The French artillery schools were in fact the only places
where science was systematically taught in the eighteenth century, and
it was in them that many of the mathematicians and physicists of the
time received their training.

## THE AGE OF TOTAL WAR

Almost two centuries elapsed before the scientific revolution of the
seventeenth century brought about a fundamental change in the economic and social fabric of Western society, and in the nature of modern warfare. Whether or not these changes had their origins in military
needs, as has been argued, is beside the point; the relationship between
the great technical developments of the eighteenth and nineteenth centuries and the transformation of modern warfare is clearly evident. The
nineteenth century witnessed an enormous expansion in the size of
armies, partly for political reasons. But these large armies or armed
hordes, as they have been called, would have been impossible without
the industrial revolution that enabled fewer men to produce vastly
more than ever before, thus releasing part of the population for military duty and at the same time providing the means for its support.
By harnessing new forms of power—steam, electricity, and internal
combustion fuels—to machines, it became possible to produce the massive quantities of food, clothing, weapons, ammunition, and countless
other items needed by the mass armies of the twentieth century, move
these armies rapidly over land and sea to the field of battle, and keep
them supplied for protracted periods of time.

This revolution in technology may not have been the product of
military necessity, but it owed a great deal, nevertheless, to military
needs. The steam engine, as we have noted, was the result in part of the
development of artillery. Railroads were first built for civilian use, but
the transportation of large armies would have been impossible without
them. The development of dyes, in part for military uniforms, stimulated chemical research and the development of a chemical industry
that ultimately produced more powerful explosives. The heavy metal
industry and large-scale production of steel, the basis of modern industrial civilization, was dependent in large measure on the requirements

of war, on orders for big guns and naval warships. The Bessemer process for making steel was the result of Bessemer's search for metal strong enough to withstand the strain of the rifled cannon he invented. Improvements in communication, the invention of the telephone and wireless, and the development of new means of transportation, the motor car and the airplane, made possible the coordination, direction, and movement of millions of men—an essential requirement of the modern army. And finally, improvements in methods of food storage and medical service made it possible to feed and maintain the health of these millions.

About midway through the nineteenth century the scientific and technological advances that had provided the basis initially for the industrial revolution produced a revolution in military weapons that has continued since. Naval warfare, which for two centuries had rested on the sailing ship of the line, underwent a profound transformation with the introduction of steam power, the use of iron, and then steel plate for construction of the hull, and vastly improved guns that could fire over the horizon. The flintlock musket, the standard infantry weapon since about 1700, was transformed into the modern rifle through a series of technological improvements that began with the invention of the percussion cap and the cylindro-conoidal bullet. Automatic and multiple-firing weapons such as the machine gun made their appearance late in the century and had a profound effect on warfare. It was these automatic weapons as much as anything else that produced the bloody stalemate of World War I. Artillery, which had remained stationary for several centuries, was also improved as a result of developments in metallurgy and ballistics to become the mobile quick-firing, accurate, long-range weapon that created the no-man's land of the Western Front. The airplane and the tank, both children of the internal combustion engine, made their appearance in World War I but were not fully effective as military weapons until World War II.

Despite the tremendous fire power made available by the new weapons, the scale of warfare remained generally limited through the nineteenth century. The next war, most men, soldiers and civilians alike, believed, would be short and could be settled by one or two decisive battles. Only a few men really grasped what the industrial revolution and increased fire power meant in terms of destruction, and to them a war fought with these weapons was unthinkable. "Humanity," wrote the Polish banker Ivan S. Bloch at the turn of the century, "has progressed beyond the stage in which war can any longer be regarded as a possible court of appeal. War between the great industrial powers, therefore, is nothing more than mutual suicide." His description of the next war was prophetic. He foresaw correctly that it would be a war of entrenchments, with the spade as indispensable to the soldier as the rifle: [27]

> At first there will be increased slaughter—increased slaughter on so terrible a scale as to render it impossible to get troops to push the battle to a decisive issue. They will try to, thinking that they are fighting under the old conditions, and they will learn such a lesson that they will abandon the attempt forever. Then, instead of a war fought out to the bitter end in a series of decisive battles, we shall have as a substitute a long period of continually increasing strain upon the resources of the combatants. The war, instead of being a hand to hand contest in which the combatants measure their physical and moral superiority, will become a kind of stalemate, in which neither army being able to get at the other, both armies will be maintained in opposition to each other, threatening each other, but never able to deliver a final and decisive attack.

Bloch was wrong in his estimate of the possibility of war, but right in his understanding of its nature. This new form of warfare had a voracious appetite and consumed supplies and munitions at a prodigious rate. Partly it was a matter of manpower, for an army of ten million men needs far more than an army of one million, while reducing the effective civilian labor force at least by nine million. In addition, the new weapons, the rapid-firing guns and the thousands of vehicles required much more ammunition and fuel. And there were more of them per man than there had ever been before. In Napoleon's time, the ratio of artillery averaged 3 per 1,000 men; in 1916, it was 6 per 1,000—and the guns were rapid-firing. A flintlock fired at most four rounds per minute, a breech loading rifle about 20 per minute, a machine gun 300 to 400 rounds a minute. The bombardment at the third battle of Ypres in 1917 required 321 trainloads of shells, the equivalent of a year's production for 55,000 workers, and on the opening day of Verdun, the Germans dropped 80,000 shells in an area of 500 by 1,000 yards.

Even more conspicuous than their appetite was the destructive power of the new weapons. In the Civil War, largest of the nineteenth century wars and first to employ the fruits of the industrial revolution, deaths on both sides numbered about half a million, with many regiments taking losses as high as 50 per cent. Between February and November 1915, in their effort to break through the German lines, the French and English lost about one and a half million men. At the third battle of Ypres, the British gained 10,000 yards at a cost of 300,000 men. The Battle of Verdun, lasting ten months, produced almost a mil-

[27] Quoted in I. F. Clarke, *op. cit.*, p. 134.

lion casualties, and, at the end, the situation was scarcely any different from what it had been at the start. Nothing more strikingly lays bare the nature of the new warfare produced by the industrial revolution than these figures, providing, as Hanson Baldwin wrote, "a preview of the Pandora's box of evils that the linkage of science with industry in the service of war was to mean." [28]

It was also in World War I that science was deliberately organized and employed for war. After a century-long separation of the scientist and soldier, marked by "a strange obtuseness about technical matters" on the part of the professional soldier, World War I witnessed the reunion of the two. Scientific talent was utilized systematically to aid the war effort, to discover new weapons, improve old ones, and to counter the work of scientists on the enemy side. The contributions of the scientist during the war came in many areas—in submarine, aerial, and chemical warfare, in the development of the tank, and in a wide range of medical problems. In all these, research was carried on with little thought of the cost. Under the stimulus of war, once the political and economic barriers had been lifted, science was able to make enormous progress.

The utilization of science in World War I was in some measure at least the result of pressure by the scientists themselves rather than of any demand for their services from the military. "All the force of scientific ingenuity and scientific organization," wrote the editors of an outstanding British scientific journal, "must be concentrated upon the military and naval operations." There were, according to the editors, hundreds of scientists whose talents were not being used, because the authorities had no understanding of the contribution that science could make to the war effort. "We should possess a scientific corps . . . ," they declared. "The necessity has arisen for surveying the whole scientific field to discover methods of destruction which we may use ourselves or from which our men look to us for protection." [29]

The role of the scientists in World War I foreshadowed the important part they played in World War II. Organized more effectively and cooperating on the international level, they scored startling achievements. The atomic bomb, incorporating the latest discoveries in science, was their most spectacular success. But there were others of first importance in the winning of the war and in new technologies afterward. Radio and electronic research was greatly accelerated during the war, and the need for light, compact equipment led to miniaturization. The application of radiation physics and information theory produced

[28] Hanson W. Baldwin, *World War I: An Outline History*, New York: Harper & Row, 1962, p. 159.
[29] Quoted in J. D. Bernal, *Social Function of Science, op. cit.*, p. 188.

a number of useful military (and civilian) devices, such as telecommunication, radar, proximity fuses, and guided missiles. Jet propulsion was a product of the war, as was synthetic rubber, plastics, DDT, penicillin, the jeep, the bulldozer, and a host of other devices and products that have become an integral part of postwar life.

The scientist served in World War II in yet another way. For the first time he moved onto the battlefield and applied his knowledge and methods to military operations, and even plans, advising the soldier on a variety of operational problems, tactical and strategic. This activity came to be called operations research, defined as "the use of scientific method, particularly that of measurement, to arrive at decisions on which executive action can be based." [30] It proved its value early in the war in meeting the German submarine threat and in the bombing of Germany, and was expanded rapidly to solve problems in other areas.

The methods of operations research, at first confined to the physical sciences, were equally applicable to other forms of activity, in fact, to almost any complex human organization. By the end of the war, it was being employed for the analysis of military plans and the evaluation of weapons systems and tactics before they had been used. The development of computer technology, which provided the means for testing mathematically any complex situation that can be stated quantitatively, increased enormously the use of operations research and led to refinements and improvements in the methods employed. The computer also made possible the application of operations research to a variety of activities, civilian and military, to industrial operations and market research, and to situations involving political and military conflict.

Except for the atomic bomb, World War II produced no new weapons. But the improvement of existing weapons such as the airplane and the tank as well as a better understanding of their use wrought a profound change in the nature of warfare between the first and second World Wars. The static trench warfare of 1914–1918 with its enormously high casualty rate gave way in 1939 to the *Blitzkrieg*, a lightning war of movement. Warfare became mobile again and ground casualties declined. But the capacity for destruction through air power greatly increased. In the allied attack on Hamburg an estimated 60,000 people died. Twice as many were killed in the bombing of Dresden in February 1945. One B-29 raid on Tokyo destroyed 16 square miles of the city and killed 84,000 people. By 1945 the destructive power of the new weapons had become so great that many began to wonder once more whether such destruction did not exceed the use of war as a rational instrument of policy. Moreover, the doctrine of

[30] J. D. Bernal, *Science in History, op. cit.*, p. 581.

strategic airpower that justified the bombardment of centers of population and industry raised serious questions about the morality and purposes of war.

The development of the atomic bomb, even as World War II was coming to an end, increased enormously the capacity for destruction, and, with the rapidly advancing technology in jet propulsion, electronic guidance systems, and nuclear-powered submarines, produced a fundamental and far-reaching change in the nature of war. It altered also the nature of diplomacy and international relations, raised grave domestic problems, and emphasized military institutions in a society that had been traditionally anti-military.

The most striking characteristic of nuclear weapons, utilizing an entirely new source of power, was the level of destruction now available to man. Less evident but equally important were the range, speed, and accuracy of the means of delivery provided by a rapidly advancing technology. For centuries the capacity for destruction and the range of weapons had been increasing, but this new increase was of such an order of magnitude as to constitute a difference in kind rather than degree. Most of recorded history lies between the spear or the bow and the flintlock musket. But there is little difference in their effective range, accuracy, or rate of fire. In the fifty years since the first successful flight by the Wright Brothers, the range has been increased from yards to hundreds of thousands of miles. As significant is the increase in the speed of delivery. In the decade since 1955, the intercontinental ballistic missile has expanded both the range and speed so radically as to destroy almost altogether the factors of time and distance.[31]

Before the advent of gunpowder, a weapon usually could kill only one soldier at a time and not a great many over a span of time. Even the rifle and machine gun, though they greatly increased the numerical capacity for destruction, could kill only one man at a time. Explosive shells and aerial bombs changed all that. A single fire raid of World War II could destroy 4,000 or 5,000 people; a nuclear attack, millions. Theoretically, there is no limit to the damage that can be wrought by nuclear weapons.

For the United States one of the most important consequences of this increased destructiveness and range of weapons was the loss of the security it had enjoyed at such small cost for 150 years—a security provided by distance and two oceans. Absolute security was no longer attainable and the price for even partial security rose to astronomical figures, accounting for more than half the annual budget. At no time

[31] This and the subsequent material is drawn from a lecture given at a Conference on the Requirements of Peace sponsored by the New Hampshire Council on World Affairs, March 31–April 1, 1967.

before 1945, except in time of war, had the cost of security been more than one per cent of the gross national product; since then it has risen to ten per cent. And the size of standing military forces has risen from less than 100,000 at the turn of the century to over two million in 1964 —before the advent of the war in Vietnam.

The loss of security and the nature of the new weapons have been responsible also for important changes in the American scene. They lie behind the strategy of deterrence that has shaped our military forces; they have led to an extension of the American frontier to the Rhine and the offshore islands of Asia, and to the intricate alliance system designed to defend this frontier; they have resulted in a close partnership of the military and industry—what President Eisenhower termed the military-industrial complex; and finally, they have given the military services—as well as the scientists—an increasingly prominent role in the formulation of national policies.

By 1945, war, horrible as it was, had achieved a relative stability. The revolution in military technology after 1945 destroyed this stability and created an imbalance between the new weapons and the military systems that had evolved over the previous century. The new weapons have also given the advantage to the offense in the age-long struggle between the offense and the defense. Historically, the defense has usually predominated, and every new weapon has been countered by another. The Russians are said to have deployed an antiballistic missile system around Moscow and Leningrad, and the Secretary of Defense has announced that the United States will follow suit, presumably as a defense against the Chinese. Nuclear weapons, as well as the more sophisticated conventional weapons, have made modern war more complex and technical—even in Vietnam. Troops must therefore be more highly trained than ever before to use and maintain the intricate and expensive weapons put into their hands.

In a very real sense, war today for the first time in recorded history is really total. Up to now, even in the two World Wars, the totality of war was only relative, limited in the final analysis by the destructiveness and range of weapons. Today, thanks to science, there are theoretically no limits except those we impose on ourselves. This fact, combined with the dangers of war by accident, miscalculation, and irrationality, has placed increased emphasis on earlier forms of warfare, since no means have yet been devised to abolish war as a way of resolving differences among nations when all other means have failed. It has also given increased urgency to the importance of reaching agreements, first on control and limitation of the production and use of nuclear devices, and secondly on the reduction and ultimate abolition of nuclear weapons. Total disarmament and the abolition of war, the dream of many, may be the only final solution if mankind is not to perish by its own hand. War has existed in every organized society we know, and generally has served a purpose considered essential for the survival of that society. It is now a real question whether war has not outlived its usefulness as a social institution and whether man, if he is to survive, must not find a substitute to provide security for the nation and to resolve international conflicts. Perhaps science, by making war so destructive that it can lead to the end of civilization, has after all created the conditions for peace.

# 3.

## LANGUAGE RATIONALIZATION AND SCIENTIFIC PROGRESS

### BY CHARLES F. GALLAGHER
*American Universities Field Staff*

Where nature shows a new principle of growth the mind must find a new method of expression, and move toward other goals.
—Santayana [1]

There is widespread agreement that language is at the minimum an essential element of the totality that goes under the name of culture: ". . . that complex whole which includes knowledge, belief, art, morals, law, customs, and any other capabilities and habits acquired by man as a member of society." [2] Linguists and anthropologists have argued for much of this century about the exact nature of the relationship—about language in culture as opposed to language and culture —and the discussion has been sharpened by trenchant hypotheses of the kind presented by Whorf and his supporters; but as to the fact that a deep involvement exists there is little dispute. On that score Kroeber puts it with clarity that, "Cultures are larger, more varied and compli-

[1] George Santayana, *Reason in Science* (Vol. 5 of *The Life of Reason*), New York: Collier Books, 1962, p. 148.
[2] Edward Burnett Tylor, *Anthropology: An Introduction to the Study of Man and Civilization*, as quoted in Harry Hoijer, "Linguistic and Cultural Change," in Dell Hymes, ed., *Language in Culture and Society*, New York: Harper and Row, 1964, p. 455.

58

cated sets of phenomena than languages, as well as more substantive and less autonomous. But the two are interrelated—in fact, language is obviously a part of culture, and probably its precondition. . . ." [3]

Standing in a central position within the framework of culture, language is holistically concerned with all facets of it, reflecting like a prism the separate elements that make up its sum. And of these, it falls into a special relationship with the branch of knowledge commonly termed science. For science we may take the fundamental definition given by Santayana:

> Science . . . is common knowledge extended and refined. Its validity is of the same order as that of ordinary perception, memory, and understanding. Its test is found, like theirs, in actual intuition, which sometimes consists in perception and sometimes in intent. The flight of science is merely longer from perception to perception, and its deduction more accurate of meaning from meaning and purpose from purpose . . . [4]

The relationship is explicit in that, as Bloomfield has written,[5] "linguistic science is a step in the self-realization of man," in which it is in harmony with the other sciences; and it is implicit in that the study of and concern for language in Western civilization developed chronologically alongside the growth of the scientific spirit in post-Renaissance Europe and was intimately connected with the founding of scientific academies and institutes. The study of language had developed out of philology, the first pre-modern flowering of which was seen at the Accademia in Florence in 1540, and it was concerned with culture in both the humanistic and scientific senses of the word. From there language and science spread in close communion to the Académie Française (1635) and the Académie des Sciences (1666), to the real Academia Española (1713), and in the same century to Russia (1725), Denmark (1742), Sweden (1786) and throughout the petty states of Germany just at the time that German was emerging as a major literary and philosophical language.

Potter points out that, "Linguistics stands in its right place in the Dewey Decimal Classification between sociology and natural science"[6] because language is a social function on the one hand and a scientific system on the other. It refines and defines at one and the same time; it classifies phenomena and puts order into them while it opens

[3] Dell H. Hymes, "Alfred Louis Kroeber," in D. Hymes, ed., *op. cit.*, p. 697.
[4] G. Santayana, *op. cit.*, p. 29.
[5] Leonard Bloomfield, *An Introduction to the Study of Language*, New York: Holt, 1914, p. 325.
[6] Simeon Potter, *Language in the Modern World*, Middlesex: Penguin, 1960, p. 175.

the imagination and generates a cloud of associations which give expression to every fleeting thought and dream. Language is, as Kroeber again points out, ". . . easily the most nearly autonomous, self-consistent, and self-contained unit which is discernible within the totality of culture." [7]

The elusive, twofold nature of language and the intricate relationship in which it stands to other facets of culture while preserving its integrity and autonomy permit another kind of confluence to be discerned between language and science; more specifically between change and development in language on the one hand, and the steady progress in the domain of scientific endeavor on the other. It is the purpose of this tentative paper to try to indicate some of the configurations of the congruence and their consequences, with special reference to some of the major non-Western languages with which the writer is familiar.

A number of basic premises can be briefly set out and then examined in relevant detail:

(1) The outstanding fact of the past two or three centuries has been the greatly increased degree of control by man over his environment, and his resultant ability to shape consciously many, but not all, elements of his culture.

(2) Those capabilities and forms of knowledge which derive from the areas of culture that are the domain of the exact sciences in the modern world have been and are those subject to the highest degree of control.

(3) As such the branches of modern science increasingly demand a precise, rational, and adaptable form of thought and a correspondingly adequate method of expressing and presenting that thought.

(4) Linguistic change has taken place continuously and gradually throughout history, but with the rarest exceptions change has been unplanned, unsystematic, and sporadic.

(5) Beginning in the seventeenth century, however, a correlation may be noted between (a) the tendency of a society to accelerate technical progress and to turn toward more modern forms of social organization, and (b) moves to control and order the structures of the language of that society in the direction of rationalization, standardization, simplification, specialization, and greater precision.

(6) Moves to control and/or restructure a language or parts of it may exist in conjunction with spontaneous movements for change. In most cases societies which feel themselves to be in the rear echelons of technical progress indicate a desire to exercise control through fairly coercive means, although that desire is not always effectively carried

[7] D. Hymes, *op. cit.*, Foreword, p. xvii.

out. In a few cases planned and unplanned changes occur in striking symbiosis.

(7) Sustained, rapid change (as opposed to faddism) tends to occur in periods of heightened intellectual activity, marked social change, and noticeable technical progress, whether the stimuli be primarily external or internal.

(8) All languages as systems are potentially equal for the expression of new thought and ideas, but as social realities they very according to the attitudes and values which underlie them and in respect of the historical circumstances that have shaped their present structures and content.

(9) As scientific progress and the modernization of society is an unending phenomenon, so the modernization of word and language is ceaseless. All languages without exception, therefore, are having and will continue to have relative degrees of difficulty in adapting to the constantly increasing complexities of modernism, depending on the social setting in which they have developed and now function. There can be found relatively "closed" and relatively "open" languages (cf. below on these categories) in roughly comparable societies, but the requirements of modernism lead inevitably from the more "closed" end to the more "open." The classic *reductio ad absurdum* in this respect has been cited by Bar-Hillel, using English and Choctaw as examples.[8]

## MODERN SCIENCE AND MODERN LANGUAGE

It is of course obvious that language and science are only partially tangential. Their area of congruence is in one respect basic, however, and that is that modern science and modern languages are both required to organize the phenomena they describe in as rational and precise a way as possible. It is in rationality and preciseness that prose differs from poetry, and that modern technical language—in which despite a currently fashionable disparagement there should be included technical jargon and "governmentalese"—differs from much other prose. Rationalization itself, however, is a spectrum at one end of which we find extreme specialization while at the other we see a very general systematization. Thus the extension of rationalization in itself opens a multitude of potentials for new arrangements and categories and becomes the basis for further flowerings of intuitive thought.

[8] Yehoshua Bar-Hillel, *Language and Information: Selected Essays on Their Theory and Application*, Reading: Addison-Wesley Publishing Co., and Jerusalem: The Jerusalem Academic Press, Ltd., 1964, pp. 56ff.

Ray has suggested that the "value" of a language can be measured only in terms of a very similar spectrum: [9] a "gain in closure" which provides semiotic uniformity and semantic solidarity, balanced by a concomitant "gain in opening" which allows for semiotic and semantic accommodation and assimilation. The task of rationalization which is assigned to a modern language—to which languages have been forced by the needs of modern society—is precisely this double one. It must provide for the systematic and logical arrangement of an ever-growing number of variables, while leaving open the maximum possibilities for both the further enlargement and the further refinement of the categories established. In fact, the modernity of a language system may be gauged by the degree to which this double rationalization is being effectively performed. It is clear that the task is not an easy one, and it will be pointed out below that some important languages have not yet made much progress in this direction. Indeed, the Whorfian hypothesis claims that from a semantic point of view the task is impossible, in that "What we call 'scientific thought' is a specialization . . . which has developed not only a set of different dialectics, but actually a set of different dialects. These dialects are now becoming mutually unintelligible." [10] This represents an extreme view taken along a quite special sighting line, and it is not subscribed to by most linguists or anthropologists.

A gain in closure, which may be termed standardization, provides a means of rational communication among all segments of a speech community, as well as among specialized subsegments of the community as viewed in the broadest terms. In early periods of standardization, through which the major European languages passed more than a century ago and in which several major non-Western languages now find themselves, the problem of modern, technico-dialectal specialization does not occur. The main effort rather revolves around the reduction of traditional dialectal differences, the reduction of diglossia,[11] and the unification of variant forms in a single "high" tradition. A gain in opening is on the other hand "a standardization of the means of introducing changes as well as an increased coincidence in dissociations and associations of forms and meanings with those of such other languages as are within reach of the speakers of the language in question." [12]

[9] Punya Sloka Ray, *Language Standardization: Studies in Prescriptive Linguistics*, The Hague: Mouton & Co., 1963, pp. 123–37.
[10] Benjamin Lee Whorf, *Language, Thought, and Reality*, New York: John Wiley & Sons, 1956, p. 246.
[11] For a definition of diglossia—"two or more varieties of the same language . . . used by some speakers under different conditions," cf. Charles A. Ferguson, "Diglossia" in D. Hymes, *op. cit.*
[12] P. S. Ray, *op. cit.*, p. 134.

This process builds into the language a sensitivity to innovative patterns of expression and a receptivity to what results from communication with members of other speech communities that may be summed up as adaptability. Both standardization and adaptability are required in reasonable balance for a language to function effectively as a vehicle for modern technical and scientific communication, although languages making strenuous efforts to rationalize themselves may show a temporary tendency toward imbalance at certain times. Modern Israeli Hebrew, for example, although it has been the object of much consciously planned change, is one of the outstanding examples in the world today of a widely open, innovating language with a high degree of adaptability. Similarly, modern Japanese has proceeded from a necessary period of standardization accompanied by innovation in the late nineteenth century, through a second phase of simplification, and has now entered an era of extremely outward-looking experimentation which stresses adaptability. Modern Arabic has for more than a century leaned heavily toward the focus of stabilization at the expense of accommodation to change through adaptability; Turkish and Persian, for quite different reasons, fall in between those extremes, while Bahasa Indonesia, emerging only in the past generation from premodern simplicity, has had little choice but to direct itself toward innovation in an effort to build a reasonably adequate body of vocabulary before it can consider the problems of standardization and stability. In addition to its almost obligatory link with innovation, however, Bahasa underscores another aspect of rationalization: that of specialization and a general "intellectualization"; i.e., a new terminology grafted onto a system not only largely devoid of specialized technical terms but—unlike the other languages just mentioned—unaccustomed to organizing thought on more complex, abstract levels until very recently.

In respect of this last point, languages of very different societies will experience different problems depending on their past experience and emphases. The difficulties of Arabic and other Middle Eastern languages in dealing with many of the abstract political terms imported in the nineteenth century—freedom, nationalism, state, nation, and such [13]—were not paralleled in Japanese where, as Dore points out (despite the well-known clamor over the translation of neologisms such as "rights" *kenri* and a few others), "The new chemists of Meiji had to develop a whole set of new words to express new ways of

[13] Cf. Franz Rosenthal, *The Muslim Concept of Freedom*, Leiden: E. J. Brill, 1960, and Charles F. Gallagher, "Language, Culture, and Ideology: The Arab World" in K. H. Silvert, ed., *Expectant Peoples: Nationalism and Development*, New York: Random House, 1963, for the problem in Arabic. For Turkish, cf. Bernard Lewis, *The Emergence of Modern Turkey*, New York: Oxford University Press, 1961, pp. 126ff.

classifying matter, but the students of politics, law or philosophy found that most of the conceptual distinctions found in their European models were already familiar and could be easily expressed in their own vocabulary." [14] But if in Arabic, Turkish, and Persian there were difficulties in the interpretation of abstract terminology reflecting a different sociopolitical system, there could at least be found abstract alternatives for describing the new ideas and these could be manipulated or modified in most cases. It was a problem of another order of magnitude when it was decided to raise the Malay *lingua franca* of the Indies to the position of a modern, international language.

Keeping in mind that language functions as a kind of internal mirror of the total culture of a society, if we consider it in a wider perspective than that of its relation to scientific progress—with which we are primarily concerned here—we observe a logical connection between the nature and quality of language rationalization and the nature and quality of over-all social development.

The modernization of society, like that of language, demands first an agreed standardizing of norms and principles: the consensus that helps shape the modern, national community. Both equally require a concomitant adaptability to change which can only come into being once the stability of standardization is achieved. And both involve a technical subspecialization which can expand its potential fruitfully and almost without limit to the degree that the two preceding basic requisites are kept in harmonious balance. In traditional societies language patterns tend to be specialized along hierarchically discrete lines consonant with the status of society members and their interpersonal, interclass relationships. The passage from linguistic traditionalism to linguistic modernity has in all cases—whether in England, Turkey, Japan, Indonesia, or elsewhere—been accompanied by a reduction both of hierarchical forms and of diglossia patterns that consecrate widespread attitudinal compartmentalization. The variant forms of traditional social communication are limited and clearly distinguish one from the others. Everyone does not "speak" to everyone else, nor is there felt the need for a common language that would allow for and further universal communication within the society. The forming of such a vehicle has historically been the companion to, and may even be a precondition for the growth of modern societies, in which the ideal is to eliminate traditional social compartmentalization in terms of class and status (and hence the compartmentalization of communication), while furthering—just as modern scientific and technical modes of

14 Ronald P. Dore, *Education in Tokugawa Japan*, Berkeley and Los Angeles: University of California Press, 1965, pp. 303-304.

expression do to an extreme with regard to language—the modern sub-specializations of role and function.


## THE TURKISH CASE

Of all major non-Western languages, Turkish probably offers the outstanding example of dramatic change associated with a preoccupation about technical inferiority and a concern for closing the material gap separating Turkey from European states. The Turkish case is instructive not only for the sweeping nature of the changes undertaken, but also because the Turks were the first non-Western people to become fully aware of protomodern European technical and scientific capacities as early as the first half of the eighteenth century. They were also the first Asian society to grasp the idea that internal language backwardness was related to technical lag, and to talk openly of basic structural reform rather than of mere surface refurbishment. The thoroughgoing nature of the Turkish reforms is shown by the fact that, even putting aside the romanization of the script, Ottoman Turkish texts of around 1900 are essentially unrecognizable foreign documents to the modern Turk. Similarly the Constitution of 1924, which contains an abundance of Arabic and Persian words and grammatical forms, must be explained to Turkish students, and even the famous speech of Mustafa Kemal (Atatürk) to the National Assembly in 1927 is so archaic that it must be accompanied by a gloss which "translates" it for present-day schoolboys. In no other society has there been effected in so short a time so drastic a transformation in both the form and content of the national language.

Although the most profound changes were made under the Republic after 1923, the reform of Turkish appropriately began during the long Tanzimat (Reform) Era (1839–76), when almost all aspects of Ottoman life were subjected to critical scrutiny.[15] In 1862 a Turkish civil servant engaged in translating Western scientific and scholarly works significantly proposed a reform of the alphabet "as a necessary pre-

[15] Cf. Roderic H. Davison, *Reform in the Ottoman Empire, 1856–1876*, Princeton: Princeton University Press, 1963; Serif Mardin, *The Genesis of Young Ottoman Thought: A Study in the Modernization of Turkish Political Ideas*, Princeton: Princeton University Press, 1962; and B. Lewis, *op. cit.* Lewis is especially valuable for a summary account of the language question, pp. 419–431, which he bases on the comprehensive monograph of Uriel Heyd, *Language Reform in Modern Turkey*, Jerusalem: 1954. Cf. also "Venticinque anni di rivoluzione dell'alfabeto e venti di riforma linguistica in Turchia," in *Oriente Moderno*, xxxiii, 1953. In Turkish, cf. Agah Sirri Levend, *Türk Dilinde Gelişme ve Sadeleşme Safhalari*, Istanbul: 1949.

liminary to the advancement and dissemination of science," and again significantly this proposal was made before the Ottoman Scientific Society, founded two years before. Controversy over the adequacy of Arabic script continued and was reinforced when the Persian Ambassador in Istanbul wrote to a newspaper in 1869 agreeing that the inadequacy of that alphabet was the basic cause of the poverty and backwardness found in Muslim countries.

In the ensuing decade questions of content as well as of form were taken up. The first moves were made to drop obscure and obsolete Perso-Arabic baggage from the vocabulary; these usages were replaced by common Turkish terms. Meanwhile a few important writers of prose broke with the "high chancery" style, and in the years just before World War I the resuscitated press played an increased role in these language changes. The Young Turk movement (1908–18) was anxious that the reform message of the government be widely understood, and the decade of their rule gave much impetus to the development of a simpler Turkish, as did the First World War. The Minister of War, Enver Pasha, invented a script of modified Arabic letters for use by officers in dispatches, a telegraphic style was invented, and the language was further shaped by propaganda delivering the word of the authorities in easy-to-understand terms to Turkish soldiers. By 1918, more or less, the old "high Ottoman mandarin style" was dead, and in its place there was coming into being a flexible and living language arising in good part from the spoken language of the urban educated classes, although it was one which still had a large foreign vocabulary, was still written in Arabic script, and contained a substantial measure of diglossia vis-à-vis the true vernacular.

Following the revolution and the proclamation of the Republic in 1923, serious attention was given to the idea of romanization, which had been discussed as far back as 1878. Political as well as purely technical questions were concerned (for the Soviet Union had at that time changed the script used by Turkish-speaking peoples in its territory from Arabic to Latin, later again changing it to Cyrillic). Nonetheless, romanization appealed to Atatürk primarily as a way of cutting off the new Turkey from what he regarded as the dead weight of the past. This objective was made easier by the fact that only ten per cent of the population was literate (1927) and participated in the Perso-Arabic Ottoman literary heritage. The new script was adopted in November, 1928, and Arabic letters were prohibited from the beginning of 1929. Atatürk himself gave public lessons in the new script and much compulsion was used, notably on members of the National Assembly itself.

Romanization was followed by a large-scale purge of the language, carried out by the government-sponsored Turkish Linguistic Society (*Türk Dili Tetkik Cemiyeti*—later restyled in "purer" Turkish *Türk Dil Kurumu*), starting in 1932. This program was executed as a quasi-military operation with bureaus dealing with linguistics, grammar, terminology, etymology, lexicography, and other areas of the language. The task of the Society—the simplification and the purification of the language—was not unique, but the radical way in which the reform was executed and the enormous pressure applied by the government in support of it was unprecedented. The remaining Arabic and Persian grammatical intrusions in Turkish were eliminated and an effort was made to remove by "deportation" all words from those languages in Turkish and not merely obsolete, rare, or archaic terms. Simultaneously scholarly committees sought to uncover pure Turkish roots from the past or from spoken dialects to serve as replacements. European terms were left untouched, and were even imported in quantity to substitute for some of Arabic or Persian origin that were displaced.

As with some other reforms early in the Republic, excess was the order of the day, particularly in the claim made for a Turkish origin for all languages, which thus justified the foreign words that had to be left in the national vocabulary. The "deportation" was only partly carried out, but reform continued at a steady pace and by the time of the 6th Congress of the Society in 1949 exotic theories had given way to a sober and scholarly attempt to continue the simplification and modernization of the language as a continuing process without nationalist bombast.

The accomplishments of the Turkish language reform can be summarized as:

(1) The creation of a simplified and clear national language, now taught to and understood by all Turks.

(2) The elimination of the last diglossia in Turkish.

(3) A nationalization of the language accompanied by a neo-internationalization, in which foreign technical terms—and a good many non-technical ones as well—were taken from the dominant culture of the age, the West, to replace learned words once borrowed from the sometime ascendant high cultures of the Middle East.

(4) A major modification of the principal aspects of the language—script, syntax, and vocabulary—in the direction of rationalization.

The question remains as to what the effects of such changes have been on modern Turkish society in broad terms and on the adoption of modern scientific thought and method in particular. As Lewis has encapsulated it, "All these changes in the manner and form of expression were, in the last analysis, secondary to the greater and infinitely more difficult process of changing the ideas expressed."

Although it is still early to pass judgment, for only one generation of scholars and scientists trained under the new system has come of age and is now mature, preliminary evidence suggests that the transference of foreign "style" is proving more difficult. The output of scientists and well-trained technicians in Turkey is still quite low. Research is scanty and the scientific mentality is far from having taken hold. In part the slowness may be attributable to the fact that the educational system even at higher levels is still mostly statist and rigid in its conceptions. Moreover, a certain "intellectual diglossia" of the spirit prevails in Turkey; popular sentiment is hesitant and current usage has not yet digested all the sophisticated innovations and borrowings injected into the language. In this respect the masses have to be led, if not pushed along, by a small élite group. In short, language modernization has not yet taken root to the extent that it proceeds spontaneously and without plan, and the intellectual processes on which scientific achievement depends are still only partly formed.

Nevertheless, advances can be seen. Turkish scholars of this generation show a self-awareness, objectivity, and capacity for self-criticism unmatched elsewhere in the Muslim Middle East, and this attitude—noticeable among social scientists in particular—is the basis for all serious future work. The new mentality exists in a number of fields and has been remarked by observers as different in their approach as Smith and Von Grunebaum.[16] Given the adaptability which the Turkish language has begun to show, added to the standardization achieved, the implantation of the Middle East Technical University in the country may produce stimulating results. At METU science is taught in English to an international but primarily Turkish student body, and its interaction with an expanding provincial university system using modern Turkish as the language of instruction will be important. All in all, even if a fully scientific mentality has not yet emerged in Turkey, the linguistic tools for proceeding to build it have themselves been forged. In terms of the analysis of this paper, Turkish has made considerable progress toward equipping itself at both ends of the rationalization spectrum, and the sparks of a firmly controlled and directed reform may at some time in the not-distant future burst into the spontaneous combustion of popular, unplanned change.

[16] Wilfred Cantwell Smith, *Islam in Modern History*, Princeton: Princeton University Press, 1957, Chapter 4, "Turkey: Islamic Reformation?". Gustave E. Von Grunebaum, *Modern Islam: The Search for Cultural Identity*, Berkeley and Los Angeles: University of California Press, 1962.

## THE CASE OF MODERN ARABIC

The development of modern Arabic presents almost totally different configurations of change from those of Turkish. To begin with, Arabic has historically occupied a position within the group of "teacher-languages" rather than "learner-languages." [17] Early in its career as a world language Arabic did borrow a number of specialized words, mainly from Greek and Persian, but it also stopped doing so fairly early on. In the high classical period, beginning in the second half of the ninth century, it became formal and rigid, setting itself into an ossified mold from which it has only recently and with difficulty begun to emerge. Even beyond that, it has at all times borne the burden of sacrality, as the *lugha*, the language of the revelation, the language *par excellence* used as the means of transmitting what was in Muslim eyes the most important and authentic and final communication from God to man. The fact that the Quran, unlike the Bible, is accepted as the direct word of God himself speaking in Arabic cannot be given too much emphasis when considering the history of the development of the language.

During the past thirteen hundred years Arabic has functioned as a largely closed, sacral language for the Middle East and most of the Muslim World beyond. The role of a closed language may be of great value, as has been that of Latin in the terminology of some fields of science—although analogies with Latin are not complete because Latin ceased to be both a spoken vernacular and a sacral language whereas Arabic still is—but it has drawbacks with regard to adaptability and receptivity. Moreover, an extremely rigid standardization of the kind

[17] Most languages have had complex relationships with other languages at varying periods of their history, and most have functioned at some time as both "learner" and "teacher" languages. To take the case of English, it "learned" from at least Norman-French, Latin, and Scandinavian on a large scale, and from other European languages on a minor one; after which it becomes a "teacher" to most of the world. A few early-developed languages such as Chinese, Sanskrit, and to a certain extent Hebrew and Greek, illustrate a process of self-teaching that is somewhat unique, but if more were known about all the details of their antecedents and their initial phases this statement would probably have to be revised as well. Arabic learned from Greek and Persian, and a bit from Latin through contacts with the Roman Empire in pre-Islamic days, but since the ninth century it has been almost exclusively a teacher until modern times. Change in status from "teacher" to "learner" appears to produce psychological troubles, as is evidenced by the attitudes taken by a great number of French writers and intellectuals today regarding the so-called "invasion" of French by English and the resulting *franglais*. French today is of course still an important teacher to much of the world, but it is assimilating a considerably body of modern English words and appears to be reacting to this with some strain.

enjoined upon Arabic for centuries by the weight of religious tradition produces fissures between the ideal norm and the living forces of the language: the result is differences of dialect in diverse regions of the Arab World and a high diglossia within each region.

By the eighteenth century Arabic had moved from rigidity to stagnation. Unlike Turkish or Persian, it was by then no longer widely used in the Middle East as a language of government and administration, and its literary production had dwindled almost to nothing. In effect, the main aim of Arabic reformers since the early nineteenth century has been to revive the language and give it new content while allowing it to keep its sacral quality and letting it benefit from the advantages with which its standardization of form has endowed it. Thus Arabic reform in the past century shows a strong reluctance to admit foreign borrowings in quantity and an often hair-splitting search for internal equivalents, combined with a defensiveness that can be found in other aspects of the culture as well. Added to this bent is the related problem of semantic anarchy in new coinings, stemming from the lack of effectively exercised responsibility and culminating in the proliferation of divergent new terminology. Taken together with the multiple dialectal differences and the diglossia already mentioned, this confusion makes for as severe a set of problems as those faced by any language seeking to modernize.

It is something of a paradox that the Arab revival of the past century began with and has always given a prominent place to a renaissance of the Arabic language.[18] Indeed, the special place of Arabic in the dreams of Arab modernizers and the limited results so far attained in opening up the language are still another indication of the painful problems presented to it. Reform began in the second quarter of the nineteenth century under the stimulus of foreign mission activity and the importation of the first printing presses in the Levant, and in Egypt with government subsidies to a translation bureau. For some time efforts by men like Nasif Yaziji and Butrus Bustani were directed toward purifying the language of latter-day involutions by returning to the pure, classical sources. A parallel to this movement in politics and religion can also be found, and the preoccupation with the classical norm of a golden age led Arab writers and linguists into the domain of history, whereas the exigencies of military and imperial affairs turned men's minds in Ottoman Turkey toward the practical and technical end of the language spectrum. In both cases, of course, as almost everywhere, language reform had some connection with nationalism, but in contrast to the Ottoman emphasis on the material and the prac-

18 Cf. Albert Hourani, *Arabic Thought in the Liberal Age (1798–1939)*, London and New York: Oxford University Press, 1962.

tical, Arab intellectuals associated linguistic renovation with an ideal life which could be hoped for in the future but could only be looked for in the distant past, and which was in sharp contrast to the powerless state they found themselves in at the time.

In another seeming paradox, the work of reforming the language was left for almost a century to a small number of individuals— writers, linguists, historians, and journalists. Private groups like the Syrian Scientific Society were formed as early as 1857, but their influence was limited. In Egypt intermittent progress was made under occasional official encouragement but the British occupation (1882–1914) meant an enlarged need for English and a slowing down of the Arabic revival in official circles. This foreign intrusion was compensated for in some measure, however, by the freedom given to an expanding press and a nascent theater. It was not until the tenure of Hishmat Pasha as Minister of Education (1910–13), however, that Arabic replaced English as the language of instruction in secondary schools, that encyclopedic works in Arabic were published, and that a series of committees for the translation of scientific terms into Arabic and for the translation of science texts were formed. The language of instruction in higher education was English or French for some time, but it has gradually been replaced by Arabic for all subjects except the sciences in the United Arab Republic today.[19] Likewise in Iraq, Jordan, and all other Arab countries of the Middle East with one exception, university-level science courses are given in English, with occasional simultaneous translation into Arabic that produces a hybrid lecture neither part of which is fully understandable in many cases. The exception is Syria, where instruction in all subjects is given in Arabic. As Qubain notes in his recent study of education and science in the Arab World,[20] ". . . This creates serious problems, particularly in the various science fields." While it is true that Syrian universities have deteriorated in quality owing to an endemic political irresponsibility and the misuse of students for political ends during the past two decades, the meager results of science education in Syria would also seem linked to the insistence on using a language not yet equipped for the tasks assigned it.

Although the Arab Academy of Damascus was founded in 1919 with the stated goals of "working in service of Arab science and language" (*hidma al'ilm wa-l lugha al 'arabiy ya*), the principal instrument of language reform in the Arab countries in recent decades has been the Arabic Language Academy (ALA) founded in Cairo in 1932 (*Majma'*

[19] This is true at this writing except for Assiut University, a relatively minor component of the Egyptian university system, where instruction in the sciences is given in Arabic.

[20] Fahim Qubain, *Education and Science in the Arab World*, Baltimore: Johns Hopkins Press, 1966, p. 448.

*al Lugha al 'Arabiyya,* originally called the Fuad I Academy). The main aims of the ALA are to "preserve the purity of the Arabic language, to furnish adequate terms for the needs of science and technology, and in general to adapt the language to modern life." Most of the Academy's work has been devoted to expanding the technical vocabulary of modern Arabic. Subsidiary activities include publishing dictionaries of technical terms, dictionaries for students, laying down the groundwork for an etymological dictionary, and making rules relating to grammar and orthography in order to simplify the language for the modern student. The question of romanizing the script has been raised and rejected. The publication of comprehensive dictionaries has proceeded very slowly, although it should be noted that similar enterprises in English and other European languages have required decades and even, in the case of the Académie Française, more than three centuries.

In 1957 the ALA published a preliminary body of technical terms adopted by it, of more than 11,300 words. Taken along with the terms adopted at various Arab Scientific Congresses held under the sponsorship of the Arab League since 1953 and the results of the work of the Arab Scientific Union founded in Egypt in 1955, a total of some 30,000 technical terms (some of which overlap or are in disaccord) have been rendered into Arabic. An analysis of the 1957 Academy corpus made by Monteil,[21] comparing it to the work of the Congresses, the ASU, the Damascus Academy, and already existing popular scientific translations, illustrates the problem of semantic anarchy effectively. The largest segment of the corpus is devoted to medicine (3,700 words), followed by law and government, natural sciences, and mathematics. Although the administrative and legal terms suggested often do not coincide with those in actual usage, problems here are of a lesser order than in the scientific domain: *qanun asasi* (basic law) will be understood by the layman as easily as *dustur* for "constitution." In medicine and the natural sciences, though, we find five words in use for "thermometer," three for "pneumonia," six for "pancreas," three for "space," four for "vertical," and five for "coefficient." [22] Examples of directly opposed usage in neighboring Arab states make exchanges of scientific work difficult. "Energy" (*taqa*) in Egypt and Lebanon is *qudra* in Syria, and "force" is the converse in both cases. Likewise, *dharra* is now standard for "atom" in all Arab countries but Syria, which reserves the word for "molecule," which is itself *juzai'* elsewhere. Interdisciplinary rivalries also have their place, with members of a committee from one field frequently ignorant that a term has

[21] Vincent Monteil, *L'Arabe Moderne,* Paris: C. Klincksieck, 1960.
[22] *Ibid,* pp. 203–209.

come into fairly standard use in another. Perhaps in no area is the confusion as great as in zoology and botany, where naturalists the world over employ Latin binomials, but where the Arabs have for over fifty years persisted in seeking tortuous equivalents for Latin terminology which they hesitate to incorporate into the language.[23]

The catalogue of terminological anarchy, excessive synonyms, and classificatory confusion could be extended almost indefinitely but without useful purpose. The problem should be viewed as the reflection of a cultural attitude which on the whole still refuses to make the profound adjustments required for linguistic survival in the technical jungle of the modern world, for the ALA and kindred organisms are falling behind the output of technical terms at the sources of science in Western countries and linguistic confusion has not decreased in the past decade.

Qubain makes a brief reference to the "Language Problem" in his study, but even he as a foreigner looking at the language from the outside argues against the use of Arabic in scientific education. He favors another language less because of Arabic's present incapacities than because of the need of scientists and engineers to read journals written in a handful of international languages, and because ". . . for the time being, science instruction in Arabic would greatly reduce the contacts of Egyptian scientists and engineers with the mainstream of scientific research," and also because such instructions ". . . would of necessity involve a rather extensive translation program . . . [requiring] the employment of topflight specialists . . . badly needed for research, teaching, and other vital activities." [24] The UAR government has recently decided to give first-year science in Arabic and couple such courses with continued instruction in English, thus continuing to pursue its policy of Arabization in all areas.

The statements of Ahmed Zaki, (then) Director of the National Research Council of Egypt, in a study of the renovation of Arabic made by him for UNESCO,[25] illustrate some of the attitudinal difficulties involved. According to the writer, ". . . the renovation of Arabic to meet modern needs has been and still is a matter of individual endeavour, and this is the natural way of growth. . . . A special prob-

---

[23] V. Monteil, *op. cit.*, p. 177ff.
[24] F. Qubain, *op. cit.*, p. 89.
[25] Ahmed Zaki, "The Renovation of Arabic" in *The Use of Vernacular Languages in Education* (UNESCO Monographs on Fundamental Education), Paris: UNESCO, 1953. A less dogmatic view is taken by Amir Boktor, *The Development and Expansion of Education in the United Arab Republic*, Cairo: The American University in Cairo Press, 1963, pp. 167-169, but the passages devoted to "The Language Problem" treat it in an offhand way and give little indication of its gravity.

lem arises with scientific terms. It is desirable that these be international, but words of Greek or Latin origin are unsuitable for popular use among Arabic speaking people. . . . Many words which have been introduced fairly recently and rather hurriedly (*sic*) into Arabic will always remain foreign to the language, either by the strangeness of their form or because they do not suggest to the Arabic mind any association between them and the thing named. Of most of these the language could well be purged." [26] Referring to the protection of sacrality, especially noteworthy is his comment that, "Apprehension lest the introduction of colloquial words into written Arabic contaminate the language of the Koran might be allayed by providing an annotated glossary of all terms in the Koran. . . . This collection would then be at the disposal of those who seek new terms, and thus give the words of the Koran a permanent place in the language of the people."

Broadly viewed, Arabic is an extreme example of a language whose closed quality derives primarily from a religious tradition akin to taboo. Therefore it is finding great difficulty in arranging some way to take advantage of its potential of adaptability. It has other real problems, too, the result of geographical diffusion and political fragmentation. But they, too, are partly psychological, in that language problems, like all problems in the Arab World, are linked with political issues and tend to become a subject for polemics and apologetics. What would be most beneficial to the Arabs as a whole and to Arabic would be for one government to plunge firmly ahead with a massive program for the translation of technical terminology by the most rapid and efficacious means possible, including direct large-scale borrowing, and to supplement this campaign with a program of textbook translation and pub-

---

[26] Cf. below for a different view. In "European Loan Words in Contemporary Arabic Writing: A Case Study in Modernization," *Middle Eastern Studies*, Spring, 1967, Charles Issawi compares the frequency of borrowings from European languages in modern, literary Arabic with those in similar prose forms of Turkish, Persian, and Uzbek. The samples are taken from modern novels for the most part and they deliberately avoid the technical terminology that is the focus of this paper. Nonetheless, the conclusions reinforce the general impression given by each language with regard to its adaptability both in general literary and in technical terminology. Issawi found Persian ". . . distinctively more receptive to European words than Arabic," and for Turkish he notes that ". . . the incidence of European words is 3 times as high as in Persian and about 10 times as high as in Arabic." Uriel Heyd, *op. cit.*, estimated the number of European words in newspaper Turkish at from five to ten per cent of the total. (Newspaper writing usually shows a higher frequency of borrowings than do more purely literary efforts.) By way of comparison, Minoru Umezaki, in *Nihon Gairaigo no Kenkyū*, Tokyo: Kenkyusha, 1963 (one of the latest and best works on the subject), evaluates the number of foreign words in modern (i.e., c. 1960) Japanese at just under ten per cent of the total vocabulary. I have no figures for Israeli Hebrew or Bahasa.

lishing. Some initial time loss would be sustained and the risk of cutting some communication temporarily with other Arab countries would have to be taken. Under the circumstances the lead could hardly come from any country except the UAR, but the present politico-psychological context is unfavorable to any move that would seem to imply subservience to Western "cultural imperialism." As Egypt has become an increasingly closed society in recent years, more and more cut off from its once extensive cultural contacts with the West, so Arabic is tending to withdraw further into itself as it is used in the pivotal country of the Arab World, and it is seeking its opening in another kind of closure. As Monteil observes, however, the price of the scientific development of the Arab World is linguistic "unity, precision, and rigor, and the alternative is *ta:ahhur*, or backwardness." [27]

## THE CASE OF ISRAELI HEBREW

A discussion of the problems of modern Arabic almost inevitably calls for a short comment on the solutions of a sister language, Israeli Hebrew, if only to note that there is no inherent incapacity in Semitic languages insofar as structural modernization or absorptive adaptability are concerned. It is well known how different the cultural and attitudinal underpinnings of modern Hebrew are from Arabic, but one has to underline nonetheless the remarkable results attained during roughly half a century in refurbishing Hebrew to the extent that borrowed elements of foreign vocabulary, morphology, and phraseology have been grafted on and absorbed, that new technical terminology has been rapidly created, and that in time a truly new and quite open language has been fashioned on the foundations of a tongue fully as traditional and sacral as Arabic.

Modern Israeli Hebrew is the outstanding example of the concurrence of planned and unplanned linguistic change of all kinds. The movement to revive Hebrew began around the turn of the century, but it was given great impetus by the efforts of some two hundred scholars in the 1920s who added 18,000 words to the traditional vocabulary, of which about 3,000 were of European origin. Since then the modern technical vocabulary has grown without cease. More than one-third of the words in a current standard dictionary are estimated to have been introduced within the past forty years. As Blanc points out,[28] immigrants from Europe brought with them large chunks of the

[27] V. Monteil, *op. cit.*, p. 223.
[28] Haim Blanc, "Hebrew in Israel: Trends and Problems," *Middle East Journal*, Vol. 11, No. 4, Autumn 1957, pp. 397–409.

abstract and technical vocabulary of Standard Average European (SAE) in a somewhat East European variant form; e.g., *stratosfera, prestiža, televizya, metafizika,* et al. Stimulated in part by this vocabulary and SAE morphology, the morphology of modern Hebrew itself has undergone changes so that it is no longer exclusively and typically Semitic. In particular, new systems of prefixes and suffixes have been devised, some taken directly from SAE: (*pro-aravi*), "pro-Arab"; (*anti-mitsri*), "anti-Egyptian"; others formed by analogy: (*tlat-regel*), "tripod"; (*beyn-leumi*), "international"; (*du-kiyum*), "coexistence," et al. And from these verbs have been formed, such as *le-van:em,* "to internationalize," or, as from *ad kan,* "up to here, now," through *adkani,* "up-to-date," there has been coined *le-adken,* "to modernize."

The important points of the Israeli achievement are two. The "establishment" went diligently to work to produce a rapid and vast transformation of the basic technical vocabulary, and in addition an alert and largely literate population, which was not isolated from intellectual developments among the élite, followed by taking control of the language and infusing into it that living, vigorous expressiveness that can only come from daily use by broad masses of the people. Granted that Israel or any state its size has unusual advantages of geographical cohesion and ease of communication amongst the intellectual establishment, the creation of a common working language well equipped for modern tasks in so short a time is proof of Blanc's statement that:

> Languages not only change over long stretches of time, sometimes beyond recognition, but have built-in devices for potential change at relatively short notice. It is meaningless to speak of some linguistic systems as "archaic" in and of themselves, or intrinsically "suited" for one type of cultural pursuit rather than another. One may speak of *cultures* as being more or less in tune with the modern West; each language can, in its own way, readjust itself to meet the cultural needs of its speakers when change occurs.[29]

In this sense, one of the most important aspects of the transformation of Hebrew is the potential it demonstrates to lie in any language, and certainly in a related, rich, and ancient tongue like Arabic.

## THE CASE OF PERSIAN

With respect to modernization, Persian has found itself in a position different from either Arabic or Turkish in the past century. Unlike

[29] *Ibid.,* p. 397.

Arabic, it continued to serve during the last few centuries as a functioning language for the government and administration of a centralized state which had a comparatively strong sense of national identity among non-Western political entities. Unlike Turkish, whose literary and cultural pretensions were limited, it had been and was still a "high" literary language with a vitality that was considerable even if not equal to that of its golden age. It had served a period of apprenticeship as a learner language in the period of the early 'Abbasid Caliphate, incorporating into its vocabulary Arabic terminology that represented about thirty per cent of the total, but it also subsequently functioned as a teacher language to Turkish and Urdu among others, and had been the vehicle of a more profound Islamification of much of the eastern realm of Islam in Central Asia, Afghanistan, and India, in which latter country it was the court and government language until the nineteenth century. Finally, it was spared the burden borne by Arabic as a primary sacral tongue indissolubly associated with the central Islamic tradition. Although the nationalizing of Shi'ism from Safavid times onward brought it into closer association with a state-supported faith, it remained essentially a language of this world. Thus it did not share the repugnance of Arabic for innovation, a fashion which was on the contrary prized among Persian writers and poets, as were wit, fantasy, fancy, and all kinds of new linguistic combinations.

The result was that Persian was functioning in the nineteenth century as a living tongue, growing and evolving slowly, drawing on a rich tradition and suffering no deep complexes. It had no dialect problems of a scale comparable to those of Arabic, and revealed less diglossia of relevance than either Arabic or Ottoman Turkish. Official or literary Persian was not the tongue of the common man, to be sure, any more than the writings of Burke and Shelley were the speech of Lancashire, but the high and low forms of Persian and its dialects all were closely bound together with common roots, something notably not found in the hybrid Ottoman mandarin style. Thus, users of Persian felt little need for reform movements of the scope and vigor entertained by their neighbors at that time.

Nevertheless, Persian was equally unprepared for the onslaught of the modern West and the educational and linguistic problems brought with it. The reaction of Persian usually followed that in Turkey and the Arab countries by a considerable margin. The total number of graduates in what were dubiously called at the time higher institutions in Iran between 1851–1923 was about 1,500, a much lower figure than in Turkey or Egypt. Most of those persons graduating from the Dar al-Funun before its demise in 1891 were receiving little more than technical-school type training, much of which was devoted to military arts. Between 1901, when the School of Political Science was founded and 1934 when the Educational Act laid the groundwork for the university, specialized training schools were established by various ministries to prepare staff. Thus the Ministry of Education founded a normal school which in 1928 split into two branches, one of which was affiliated with a newly founded Faculty of Science. Progress was steady but slow during this period, and it should be remembered that the initial level was not high. The autobiography of an official admitted to the School of Political Science early in the century records his entrance examination in this way:

> We stood before teachers. The first examiner opened a Koran and read a passage. I recited the rest and interpreted it in Persian; then I explained its significance and also gave authoritative references for it. I went to another examiner who asked me about history. This was followed by dictation, composition and basic mathematics. In two weeks a dozen of us had received acceptances.[30]

However, the modest pace of modernization in Iran and the small-scale, integrated nature of the intellectual establishment were factors that helped Persian to keep its balance during the first three decades of this century while it underwent a partial modernization through assimilation and translation. Even so, by 1935, when the university was formally opened, a strong need was felt for language reform on a broader scale. This was typically thought of as a "purification" process and the task of carrying it out was assigned to the Iranian National Academy founded in the same year. The Iranian approach was not identical to the Turkish model, though it drew some inspiration from it. In both cases the needs of modernization were veiled by a rampant linguistic nationalism, and in both Arabic terms were rejected in large numbers as outworn intruders. But the incidence of Turkish appropriation of Western technical terms was very much higher than the Persian. Thus, for example, random selections from a comparative list prepared by the writer over a period of time reveal that for the Turkish *teleskop* we find the Persian *durbin* (lit. "far-see"); and similarly, T. *tyatro* and P. *tamašakhane;* T. *teknik* (adj., technical) and P. *fanni;* T. *teknisyen* and P. *fanni;* T *elektriki* and P *barqi*. It will be seen that by no means all Arabic words were removed from Persian (cf. *fanni* and *barqi*), but the principal recourse of the Academy purgers was to substitute old, Indo-European root forms of Persian for latter-day Arabo-Persian formations. In this way most governmental vocabulary was reworked, and the various ministries, for example, were renamed

[30] Reza Arasteh, *Education and Social Awakening in Iran*, Leiden: E. J. Brill, 1962, p. 24.

and Persianized: the *vezārat-e tejārat* (Ministry of Commerce) became the *vezārat-e bāzārgāni;* the *vezārat-e mǎʿaref* (Education) was the *vezrāt-e farhang;* the *vezārat-e adliyeh* (Justice) became the *vezāret-e dādgastari,* and so on. The process may seem somewhat akin to English in the twentieth century reneging its French and Latin heritage and returning to Anglo-Saxon roots, but the analogy is not exact. For the Iranian reformers, consciously or unconsciously, have equipped themselves with devices—such as the ability to prefix and suffix with ease and almost indefinitely—which favors the rapid formation of technical terminology. Taken together with the morphological similarities of Persian, the basic grammar of which remained virtually unchanged despite the flood of Arabic words, to other members of the Indo-European family, this return to the sources is a potential means of greater rapprochement with those languages that are producing the bulk of scientific vocabulary today, and provides a hook-in that can be effectively used.

Moghdam, who has been active in this field,[31] gives a model prefixing system for the verb tāšīdan (to form): hamtāšīdan (to conform); deštāšīdan (to deform); bāz tāšīdan (to reform); tarātāšīdan (to transform). The similarities with Greek prefixes are obvious. Direct analogy with Greek gives combined forms such as mardomšenasi (anthropology), and forms such as dādgāh (hall of justice, or court), danešgāh (hall of knowledge, or university), etc.

Modern Persian has been spared the special problems of Arabic and it has managed so far to avoid the necessity of opting for forthright solutions of the Turkish type. This evasion has been possible, though, only because of the somewhat leisurely approach taken to the question of ingesting and transmitting information.[32] There is no real scientific research in Iran comparable to that being carried out either at the Middle East Technical University in Ankara or at an institution like the Atomic Energy Commission in Egypt—in both these cases the working language is a European tongue. Moreover, the Iranian scientific establishment, which is almost entirely confined to Teheran University, is headed by senior men who were among the first Iranians to receive training in Western institutions. Their courses, laboratories,

---

[31] Mohammed Moghdam, *Ayande Zabān-e Fārsi,* Teheran: 1341 (1963).

[32] By way of example, in 1967 no single body of scholars could be named as responsible for the work of coining or translating new technical terminology. The Iranian Academy could hardly be considered to be functioning, and responsibility seemed to be divided between Teheran University and the Institute for Iranian Culture on an informal basis. The former had a committee for medical terminology, composed of five physicians and three linguists, which produced about one hundred terms in 1967. In addition a military committee was just starting to work. In most other fields terminological decisions appeared to be left to individual initiative.

79

and texts have perpetuated a low-keyed state of affairs in which old-style translations and approximations of often dated Western sources are still numerous. The ultimate impression given by modern Persian, then, is that because of all this cultural slowness it is just keeping its head above water as a functioning scientific language, but that the increasing problems of communication threatened to overtake it in the near future if greater adaptability is not evidenced. On this score many Iranian scientists would rate script revision as an essential, along with a more resolute pattern of decisions relating to the incorporation of new technical terminology.

## BAHASA INDONESIA AND JAPANESE

Two other very important non-Western languages might be briefly considered here: Bahasa Indonesia and Japanese. Our interest in them lies in the fact that they illustrate extremes of language adaptability which start from completely different points of departure. Bahasa is probably the world's outstanding example of the planned creation of an "artificial" national language, derived from a *lingua franca* that was only one of a great number of dialects used throughout Indonesia. The new language was given a normative grammar, there is being attached to it an abstract vocabulary and a battery of technical terms, and an effort is now under way to instruct some 100 million persons, adults and children, in its use.[33]

The tasks facing the various Indonesian Language Commissions that have functioned since 1942 have been manifold and awesome, and the time span within which Bahasa has had to become fully operational has been foreshortened by political urgencies. The point of departure for Bahasa was Malay, which had served as the main vehicle for interisland and European-native intercourse in the area for many centuries. But Malay differed from the higher traditional languages previously discussed here in its almost total lack not only of modern technical terms, but of an abstract literary and philosophical vocabulary. Balancing this lack in part was its extreme grammatical simplicity, especially in its pidgin (*malaju pasar*)—literally "bazaar Malay"—form often used by foreigners. Javanese had more than five times as many speakers as Malay when the choice was made, but it also had complex speech stratifications, the vocabulary of which differed according to the age,

[33] On the development of Bahasa Indonesia, cf. S. Takdir Alisjahbana, *The Development of the Indonesian Language and Literature* [undated English translation of "Le Développement de la langue et de la littérature indonésienne"], in *Cahiers d'histoire mondiale*, Vol. II, No. 3, 1955, pp. 602–703.

rank, and social situation of the person addressed. Thus Malay as the base for Bahasa reinforced a democratic ideal that was being sought for the emerging Indonesian state.

At the same time that Dutch was suppressed by Japanese occupying forces in 1942 during World War II, a Komisi Bahasa Indonesia was formed, and by the end of the war 7,000 new terms had been added to the basic vocabulary. The task of inventing new scientific terms was formidable enough—the flora and fauna of Indonesia are still not adequately named in Bahasa—so that a special working committee was established in 1947, and its work was continued by the Committee for Technical Terms (*Komisi Istilah*) founded in 1952 and now functioning as part of the Institute for Language and Culture of the Faculty of Letters of the University of Indonesia. To date more than 20,000 technical and scientific terms have been added to the Bahasa storehouse, the overwhelming majority of them by outright borrowing. Direct borrowing, moreover, is not limited to technical terms, but includes many general abstractions; *konsepsi, konfrontasi, universitet, komisi, pakultet* come immediately to mind. Final results cannot be judged at this still early stage of development, but enough is known to suggest that the chaos endemic in Indonesian language patterns at the moment will continue for a considerable time. Bahasa is still to most Indonesians a foreign language which has to be studied before it can be mastered. (In fact, by creating it, Indonesia is deliberately setting up a form of diglossia, for the Javanese speakers in particular, in order to overcome the handicap of having to handle six major related languages and more than one hundred minor ones, some of which have no connection with the Indonesian subgroup of the Malayo-Polynesian group.) In Indonesian schools it supplants the vernacular after a certain number of years —usually three, but in some areas it is introduced at once. University lectures are legally required to be given in Indonesian, but in practice they often have to be supplemented by a foreign language, usually English. The basic terminology is still spotty in very specialized fields, and advanced work in the sciences is handicapped.

Nonetheless, although the near future does not hold much promise, in the long run the forthright attitude taken in Indonesia toward adaptation by borrowing may prove to be a permanent benefit to the country by helping it to integrate itself into the mainstream of world thought. Today it is often possible to manipulate Bahasa via a combination of foreign-derived abstract nouns and a simple verbal and auxiliary system. The results are an understandable vehicle of communication among Indonesians and between Indonesians and foreigners. The level is low, the manipulation often graceless, but there is communication and, most importantly, the language because of its openness is not so cut off from the community of world languages as it otherwise would be. Finally, the teaching of English as a second language is much facilitated by the similarity—in some cases almost total identity—of a vast array of newly-imported technical vocabulary. Bahasa Indonesia today can hardly be said to be an efficient linguistic vehicle for any complex technical or scientific purpose, but it has moved forward quickly, and it is possible that it may catch up with some of its currently better-placed rivals in the race to attain adequacy.

Looked at in one way, modern Japanese could be said to be doing just the same as Bahasa at an infinitely higher and more sophisticated level. In fact, Japanese today can be credited with being the one non-Western language that has performed all the tasks without exception for which a modern language is called upon, no matter what the specialized field. This conclusion is somewhat surprising given the general reputation of Japanese, even among the Japanese themselves, for a supercomplexity that ends in vagueness and reduced intelligibility.[34] The language has only achieved its present condition, however, over a considerable period of time, with rearrangements in several stages, the last of which has produced a unique *tour de force* of continuing dimensions and seemingly increasing proportions.

Like Ottoman Turkey, Japan took an interest in Western science from an early period and already by the start of the nineteenth century a sizable body of standard translations of Western technical terms existed. Japan also had at that time a significant literacy level, which can be estimated from a school attendance rate placed at forty-three per cent for boys and ten per cent for girls by 1868;[35] a standardized spoken language without important dialectism, rich traditions in literature and philosophy, a differentiated and semispecialized intellectual class, and an extensive publishing industry. From our point of view it was perhaps most important of all that the "indigenous vocabulary which could be mobilized for the new translations [of Meiji] was not the esoteric language of a small intellectual coterie, but the common property of a relatively large section of the nation. If one takes, as an example, a random page from an official memorandum justifying the imposition of compulsory education by arguments clearly derived from Western sources, a few of the new words stand out: 'the rights

[34] Cf., for example, Masao Maruyama, *Thought and Behavior in Japanese Politics*, London and New York: Oxford University Press, 1963, pp. 84–134, and especially pp. 102–103, where in his analysis of the "vagueness and complexity" of the defendants' often seemingly evasive answers to questions put to them at the International Military Tribunal for the Far East, he cites the linguistic problems of Japanese as having "aggravated the obscurity of the replies and added to the bewilderment of the court."
[35] R. P. Dore, *op. cit.*, pp. 317–322.

[*kenri*] of minors,' 'the government,' i.e. 'the collective force of society,' 'in the eye of the law.' But these are few in proportion to the indigenous abstract vocabulary: 'to state a reason,' 'fixed interpretation,' 'impose a responsibility,' 'evasion,' 'essential criterion,' 'minimum period,' etc." [36] Thus, Japan was able to carry on her educational system in her own language during the first crucial transition period when large quantities of imported learning had to be absorbed. This advantage contrasts sharply with the situation prevailing in the Middle East in the nineteenth century, and in Southeast Asia and most of the rest of the underdeveloped world in the twentieth.

Even so, Japanese scientists were hard put to coin new terms in scientific fields, and the fact that they kept abreast was due not only to the basic equipment in the linguistic culture and to their diligence, but also to the relatively slow rate by today's standards at which scientific innovation was progressing in the nineteenth century. The Japanese thus had time to absorb new ideas and terms and, although they had to quicken their pace, they were not forced to choose between the dilemmas of falling hopelessly behind or rushing pell-mell into large-scale borrowing that face most latecomers today.

During this same early period, roughly from 1870 to 1890, Japanese reduced the relatively minor diglossia it offered in the coexistence of a literary language and a spoken tongue through the so-called *gembunitchi*, the unification of spoken and written forms that is generally considered to have been accomplished with the appearance of Futabatei Shimei's translations of Turgenev in 1889. From that time forward, with the exception of a few archaic forms like the *sōrō* epistolary style and certain literary and stylistic efflorescences in the *bungotai* used by the Imperial Government until 1945, a unified, modern Japanese of great expressive range and versatility posed almost as few problems with respect to modernization and adjustment as did any European tongue at the time.

Japanese did present a problem in the complexity of its orthography, however, which can perhaps best be illustrated by noting that blind Japanese children who learned the national language via Braille completed in four years what Japanese children with normal sight using characters and *kanamajiri* did in five. At the partial instigation of occupation authorities after World War II, the Ministry of Education took important measures to simplify the extraordinarily difficult multiple writing systems of the language. The number of Chinese characters (*kanji*) prescribed for normal use was limited to 1,850, as opposed to a pre-war average Tokyo newspaper stocking of over 7,000. Many characters were abbreviated or otherwise simplified in form and in diction-

36 R. P. Dore, *op. cit.*, pp. 303–304.

ary classification. Phonetic combinations of the *kana* syllabary used to form diphthongs and long vowels were also simplified; alternative spellings were dropped and new rules were provided for the use of word endings and inflections written with declensional *kana* (*okurigana*).

These government-directed changes were important in the area of orthographic simplification, but they were modest compared to the uncontrolled, popular evolution of modern Japanese in the past two decades. This evolution is a structural one involving the incorporation of foreign, usually English, words directly into the body of the language, where they are now beginning to function as a new equivalent of the Chinese-type compounds that formerly provided the bulk of the literary and abstract vocabulary of classical Japanese.[37] The evolution of Japanese in this direction has been likened to the phenomenon of a similar massive introduction of Chinese vocabulary in the Nara Period (710–94), a step that completely changed the structure and development of the language. A random page taken from the Kenkyūsha Japanese-English Dictionary as early as 1954 reveals how far the penetration of foreign words and phrases, often in abbreviation, had gone and since then incorporations have proliferated even more.

Moreover, the fact that English is taught universally and for long periods in secondary schools (lower secondary schooling to the ninth year is compulsory and in 1966 more than seventy per cent of those graduates went on to upper secondary school) has led to a growing tendency on the part of educated Japanese to introduce English words throughout their discourse in Japanese, often in substitution for, or in explanation of Chinese compounds that, as homonyms, are difficult to understand aurally. In short sentences, in cases where only the verbs and inflecting particles are retained in Japanese, it becomes difficult at times to tell whether the interlocutor is speaking a somewhat broken English or the most modern Japanese, as can be indicated by the following sentence read out by a television news broadcaster in this writer's hearing in the summer of 1967: *torakku* ga *supīdo* shite *sentā rain* wo *ōba* shita. (The *truck* was *speeding* and *crossed over* the *center line*.)

Habits such as these, increasingly ingrained among millions, indeed tens of millions of educated persons, make easier the rapid adoption of foreign technical and/or modern jargon terms almost as soon as they appear. Japanese today use without second thoughts such words as counter-productive, escalate, and so on in the midst of their Japanese conversations. Furthermore, given the rapidity of the appearance of such terms and their often brief life span, Japanese are tending (a) to

[37] Personal communication from Herbert Passin on work in progress. I am indebted to him for the entire concept of "English-type *kanji*."

translate less and to take the foreign phrase as is, or (b) to use the foreign word alongside a Japanese translation which serves for a time as an explanation of the meaning of the borrowing while the latter is being digested, and *simultaneously* to use the foreign word (among those who have already grasped the meaning) as a gloss for a constructible Sino-Japanese phrase which might not be perceived at once by ear. Thus *higyō* (strike, walkout) glosses the popular and common term *suto* (short for *sutoraiki*) and vice versa, but—operating as "new English-type" *kanji*—*zenesuto* (for *zeneraru sutoraiki*, or "general strike") is apparented to *zenhigyō* (a complete labor stoppage), in which the Sino-Japanese character *zen/mattaku* means "total, all." *Zenesuto* offers a much more comprehensible aural pattern than does *zenhigyō* and has the orthographic advantage of being written in *kana*.

## CONCLUDING OBSERVATIONS

Aside from the more abstract considerations of the interrelationships between language and science, the basic practical tasks of modern language with respect to science are three: to allow the easy, rapid translation of material embodying the most up-to-date information; to function as a vehicle for the transmission of that information through instruction to members of its linguistic community; and to provide the means for expressing the scientific work and research of members of that community for the benefit of its members and to be potentially available to those outside who desire it. The summary survey of six non-Western languages made here suggests that only two of them, Israeli Hebrew and Japanese, are adequate to all three tasks. Turkish and Persian, in that order, can fulfill the first two requirements reasonably well, but do not in fact fulfill the third. Arabic is largely inadequate for the first task, fulfills the second with difficulty, and does not comply with the third. Bahasa barely functions with respect to the second and is otherwise insufficient.

   In order for those languages that are still "underdeveloped" at this time and in this special frame of reference to come abreast of the major, modern languages in the international community, we have seen that they must take two important steps: (1) the rationalization of the language through internal standardization or closure, and (2) the adoption of an attitude of adaptability and receptivity to foreign culturolinguistic influence. In other terms the first step means that the gap between a "high/élite" culture and a "low/popular or peasant" culture within the society must be closed, and that the social cohesion of the linguistic community must be reinforced as a precondition to its modernization. As to adaptability, the lesson is that if the time span has been sufficient, and the preparation extensive enough, as it was in the Japanese example, a leisurely method of independent invention and translation would be possible, but that—as things stand today with the mushrooming of information and technology—independent formation is more and more difficult. Direct borrowing is becoming the more usual pattern.

Formation by direct borrowing can be said to be not only inevitable but also desirable. Beyond the immediately apparent reason of efficiency with regard to the rapid availability of the term for working purposes, there are two other reasons. It is first of all advantageous to people of a given language community that the formations of their language, especially in the domains of science and technology which, however vaguely, are tending to form a single tradition, should correspond to the formations of other major languages, and it is useful to them to have "prefigurations" of these formations as points of solidarity. Secondly, borrowing technical terms is not merely the most economical solution but it is also the most satisfactory one psychologically, for it rightly frees the technical domain from the burden of unwanted and unnecessary associations and subsidiary meanings that accompany common, indigenous formations. The more common a term the greater is the sum of associations it carries, and the more exotic it is to the language the fewer they are. English speakers do not feel monotonous to be as simply "one-toned" as the German *eintönig* so directly suggests, nor do they think so immediately of a distant sound when they use the telephone as the Germans are obliged to do when they employ *Fernsprecher*. As Ray points out, no one is upset because oxygen does not produce sour liquids, and schizophrenia not only denotes something more specific than the "crackpot" which it translates subtly (another value in itself) but, most importantly, it carries none of the folksy, gossipy, and pejorative overtones of the popular phrase.

Finally, formation by borrowing makes it easier for fairly sizable numbers of persons engaged in technical areas to do something which they are seemingly condemned to do for some time to come: to move back and forth between their native language, in which they have acquired the bases of their scientific knowledge in most cases, and a major scientific language, in which they have been trained at higher levels and from which they continue to receive important current information, and in many cases through which they transmit their own research information. Almost all societies show some examples of this process, but it is noticeably marked among the advanced countries of northern Europe with minor languages—Denmark, Sweden, The Netherlands—and among the languages mentioned here it has been one of the secrets of success of the Israelis and the Japanese.

At the highest level, however, the case for adaptability can be argued on broader grounds. If language is, in Kroeber's suggestive phrase, "probably a precondition" of culture, then the increased number of crosslinks of all kinds between languages and a heightened sense of interparticipation among those who, like most scientists, are using more than one language, will prefigure and sketch out more vividly the still nebulous area within which that single, unified scientific tradition is slowly shaping itself. And the drift toward linguistic solidarity as opposed to nationalistic atomism has many influential supporters in the modern world; for, as has been remarked, ". . . in the question of scripts, sources of borrowing, etc. . . . whichever alternative matches most closely the practice of the most accessible of the leading languages of science will always have the entire communion of scientists urging its adoption." [38]

Ultimately the interconnected problem of language and science reduces itself to the fact that it is impossible for a broadly scientific mentality to grow up in a society which has not become reasonably modern, that is to say, which has not at least gone some considerable distance along the road to modernism. And it is impossible for a society to go very far along the road to modernism unless it possesses rationalized linguistic equipment that can be utilized in the journey.

[38] P. S. Ray, *op. cit.*, p. 60.

# II  *Case Studies*

In its early days, science was distinct from technology, springing rather from thought and philosophy than from craftsmanship. Nowadays, however, and indeed for the last century and more, science has merged ever more intimately with technology, so arming it with power, so enhancing its capacities, that no words, nor any fears or dreams, may exaggerate what depends upon the employment. Nor is the future of our own world of the West alone in play through this, its great invention. . . . Anxious though our moments are, today is not the final test of wisdom among statesmen or virtue among peoples. The hard trial will begin when the instruments of power created by the West come fully into the hands of men not of the West . . . what will the day hold when China wields the bomb? And Egypt? Will Aurora light a rosy-fingered dawn out of the East? Or will Nemesis?

Charles Coulston Gillispie

*The Edge of Objectivity: An Essay in the History of Scientific Ideas*, Princeton: Princeton University Press, 1960, pp. 8–9.

# 4.

# SCIENCE AND POLITICS IN BRAZIL:

## BACKGROUND OF THE 1967 DEBATE ON NUCLEAR ENERGY POLICY

## BY JAMES W. ROWE

*American Universities Field Staff*

At the Punta del Este meeting of the American Chiefs of State in April, 1967, Brazil's President Artur da Costa e Silva called for a crash program of scientific and technological development for his and the other Latin American states as an essential means of breaking the shackles of underdevelopment. This theme, already hinted at in his inaugural statements a month earlier, had been spelled out a few days before:

> Brazil and all Latin America should now make a clear and decided option, engaging itself in a rational but daring program of promoting research and practical applications of science. In this context, nuclear energy will fulfill a transcendental role and is, without doubt, the most powerful resource to be put at the disposal of developing countries to reduce the distance that separates them from industrialized nations. We repudiate nuclear arms and we are conscious of the grave risks which their dissemination can bring to humanity. It is imperative, nevertheless, that no immediate or potential restraints be created to the full utilization by our countries of nuclear energy for peaceful ends. Otherwise we should be accepting a new form of dependence certainly incompatible with our aspirations for development.

Later he added, "The development of scientific research in the field of nuclear energy includes, inevitably, at a certain stage, the use of explosions; to veto access to explosions would be equivalent to impeding the development of the peaceful uses of nuclear energy." [1]

Two and a half months later, on the eve of an official visit to Brazil by Dr. Glenn Seaborg, Chairman of the United States Atomic Energy Commission, President Costa e Silva made a fuller statement on his administration's nuclear energy aspirations at the site where a vast new hydroelectric power project is planned, in São Paulo state. He explained that Brazil's reservation to the Mexico City Treaty banning nuclear weapons in Latin America and its position at the Geneva 18-Nation Disarmament Conference were in strict accord with this basic policy, adding, "The Brazilian Government reserves to itself exclusive rights regarding the installation and operation of nuclear reactors, as well as the prospecting, mining, industrialization, and commercialization of nuclear minerals and ores, and of fertile and fissionable materials." The President stated specifically, "I announce herewith that I have already instructed the Minister of Mines and Energy to elaborate, in close collaboration with the National Atomic Energy Commission, a program for the commercial production of electric power based on atomic energy, including specific recommendations regarding the feasibility, dimensions, and location of the first nuclear-powered electric generator." [2]

Following these statements, all made in the first hundred days or so of the Costa e Silva administration, came a succession of events—the Seaborg visit, a widespread and vocal reaction to the visit by Brazilian scientists and the press, important pronouncements by Foreign Minister José Magalhães Pinto before Brazilian scientists and at the Superior War College, the testimony before Congressional Committees in Brasília by high administration officials and research scientists regarding nuclear energy matters, the announcement by the Foreign Office of its plan to seek the collaboration of Brazilian scientists working abroad, and the presentation, on August 24, 1967 in Geneva, of the United States-Soviet draft of the long-discussed nuclear nonproliferation treaty—which have aroused interest and comment perhaps as never before on the question of Brazilian capacities and intentions in the field of nuclear energy. The discussion and debate surrounding these events called attention to important questions concerning the level of science and technology in Brazil, as well as the formulation of science policy— and for that matter, public policy in general, since fundamental questions regarding education, foreign policy, and levels of government spending are involved. The debate over the options available to Brazil,

[1] Address at the Foreign Ministry, April 4, 1967, cited in Ministério das Relações Exteriores, *Política Nuclear do Brasil*, Rio de Janeiro: August 9, 1967, p. I-1.
[2] Speech at Ilha Solteira, *ibid.*, p. I-3.

both as to diplomatic and domestic policies concerning nuclear energy, is far from complete as this is written in late 1967. Sufficient authoritative pronouncements and official actions have ensued, however, to suggest that the Brazilian government's basic position will not easily be changed in certain important respects. This policy affects matters of great interest to the international community as well as to Brazil, and is at variance with many views held in the United States. The timeliness of this debate, as well as the ways in which it is peculiarly linked to problems of political capacity and over-all development strategy, make it an appropriate topic for a discussion of "Science and Social Change," despite the risks involved in treating a process still unfolding, and the impossibility of more than a partial examination of many issues involved.

The purpose here is twofold. One is to recount some of the highlights of the evolution of institutionalized science in Brazil, which strongly suggest the two-way interaction of science and social change, and more specifically, science and politics. Such an account also points up the quite respectable achievements of Brazilian science in certain fields, the capacity for adaptive research in others, and the gradual, but fairly consistent increase in the pace of scientific institution-building and national commitment to the promotion of science. The second is to depict the major institutions and issues involved in the 1967 pronouncements on science and technology, especially nuclear energy policy, and to show that there is an especially strong interaction between science and politics in the unfolding of science policy in the Costa e Silva administration. It is our contention that, while this interaction is especially noticeable in the present case, the situation is not unique, when compared either with the Brazilian past or with the science policy-making experience of other countries. (The term politics, within this discussion, is used in the neutral or Lasswellian sense, without the pejorative connotations of conniving, self-serving behavior sometimes found in the early literature of economic development, where "politics" is viewed as an "obstacle" to development. Thus the present interpretation of science policy evolution, which admittedly stresses the political factor, is not a contradiction, but rather a complement to a more orthodox interpretation, voiced by at least some Brazilian scientists, which holds that the evolution has come about primarily through the "educational work" of the Brazilian scientific élite.) However, it seems likely that in a political system such as Brazil's, which in recent years has been marked both by high instability and the more chronic, deep-seated difficulty shared by other Latin American governments in maintaining, administering, and enforcing major policy decisions, the bargaining and trade-off between political and scientific élites is even more important and conspicuous than in some other types of political systems.[3] Even so, some problems facing Brazil in the interaction of science and politics are familiar elsewhere. The two quotations which follow are the remarks of North Americans regarding situations in the United States context, yet they seem remarkably appropriate to the Brazilian situation. In a paper written for the Center for the Study of Democratic Institutions several years ago, Lynn White, Jr. pointed out: [4]

> Science must have a positive emotional context to thrive, as well as economic and political encouragement. Legislatures and corporate bodies must reach decisions favorable to science and investors and voters must approve what their representatives do. Parents must want science in the education of their children. Above all, a significant proportion of the ablest minds must choose to dedicate themselves with passion to scientific investigation if the movement is to succeed.

And the political scientist Wallace Sayre, writing in *Science* magazine in 1961 remarked: [5]

> Talk of a single, comprehensive American science policy has an essentially fictitious quality. There will be many science policies rather than a master science policy. Diversity, inconsistency, compromise, experimentation, pulling and hauling, competition and continuous revision in science policies are more predictable continuing characteristics than their antonyms. This has been the history of American science policies and this describes their present state. . . .
>
> Scientists in politics share the problems of other participants in the political process. No special dispensation exempts the scientists from the hard choices and continuing difficulties which the political process imposes upon all those who aspire to shape public policy. . . . The scientists are now inescapably committed to politics if they hope to exercise influence in the shaping of public

[3] In his study of nuclear energy policy under the Fourth French Republic, Lawrence Scheinman found that ministerial instability enhanced the influence and policy-making role of administrative and technocratic services. *Atomic Energy Policy in France Under the Fourth Republic*, Princeton: Princeton University Press, 1965, p. 210. It is generally conceded, however, that the French system has been characterized by a strong administrative subsystem, with considerable stability and strong institutional norms.
[4] "Science, Scientists, and Politics," reprinted in Alexander Vavoulis and A. Wayne Colver, eds., *Science and Society, Selected Essays,* San Francisco: Holden-Day, Inc., 1966, p. 70.
[5] "Scientists and American Science Policy," *Science,* Vol. 133, No. 3456, March 24, 1961, reprinted in Robert Gilpin and Christopher Wright, *Scientists and National Policy-Making,* New York: Columbia University Press, 1964, pp. 104 and 111.

policy, including science policies. . . . As politicians . . . they are
effective in the degree to which they understand the political process, accept its rules, and play their part in the process with more
candor than piety.

These comments are cited not merely to point up problems common
to science policy in widely differing systems. The three points made—
the emotional dimension of a favorable societal context for science, the
frequency of inconsistent, pluralistic, and zigzag courses in the evolution of science policies, and the necessity for scientists who want to be
policy-makers to learn and play the political game with all its arts and
cunning—seem extraordinarily appropriate to an understanding of recent developments in Brazil. Without an appreciation and constant
recollection of their relevance, an observer of the Brazilian scene might
be tempted to see in the evolution of policy less of science than science
fiction.

## BRAZILIAN SCIENCE, STAGE ONE [6]

A useful guide for discussing the progress and present state of science
in Brazil and comparing it with that of other areas is the model developed by George Basalla describing the diffusion of Western European
science through other parts of the world after the sixteenth and seventeenth centuries.[7] The model contains three overlapping stages: the
first, during which the nonscientific society provides a source for
European science; the second, of "colonial science," or that dependent
on foreign institutions and training, though not necessarily that of the
"mother country"; and the third, in which an independent scientific
tradition evolves. The length of these stages and the patterns of overlap
vary a great deal from country to country. Brazil today offers an
example of a predominantly colonial or dependent science, but which
has spectacularly entered the third, or "independent" stage in a few
disciplines, and still is in stage one in some respects, as suggested by the
continuing importance of non-Brazilian natural science expeditions
into the Amazon basin, contrasted with the limited and precarious state

[6] Apart from published scores cited in subsequent footnotes, this section is based
on interviews with research scientists of the Federal University of Minas Gerais
(Belo Horizonte), the Pontifical Catholic University (Rio de Janeiro), the Brazilian Center of Physics Research, and the Federal University of São Paulo; present
and former personnel of the National Atomic Energy Commission and the National Research Council in Rio de Janeiro; and the Rectors of the Federal University of Minas Gerais and the Federal University of Rio de Janeiro.
[7] "The Spread of Western Science," *Science*, Vol. 156, No. 3775, May 5, 1967,
pp. 612–619.

of Brazilian research activities in geology, botany, and zoology in that region.[8] The present bid of Brazil's leaders for a "big push" in science and technology, spearheaded by a drive toward the development of nuclear energy, may be seen as a self-conscious effort to accelerate the process of transition between stages two and three. The Basalla model, it should be noted, was developed out of the historical experience of diverse nations, including those such as the United States and Japan whose transition between the latter phases considerably preceded that of Brazil. Brazil's effort to expand and speed up its transition from dependent science to an independent tradition comes at a time when (a) the pace of scientific discovery in many fields is so rapid as to give rise to the term "New Scientific Revolution," a situation imparting an even greater sense of urgency than that which prevailed in the nineteenth century; and (b) the principle of heavy government intervention in developmental activities, whether as stimulator or direct participant, has been firmly established in Brazil since the end of World War II, a situation that hardly prevailed in nineteenth-century North America.

With allowance for these special conditions, the Basalla model provides a fair portrayal of the basic lines of the development of science in Brazil. As for stage one, the role of this vast country as a data source for European science, especially after political independence, is justly celebrated. The findings of non-Portuguese observers and expeditions concerning Brazilian natural history are better known than the accounts of Portuguese colonials, because of the wider currency of the languages in which they were published. But a tradition of data collection and publication by settlers goes back to the permanent settlement of Bahia in 1549 and the arrival of Jesuits such as Padre Nóbrega, who described the nature and uses of the tobacco plant. During the Dutch occupation of Pernambuco in the seventeenth century, Prince Mauricio of Nassau gave an impetus to scientific observation, founding the first astronomical observatory in South America and encouraging the scientific work of the Amsterdam physician Willem Pies and the German naturalist George Marcgrave, whose findings were published in *Historia Naturalis Brasilae*, the first scientific book published in Brazil, in 1648. (Incidentally, this work was translated into Portuguese only in 1942.) Scattered efforts by colonials and foreigners continued during the eighteenth century, but it was with the transfer of the Portuguese Court from Lisbon to Rio de Janeiro, and the opening of Brazilian ports to foreign navigation after 1808 that the great era of naturalists' expeditions to Brazil began, and with it the large-scale export of scien-

[8] The latest such venture is the joint Royal Society-Royal Geographical Society expedition which began studies of the natural environment in Mato Grosso in 1967.

tific data. A kind of prototype activity was that of Baron von Langs-dorff, diplomat-naturalist in the service of the Tsar, whose expeditions over more than a decade penetrated the states of Pará and Mato Grosso as well as Bahia, Minas Gerias, and São Paulo, and resulted in the organization of a herbarium of some 60,000 Brazilian plants in St. Petersburg.

Others who followed included the French naturalist Auguste de Sainte-Hilaire (1816), Prince Maximilian of Wied-Neuwied (1815), and Germans such as Friedrich Sellow (1814), the geologist Wilhelm von Eschwege, and the members of the famous 1817 expedition sponsored by the King of Bavaria, which included Johann von Spix and Karl Friedrich von Martius. From the latter expedition, which provided a basis for the description of more than 20,000 plant species, came the epic work *Flora Brasiliensis*, whose forty folio volumes required the collaboration of sixty-five botanists, and took sixty-six years to publish, and until present times has been the basic work in the field. Of the many British expeditions during the nineteenth century, that led by Alfred Russell Wallace and Henry Bates up the Amazon and the Rio Negro (1848–52) was perhaps more significant for Brazil, if less heralded, than the Brazilian stopovers of Darwin's expedition aboard the *Beagle* (1832 and 1836). In 1865 came the Thayer Expedition from the United States, led by Louis Agassiz, which gathered specimens of flora and fauna for two years on the Amazon, its tributaries, and other rivers. (Aboard was William James, age twenty-three, whose letters and drawings from Brazil, consulted today, provide a forceful reminder of how little things have changed along the Amazon in a century.)

These and other expeditions too numerous to mention shared certain basic features—foreign patronage and financing, often by the rulers of lesser German principalities; the removal of plant, animal, and mineral specimens and data to European cities for classification and display; the publication of findings in languages little-known in Brazil; limited relationships with local scholars or naturalists which, if they sometimes served to stimulate interest in and bring new techniques to the study of natural environment, nevertheless were temporary and often marginal. Important exceptions occurred from time to time, when foreign naturalists settled permanently in the country, as in the case of the Danish paleontologist Peter Wilhelm Lund, who made notable contributions to the study of fossils and minerals during half a century in Minas Gerais, and who demonstrated that an orthodox working environment is not indispensable to first-rate research. Another case was that of the German naturalist Fritz Mueller, who settled in Santa Catarina in 1852 and spent the last forty-five years of his life in Brazil; Darwin is said to have dubbed him "the prince of observers." Such figures demonstrate the linkage between stage one and the colonial stage of Brazilian science.

## BRAZILIAN SCIENCE, STAGE TWO

In the Basalla model, stage two—colonial or dependent science—begins later than stage one, but in the Brazilian case, some colonial science existed before the great flowering of data-collecting for European science in the nineteenth century. The sparseness of colonial science in Brazil during the early centuries and its thin achievements prior to maturation in the nineteenth and twentieth centuries, however, suggest that the Brazilian case, nevertheless, reasonably resembles the model. Special features of Brazilian colonial science derive from its matrix in the Portuguese culture of the sixteenth through nineteenth centuries. The scientific awakening, with its diffusion of the critical spirit and experimental method, blossoming throughout most of Western Europe during the sixteenth and seventeenth centuries, appeared to stop at the Pyrennees. The Portuguese essayist Antonio Sergio has called the seventeenth century "the century of light for the rest of Europe, a century of darkness for Portugal." As for the eighteenth and nineteenth centuries, he concluded that the Iberian Peninsula "did not produce a single superior individual who could be put alongside the great creators of modern science; there came from the Peninsula not a single one of the great intellectual discoveries that honor the modern spirit." [9] A clear grasp of the causative factors—a debatable mix involving geography, economics, and the concepts of late medieval philosophy in the Peninsula—must await further research by the historians of science and culture, but the cultural legacy from its two principal motherlands would seem to have something to do with the fact that Latin America has produced only one Nobel Prize winner in science since the awards began in 1901. [10] In the New World, Portugal's colonial policies seemed on the surface more culturally obscurantist than those of Spain, insofar as the Portuguese permitted neither universities nor printing presses in colony. The Portuguese language became known as the "Tomb of Thought." Gradually, as an awareness grew of the contrast between Iberian and Western European thought, came an inferiority complex which was long to plague Iberian and Ibero-American intel-

[9] Cited in Fernando de Azevedo, ed., *As Ciências no Brasil,* Rio de Janeiro: Edições Melhoramentos, 1955, 2 vols., Vol. 1, p. 13.
[10] It went to Dr. Bernardo Houssay of Argentina in 1947 for achievements in physiology and medicine.

lectual endeavor. Once Iberian critics and publicists began to acknowledge inferiority in this field, there was a variety of attempts to explain it, such as Juan José López Ibor's concept of the "ethical man" of Spain and Portugal, with his intense focus on personality and individualism, unattracted to the objectivity and impersonality of natural science.[11]

Against this background colonial science grew slowly in Brazil, but over about three centuries it developed a substantial body of achievements. As one would expect, the period of colonial science is marked by individual accomplishments, sometimes of a high order and occasionally surpassing work done by European science (like North America's Benjamin Franklin in electricity), but there is no institution-building, poor formal and no informal communications among the scientific community, and an insufficient number of such gifted individuals to promote "self-sustaining growth." Thus in 1709 Padre Bartolomeu Lourenço in Brazil preceded the Montgolfier brothers in launching a hot-air balloon, but the question arises, what came of it? Joaquim Gomes de Sousa, who began lecturing at the Escola Militar in Rio de Janeiro in 1848, has been called Brazil's first "mathematician-physicist," and the country's finest expression in pure mathematics, but he was a solitary figure, and later scientists have pointed out his lack of interest in the empirical, as well as excessive reliance on intuition.[12] Astronomy has a long history in Brazil, dating from the Dutch installation of an observatory in the seventeenth century; numerous *savantes*, experiments, and observations of considerable significance are recorded; institutional prestige and continuity of effort were united at the National Observatory during the long directorship of Henrique Morize (1908–30). Yet a key ingredient in the transition to independent science has been missing until now: even those in the profession recommend that advanced training be taken abroad. In other disciplines the picture is similar. Almost every field has had a few distinguished names and original contributions, and some have many, such as the life sciences following the impetus given by nineteenth century naturalists' expeditions—names such as Miranda Ribeiro in zoology and Barbosa Rodrigues in botany would merely begin a long list. But until the twentieth century essential elements of stage three, or independent science, were missing in almost all disciplines. Institution-building had not begun; scientific societies were not yet formed; advanced training was not available in Brazil; teamwork was unknown; numbers were small. The situation at the turn of the century is suggested by the publication of a significant article by the mathematician-physicist Oto de

---

[11] Cited in F. de Azevedo, *op. cit.*, p. 14.
[12] F. de Azevedo, *op. cit.*, p. 168.

Alencar in 1901—it appeared in a Portugal journal, and in the French language. At the time, and for more than two decades thereafter, Brazil did not possess a single university.

It is frequently asserted that Brazil first achieved an independent scientific tradition in the bio-medical sciences, in the first decade of the twentieth century, primarily as a result of the achievements of the brilliant young physician Oswaldo Cruz (1872–1917) and a group of his associates. Cruz is best known for his successful fight against yellow fever and other epidemic diseases, but this part of his work was intimately related with his transformation of the Manguinhos Serotherapeutic Institute in Rio de Janeiro into a modern school of microbiology and experimental pathology. Other individuals figured prominently in this flowering of Brazilian science: Adolfo Lutz and Vital Brazil, who along with Cruz were called upon for a response to an outbreak of bubonic plague in Santos, some two hundred miles from Rio, and are associated with the rise of the famous Butantã Institute in São Paulo to a leading world center of research on snake venoms and serum production; Carlos Chagas, the distinguished associate and successor of Cruz at the Institute, whose work on malaria prophylaxis led to his discovery in 1909 of the malady *Trypanosomiasis americana* (Chagas' Disease); and President Rodrigues Alves, whose administration (1902–6) was responsible for the recruitment of Cruz to his posts as director of the serum institute and later as Director General of Public Health, and for providing him with understanding and strong backing in the face of a hostile reaction by public, press, and even the scientific community. But the role of Oswaldo Cruz himself was crucial. In 1899 he had returned to Brazil after three years at the Pasteur Institute in Paris, taking charge of the production of serums and vaccines at the Manguinhos Institute, and in 1902 became its director. With the outbreak of bubonic plague in 1899, Brazilian authorities faced a major public health crisis: in the capital, 295 deaths were attributed to the plague in 1900, and a recurrence of yellow fever claimed 584 lives in 1903. In the latter year, following the inauguration of the Rodriguez Alves administration a year earlier, Cruz was appointed Director General of Public Health by the new government, which was pledged to give increased attention to public health problems. Although Cruz was a gifted scientist, his great twin achievements were in devising and pushing through an eradication campaign against yellow fever and concurrently building the Manguinhos Institute (renamed the Institute of Experimental Medicine, and later known as the Oswaldo Cruz Institute) into a world-famous center of research.[13]

---

[13] Nancy Stepan, who has done extensive research on Oswaldo Cruz and his Institute, maintains that Cruz's prime role in the transformation of Brazilian

Cruz's task was not to discover that the fever was transmitted by *Aedes aegypti*—this had been demonstrated previously in Cuba and re-proven in São Paulo in 1902—but to convince nonscientists of it, secure funds and backing from the wielders of power, and initiate the measures necessary for control, all against the widespread initial opposition of legislators, press, public, and even a sizable sector of the local scientific community. He was successful in these endeavors, and by 1907 was able to report that yellow fever no longer existed in Rio in epidemic form; by 1909 there were no deaths from it in the city. Thus Oswaldo Cruz made an unmeasurable contribution to Brazilian science mainly through the use of political and administrative talents. Ridding Rio of yellow fever was an accomplishment that brought respect for Brazil abroad, and for science and its practical applications at home, and an enormous prestige for Cruz, which he used to build up his Institute. From a pair of primitive buildings it grew into a large modern laboratory and in five years or so was internationally respected as a research center for bacteriology, pathology, immunology, and hematology.[14] Cruz encouraged group research and built a fine staff, which included some thirty scientists in the early years (it has about 140 today). Quite remarkable was the smooth transition and maintenance of high-quality research when leadership passed, following Cruz's untimely death at age forty-four, to Carlos Chagas, the associate who in 1909 had discovered the nature and transmission of the parasitic malady that now bears his name. When the first Brazilian universities were created in the 1920s and 1930s, advanced bio-medical training was already well established at the Institute, and had a profound influence on teaching in the biological sciences. Training in the biological disciplines in Brazil has been considered to be up to the "world level" in recent years—the most important criterion of independent science.

A second landmark in the struggle to create an independent science consists of events in São Paulo in the late 1920s and early 1930s. Again the case involves a major political component and a response to an urgently felt public need arising out of a natural plague. The plague was the coffee-borer, a threat to the principal source of wealth of Brazil's most advanced and populous state. The response was the creation, in 1927, of the Biological Institute of São Paulo whose scientists, under

science to a new and independent status is based on his success in meeting three basic problems in building the Institute—establishing the legitimacy of its activities, solving the problem of recruitment and training, and developing leadership to insure survival of the Institute independently of Cruz himself. Unpublished ms., Los Angeles: 1967.
[14] The Institute, the only Latin American entity invited to participate in the XII International Conference of Hygiene in Berlin in 1907, won the gold medal, highest prize of the Conference. N. Stepan, *op. cit.*, p. 25.

the leadership of Artur Neiva, identified and made possible control of the pest. The Biological Institute was backed by two outstanding governors of the state. Its success added not only to the prestige of biology but to the interest in science in general in a prosperous state which, through immigration, had somewhat closer ties with European culture than much of the rest of the country.

Meanwhile, other problems related to the economy were arising. The long process of import substitution had begun with World War I and was speeded up by the world depression; São Paulo was the center of a growing shift from commodity exports to manufacturing. Even in its early stages this process created a demand for mechanical and metallurgical engineers and for a considerable number of persons adequately trained in chemistry—yet, Brazil had theretofore graduated mostly civil engineers, and chemistry was said to be twenty years behind world standards. In this *milieu* there appeared an exceptionally able governor of São Paulo, Armando de Salles Oliveira. His decree in 1934 creating the state University of São Paulo and with it the Faculty of Philosophy, Science, and Letters marks the beginning of modern university education in Brazil. (Individual professional faculties of law and medicine, along with schools and institutes teaching science and mathematics, had existed since the nineteenth century, and in 1921 the University of Brazil in Rio de Janeiro had been created on paper by a decree simply uniting a dozen or so separate institutions.) The same year, a National Institute of Technology was founded in Rio, preceding by five years the formation of the Faculty of Philosophy (in which science training was centered) of Rio's University of Brazil. These three institutions provided the nucleus of almost all subsequent scientific training—outside of biology and medicine—in Brazil. In physics, present Brazilian capacities can be traced back directly to São Paulo, 1934.[15]

The contribution of Armando Salles was not limited to his early perception of the link between industrialization and a supply of brainpower and trained technicians, but in such follow-up steps as assuring reasonable funding and active participation in a talent search to staff the new institutions. The early years of the University of São Paulo coincided with the gathering storm in Europe and facilitated the recruitment of quality faculty. The Governor and Gleb Wataghin, the first director of the São Paulo Faculty of Philosophy, recruited vigorously, bringing chemists from Germany and mathematicians from Italy. Wataghin, himself a physicist, and Italian recruit Giuseppe Occhalini trained the first group of contemporary Brazilian physicists, including Marcelo Damy, Mário Schoenberg, César Lattes, P. A. Pom-

[15] J. Costa Ribeiro, "A Física no Brasil," in F. de Azevedo, *op. cit.*, Vol. I, p. 181.

peia, and a half-dozen others. The São Paulo physics group was nearly evenly divided between theoretical and experimental work; the first two areas of research entered were nuclear physics and cosmic rays. In a subsequent paragraph we will return to the development of physics. Meanwhile, it appears to be the opinion of many scientists and educators that physics—cradled so recently in São Paulo—is nearing the point of national self-sufficiency, although this goal may still be some years away. This assessment does not mean that the supply of physicists is adequate, but that research orientation and teaching level are such that most types of training through the doctorate level will be possible within the country in the not-too-distant future.

In a final comment on the general state of Brazilian science as of the beginning of the Costa e Silva "big push," we may list a few rough indicators. There are very few statistics readily available, and comparisons with other countries may be inaccurate because of varying definitions. According to the Organization of American States, Brazil has a total of 104 national organizations operating in science and technology, public and private, including universities, research institutes, and promotion organizations. This total compares with 137 in Argentina and 39 in Venezuela.[16] A research branch of the Ministry of Planning reports that Brazil has 0.3 scientists per 10,000 inhabitants, compared with 23.4 in the United States, 11 in England, and 7.3 in West Germany.[17] Total university matriculations as a percentage of population were .14 per cent in 1962, compared with .9 per cent in Argentina and .44 per cent in Venezuela.[18] Of the 110,000 students this percentage represented, fewer than half were studying either pure or applied sciences. Total Brazilian investment in scientific and technological activities has been estimated at about .18 per cent of gross national product, compared with .35 per cent for Argentina and a goal of one per cent set by the Organization of American States.[19] A different kind of indicator was obtained by attending the 19th Annual Meeting of the Brazilian Society for the Progress of Science, held in Rio, July 9–15, 1967. About 1,800 persons registered for the meeting, most of them scientists. No fewer than 623 papers were read in the seventeen sections [20] com-

[16] Organization of American States, *Report of the Meeting of the Inter-American Ad Hoc Science Advisory Committee,* Washington: 1966, p 55. Science experts at O.A.S. suggest that these figures are quite rough and should be used only to suggest orders of magnitude until a fuller survey, presently under way within that organization, can be published.

[17] *Jornal do Brasil,* February 26, 1967.

[18] Ministério do Planejamento, *Plano Decenal de Desenvolvimento Econômico e Social, Educaçao (I). Diagnóstico Preliminar,* Rio de Janeiro, 1967, p. 44.

[19] Organization of American States, *op. cit.,* p. 57.

[20] These sections were: Mathematics, Physics-Astronomy, Chemistry-Physical Chemistry, Geology-Minerology, Biology-Genetics-Paleontology, Anthropology-

plemented by twelve symposia and five round-table discussions. Seasoned conference-goers commented that the quality of the papers was reasonably high, and although no startling discoveries were announced, most of the papers were creative and original, a great improvement over the rehash of world literature that plagued such sessions in the Society's early years. One aspect of the meetings which even a lay observer could appreciate was the considerable attention devoted to information systems, new teaching techniques (such as nondirected learning in biophysics at the Minas Gerais Medical School and the promotion of science clubs in São Paulo State), science journalism, and political questions related to science. As might be expected, much of the latter discussion included criticism of low salaries and prestige, and lack of research funds and facilities, and stressed the need for clearer, more consistent public policies on science. The meetings received surprisingly good coverage in the press of Rio, São Paulo, and Belo Horizonte.

No word on the present state of Brazilian science would be complete without mention of the crisis that has beset and sorely retarded the promising University of Brasília since the military-backed government seized power in 1964.[21] The University, which opened in 1962, represented an entirely new departure in Brazilian higher education, the fulfillment of many ideas of university reform espoused two decades earlier in the abortive attempt to create a University of the Federal District in Rio, and above all, a model for the future. As one of the former professors there puts it, "It was a light, a hope, in the dim landscape of the Brazilian university system." The innovations it embodied were many, but chief among them was a system of basic Institutes (Mathematics, Physics, Chemistry, Earth Sciences, Biology, Social Sciences, Arts and Letters) for the "undergraduate" years, used in common before professional specialization, so as to improve quality and cut costs, avoiding the duplicate facilities found in the traditional system of separate faculties. Other features included the intent to have only full-time professors with decent pay—still the exception rather than the rule in Brazil—and independent funding based on patrimony and earmarked appropriations, and compulsory research. With the advent of the mili-

Sociology-Psychology, Engineering-Technology, Agronomy, Science Education, Botany-Phytochemistry, Zoology-Parasitology, Cytology-Histology-Embryology, Physiology-Biophysics-Biochemistry-Pharmacology, Microbiology-Epidemiology-Preventive Medicine, Pathology-Therapeutics, Documentation-Scientific Information, and Oceanography-Marine Biology.
[21] This interpretation is derived from interviews with Professors David Carneiro and Roberto Salmeron, former faculty members of the University; Professor Laerte Ramos de Carvalho, then Rector of the University, and accounts in the daily press of Rio, 1965-67.

tary government in 1964, despite dismissal of the rector and the confinement of the former rector and several professors for a few days, many associated with the University held out hopes that the institution would continue much along the same lines or even improve, since there had been structural and staff problems from the beginning. Except for the extreme militants affected in the beginning of the Castelo Branco regime—some of whom, although academic modernizers, perceived the University more as a vehicle for political mobilization and eventual reform of society than as a standard of academic excellence performing a more limited reform role—there was not the kind of undeclared war between teachers and regime found, say, in the University of Buenos Aires during the first month of the Onganía government in 1966. In late 1965 this live-and-let-live state of affairs broke down, ostensibly because of the Rector's removal of a sociology assistant, but for many underlying causes, including the weakness of Rector Laerte Ramos de Carvalho, who allowed meddling by the local military commander; an insensitive central government influenced by traditional academicians who nourished a deep grudge against Brasília; delay in putting into force a basic university statute and resultant ambiguity and confusion regarding tenure of faculty, many of whom had been borrowed from government ministries as well as other universities; an aggressive, ambitious, and heterogeneous faculty accustomed to a good deal of free-wheeling, some of whose elements preferred a showdown over survival of the institution; and the lack of political skill by the faculty spokesman, Roberto Salermon, himself a moderate. In November nearly all faculty members—over two hundred—resigned, including some of the most distinguished names in all disciplines who had been attracted from all parts of Brazil. Predictions were that this would mean the end of the University.

From the standpoint of science development in Brazil, the setback at Brasília was a tragedy, but a relative one, and several points should serve to put the event in perspective. (1) What was dismantled, at least temporarily, was a set of symbols and aspirations more than a well-developed institutional base of the kind that was devised in Buenos Aires. The University had been functioning only three years, and its size (about 200 faculty members and 2,000 students) was small compared with that of São Paulo (3,000 faculty members and 13,000 students). There was no great emigration abroad, since most of those resigning simply returned to their previous positions. The University never formally closed, its basic structure and concepts remain, and despite a deep plunge in teaching quality in the interim, there are signs of a slow and painful recovery. (2) Blame for the crisis must be divided several ways, and the collapse should not be viewed as solely the result of obscurantist policies of the central government. (3) Judging by the views expressed at a recent meeting in Washington, D.C. of several dozen Brazilian scientists working in the United States, it would appear that salary levels and working conditions are more important than questions of principle (i.e., academic freedom and tenure) among the reasons why scientists leave Brazil for other countries; the events in Brasília were hardly mentioned. (4) An intact institution does not compensate for the loss of human talent, but it is important. The University today has 2,100 regular students and a faculty of over 500, and while many of the latter are said to be second-rate, some departments, such as mathematics, are rebuilding rapidly. Most signs suggest that the University of Brasília, brightest symbol thus far in university modernization, was damaged severely but not fatally.

## DEVELOPMENT IN PHYSICS

We will now narrow our narrative of science development to physics and the institutions most directly related to it, since it is one of the fields said to be closest to self-sustaining growth and the most germane to the nuclear energy debate. Just fifteen years after the founding of the São Paulo group, the Brazilian Center of Physics Research was established in Rio in 1949. Its first director, César Lattes, had worked with the Bristol group in England during the 1940s and later in California, where his work in cosmic rays and the discovery of the pi-meson gave him great prestige among Brazilians. The status of the Center is unique in that its funds are largely public, but it is an autonomous and theoretically "private" body, operating in loose conjunction with the Federal University of Rio de Janeiro (formerly the University of Brazil). Dedicated exclusively to research and postgraduate training, the Center soon became the principal center for physics research in the country, with the largest number of theoretical physicists in Latin America. With an annual budget of about $300,000 in recent years, the Center normally has five full professors and 25 to 35 associates and assistants. Among these are ten Ph.D.'s from top physics departments such as Princeton, Berkeley, Birmingham, Columbia, and M.I.T. The Center houses a Cockroft-Walton generator and other modern laboratory equipment; the best-known experimental work done there has been on high energy particles, cosmic ray recording, and solar ray noise.[22]

[22] National Academy of Sciences, Office of the Foreign Secretary, *Background Information for Brazil-U.S. Workshop on Science, Technology and Development,* Washington: Mimeo, 1966.

The Center of Physics Research in Rio and the Department of Physics in São Paulo are the two most important research and teaching centers, differing most sharply in that the latter has a large undergraduate (350 students) program. The São Paulo budget was running to half a million dollars by 1963, and there were sixty scientists on the faculty. But these institutions are not the only academic physics centers in the country. Promising physics institutes exist at the University of Rio Grande do Sul and the University of Pernambuco. Worthy of special mention is the Institute of Physics of the Pontifical Catholic University of Rio de Janeiro, founded in 1959 and directed thereafter until his death in 1966 by Father F. X. Roser, S.J., who had gone there from Fordham. It is the only private university with an ambitious program in physics. The Institute is still relatively small (95 students and 23 professors) and does not offer a doctoral program, but its operating budget increased from $75,000 in 1962 to around $135,000 in 1966, its professors are full-time, the research style is vigorous and modern, and the equipment is improving, with a four megawatt Van de Graaf accelerator to be installed shortly.[23]

Parallel to the maturing of Brazilian academic physics with the formation of the Center for Physics Research, another process was evolving that, although on a small scale, was greatly to stimulate Brazilian science and physics in particular. This was the entry of the national government into the promotion and subvention of research. It should not be imagined that this move came about easily in the 1940s. Only recently had the *Estado Novo*, Getúlio Vargas' mild dictatorship, yielded to the so-called "re-democratization" of 1945. If the Vargas period had been modernizing in certain respects, it had not been a political regime characterized by a sophisticated attitude toward science. One of Vargas' closest political associates, Gustavo Campanema, had virtually scuttled the forward-looking, scientifically oriented University of the Federal District in 1939, first by federalizing it because "no municipal university should be superior to a national body," and then by calling for a "return to humanism." It is not surprising that the military took the initiative in leading the government into the "new science." Military officers directed various industrialization efforts, such as the Volta Redonda Steel Mill built in the late forties, and were increasingly aware of the demands of modern technology for engineers. The Army, long under the influence of classical French training, had sent an Expeditionary Force to Italy and seen firsthand the place of technology in modern warfare. And the Hiroshima bomb more than anything else suggested the relationship between technology and theo-

[23] Interviews with Father Thomas J. Cullen, S.J., Director of the Institute, August, 1967.

retical science. Furthermore, hardly had the Smyth Report reached Brazil before a young Brazilian was winning laurels for his exploration of the atomic nucleus. Perhaps those in underdeveloped countries could "make magic" too.

Thus an atmosphere increasingly favorable to scientific investigation preceded creation of the National Research Council in January, 1951— a step unsuccessfully proposed on previous occasions by the Brazilian Academy of Sciences. The "father" of the Research Council was Admiral Alvaro Alberto, a former professor of thermodynamics at the Naval Engineering School and during the late 1940s Brazil's representative on the United Nations Atomic Energy Committee. His prestige and recent close association with United States nuclear authorities were great assets as he lobbied among public authorities. The Council, known in Brazil as the Conselho Nacional de Pesquisas (CNPq) is an independent agency directly responsible to the President of the Republic, its principal mission to "promote and stimulate the development of scientific research in all fields," and to advise the President on the formulation and execution of science policy.[24] Specifically, the Council is authorized to provide grants and scholarships for doctoral and post-doctoral training and research projects, grants for acquisition of scientific equipment and contract of specialized personnel, subventions for the total or partial support of research institutions, special training courses organized by the Council, and travel grants for study and conferences abroad. The basic legislation was not revised until 1964, when the Castelo Branco government attempted to revitalize the Council and give it wider authority.[25]

From the beginning, the CNPq was "nuclear-oriented." The original law gave the Council competence in the "research and industrialization of atomic energy and its applications, including acquisition, transport, protection, and transformation of raw materials." (Brazil was known to possess large deposits of thorium and of monazite sands, from which rare earths, uranium, and thorium are extracted. Awareness of these deposits, together with the country's aspirations toward major-power status and pride in the achievement of César Lattes and others, were major factors in the early postwar Brazilian interest in atomic energy.) Shortly after creation of the Council, it authorized purchase of an accelerator from Chicago at a cost of some $250,000; soon after, it approved the construction of a larger accelerator within the country. Even in the early years, Council policies displayed a strong interest in nuclear science collaboration with technologically more advanced nations—with France on uranium fabrication, and with West Ger-

[24] Law 1310, January 15, 1951.
[25] Law 4533, December 8, 1964.

many on the possible utilization of the "ultra-centrifugal" process for isotope separation. Admiral Alberto, the first President of the Council, secured a $350,000 commitment from the United States Atomic Energy Commission for financing half the cost of Brazil's first reactor, installed in São Paulo a few years later. (Principal Brazil-United States dealings on nuclear energy during the early 1950s, prior to the U.S. Atomic Energy Act of 1954 or the creation of Brazil's National Atomic Energy Commission, were limited to United States acquisition of small stocks of atomic raw materials, a matter in which the Brazilian Ministries of Agriculture and Foreign Relations took the policy lead.) The structure of the Council in its early years is indicative of priorities —of its two subdivisions, one was devoted to nuclear energy, the other to all the rest of science and technology. It was within the Council, whose direction was shared by military bureaucrats and scientists,[26] that Brazil's first policy statements on nuclear energy were prepared.[27]

A confidential memorandum prepared by the Council dated October 12, 1952, defined six goals for Brazil. These were capacity in: (1) prospecting, mining, and processing of atomic raw materials; (2) chemical treatment of atomic minerals; (3) metallurgy for high-grade uranium for use in reactors; (4) production of enriched uranium; (5) reactor construction, both for research and electric power; (6) increased cadres of scientific and technical personnel, and access to technical assistance from the major Western powers and possibly India and Japan.[28] This memorandum was approved by the National Security Council, and later by President Getúlio Vargas, apparently without discussion. It should be noted that at this time and for the next few years, little interest was attracted by such proposals outside of a narrow group of technicians. Politicians, press, and public in the mid-1950s were much more interested in a different question, only peripherally related to the building up of Brazilian resources in research, technology, and raw materials. This was the nationalists' charge concerning the agreements the Brazilian Government had signed with the U.S. Atomic Energy Commmission providing for Brazilian sale of monazite sands and rare earths for the United States stockpile program at the time when the United States was involved in the Korean War, and its acquisition policies did not yet reflect the growing abundance

[26] Of the Council's seven presidents from 1951 to the present, four have been military officers. A representative of the Armed Forces General Staff is an *ex-officio* member of the Council's Deliberative Assembly, its policy-making organ, presently numbering 25 members.
[27] As this is written, the CNPq is completing preparation of a five-year plan for science and technology in Brazil, but it was not available to the writer.
[28] Cited in Olympio Guilherme, *O Brasil e a Era Atómica*, 2nd ed., Rio de Janeiro: 1957.

of atomic raw materials. Essentially, economic nationalism and not nuclear strategy was at issue, and in retrospect the "scandals," like the Chamber of Deputies investigation which ensued, look like a tempest in a teapot.[29]

## CREATION OF THE ATOMIC ENERGY COMMISSION

In October 1956 the Council was shorn of most nuclear energy responsibilities upon the creation of a separate independent agency, the Atomic Energy Commission (known first as C.E.A. and later as CNEN, or National Nuclear Energy Commission). The Council is still an important part of the institutional framework conditioning nuclear development as well as other science policies through its subsidies for basic research. When the Nuclear Energy Commission was formed, no Federal appropriations were provided for a time, and the Council "loaned" its offspring 40 million cruzeiros to get started. The Council's own funding remained extremely modest from the beginning. Its budget has increased very little in constant terms over the years; for the last three years it has ranged between $3 million to $3.5 million.[30] Despite the modest beginning of the Council, the late J. Robert Oppenheimer, who took an interest in it while visiting Rio, declared that its creation was the most important step thus far in the evolution of Brazilian science.

Meanwhile, the Atomic Energy Commission grew rapidly in the first eleven years of its existence. Its creation in 1956 followed the recommendations of an Inter-Ministerial Commission on Brazilian Nuclear Policy and had strong political overtones. Nationalist sentiment had been galvanized as never before during the debates concerning the cre-

[29] The charges variously asserted that the Brazilian government was too permissive in selling, the United States was too niggardly in buying, the price was too low, and Brazilian demands for recompense in the form of still-secret technological information were not heeded. Actually, the amount of Brazilian minerals acquired was very small. The "exposure" coincided with the eruption of economic nationalism in many sectors, the classic example being that which produced Petrobrás, the national petroleum monopoly.

[30] In 1966 the Commission spent 6.4 billion cruzeiros, of which about 25 per cent went toward maintenance of subordinate entities—the Institute of Pure and Applied Mathematics, the National Institute of Research of Amazonia, the Brazilian Institute of Bibliography and Documentation, the Institute of Highway Research, and the National Commission on Space Activities. About 50 per cent went into direct research grants in ten disciplinary sectors—biology and medicine (887 million), physics and astronomy (735 million), technology (525 million), chemistry (445 million), earth sciences (433 million) and five other sectors with smaller sums. See Conselho Nacional de Pesquisas, *Relatório 1966*, Rio de Janeiro: 1967.

ation of the state petroleum monopoly (Petrobrás) after Getúlio Vargas' comeback to the Presidency in 1951. After Vargas' suicide in 1954, the subsequent caretaker government of President Café Filho followed more orthodox economic policies, and was more conciliatory to foreign investment, leading to a revival of nationalist charges of *entreguismo*.[31] Public figures active in the discussions leading to the formation of the CNEN have indicated that resurgence of a feeling that could be described as "pro-Petrobrás and anti-Café Filho" was partly responsible for the interagency Commission's recommendations, which led not only to separation of atomic energy responsibility matters from the Council, but tightened the government's monopoly over the whole field. A number of scientists, including the then President of the Research Council, Professor Cristovão Cardoso, did not favor the truncation, believing it to be a "precocious" development, and that the overriding task of the next few years should be "development of human infrastructure in science, not engaging in nuclear fantasies." [32] But this view did not prevail. Originally the Commission was directly subordinate to the President of the Republic, but was given autonomous status in 1962. In the general administrative reform of the government in 1967, the Commission was placed within the Ministry of Mines and Energy. Its principal activities from the beginning have been directed toward (1) uranium (and other nuclear fuel), prospecting, processing and research on uranium enrichment; (2) training and improvement of scientists and technicians; (3) direct research and contract research in nuclear physics, reactor physics, heat transfer, and nuclear engineering; (4) studies on the production of heavy water and graphite for reactor moderating and coolant elements; and (5) encouraging Brazilian industry to acquire nuclear energy capacity.[33]

It should be noted that Brazil's avowed aspirations in nuclear energy have never included military weapons capacity, and there is no evidence to suggest that a military capacity, even in the distant future, has figured even tacitly among the goals of responsible Brazilian authorities. (Apart from a modest participation on the side of the Allies in World War II, Brazil has not taken part in a foreign war since that of the Triple Alliance against Paraguay a century ago; the principles of pacific settlement of disputes, disarmament, and the like have long been keystones of the country's foreign policy.) Priorities in atomic energy,

---

[31] *Entreguismo*, derived from the verb *entregar*, to deliver, is widely used by economic nationalists to denote and disparage the policies of those (*entreguistas*) who "sell out" to foreign capital, especially by permitting exploitation of natural resources such as minerals by foreign or foreign-connected capital.

[32] Interview, August 26, 1967.

[33] Conselho Nacional de Energia Atômica, *Nuclear Energy in Brazil*, Rio de Janeiro: 1967.

during the exploratory years of 1951–67, were assigned to nuclear ore prospecting, research, training, and radioisotope production with small reactors, and plans for power generation reactors—roughly in that order. Expenditures by the Commission, which account for a large share of the total Brazilian investment in atomic physics, nuclear engineering, and related fields, have increased in recent years, with outlays of 8.6 million New Cruzeiros in 1966, 19 million in 1967, and over 25 million projected for 1968. (These sums are roughly equal to 4, 6, and 9 millions dollars, respectively.) Persons directly employed by the Commission numbered over 1,100 in 1967, more than half of them in high and medium grade positions.

The President of the Commission and its other four Members, appointed by the President of the Republic for five-year terms, provide operational direction as well as the policy-making function of the entity. Commission headquarters consists of six functional departments in addition to the normal staff units. Under Commission jurisdiction are several decentralized and relatively autonomous operating institutes, chief of which are the Atomic Energy Institute in São Paulo, the Institute of Nuclear Engineering on Fundão Island near Rio de Janeiro, the Institute of Radioactivity Research on the campus of the University of Minas Gerais in Belo Horizonte, and the Monazite Production Administration in São Paulo. There is a degree of overlapping activity within the first three of these institutes, and according to the accounts of some Brazilian scientists, a considerable rivalry based on divergent research priorities and technical strategies; i.e., which particular combination of fuels and reactor types is Brazil's best option in the quest for thermoelectric power and other peaceful uses.

All three institutes possess research reactors, two of them procured in the United States and all three fueled with enriched uranium acquired from the U.S. Atomic Energy Commission, subject to the standard inspection and safeguards procedures. The five-megawatt "swimming pool" reactor of the Atomic Energy Institute in São Paulo, which went critical in September 1957, was the first in the Southern hemisphere. In Belo Horizonte, at the Institute of Radioactivity Research a Triga Reactor of 14 megawatts became critical in November 1960. On Fundão Island, the 10-megawatt Argonaut Reactor (water-cooled and moderated) which went critical in February 1965, was constructed in Brazil—of over 90 per cent Brazilian-made components—by the Institute of Nuclear Engineering.

Although some of Brazil's top nuclear physicists and engineers have moved freely between these institutes, particular technical strategies have come to be associated with the different institutions. Experts of the São Paulo Institute, for example, advocate technology involving natural uranium fuel and heavy-water or graphite reactors. The Radio-activity Institute at Belo Horizonte has long been the home of the so-called "Thorium Group," a cluster of fifteen to twenty experts who have been searching several years for a viable process to utilize thorium and its fissionable derivative (U-233) in a power reactor. A notable fact about the Thorium Group experience is not merely its pioneer quality (no country has yet produced such a reactor technology on a practical scale), but that the original research proposal in 1964 was ig-nored and in effect rejected by the parent Commission, yet the group proceeded on its own, gradually "legitimizing" its status with the Commission. The experience is cited to illustrate the loose, permissive direction of the government's atomic energy efforts, as well as plural-ism and competitiveness within the scientific-technical establishment. Diversity of approach has also been characteristic of the Commission's five successive Presidents, three of whom (including the present Presi-dent, General Uriel da Costa Ribeiro) have been military officers. The eclectic, moderate orientation of Admiral Otacilo da Cunha (1956–61) and General Ribeiro (at present) contrast considerably with that of Professor Marcelo Damy (1961–64), a vigorous nationalist who pushed geological exploration extensively during his tenure, and who today (as a top official of the São Paulo Institute) is one of the most vocal proponents of the "independent entry" of Brazil into the "Atomic Club"—that is, avoiding reliance on external sources for atomic fuels, and insistence on the right to develop nuclear explosives for peaceful ends.

The modesty of budget and personnel figures mentioned above, as well as the organizational and policy looseness characteristic of Brazil's nuclear energy program to date appear as a rather unpretentious back-ground for the bold policy statements of 1967. Nevertheless, the coun-try is Latin America's most advanced in nuclear research facilities and in over-all industrial capacity. There are an estimated 300 graduate physicists in Brazil, of whom about 150 are in research and perhaps 100 have training relevant to nuclear programs.[34] Approximately one hun-dred nuclear engineers have been graduated from local institutions or trained abroad.[35] Salaries are low—around $400 a month for top men. United States authorities, from J. Robert Oppenheimer to Glenn Sea-borg, have nevertheless paid tribute to Brazil's beginning and its poten-

---

[34] No official figures have been published to the writer's knowledge, although both the Ministry of Foreign Relations and Ministry of Planning are apparently engaged in surveying the country's professional and technical manpower. The above figure is cited frequently by Brazilian scientists.

[35] According to Engineer Carlos Werth Urban, Chief of the "Thorium Group" of the Radioactivity Research Institute, in an interview published in *Estado de São Paulo*, August 2, 1967.

tial in nuclear planning and development. The entry of the French and the Chinese into the "Atomic Club" has had a considerable impact on influential Brazilians, whose conversations reflect a sense both of encouragement and challenge from the two examples, despite the fact that Brazil lacks France's industrial-technological base or China's capacity for regimentation. Apart from the original considerations (major-power aspirations and the possession of thorium) two additional incentives to the development of nuclear technology have gained widespread attention recently. The first relates to the electric energy needs of a rapidly growing nation. Despite Brazil's enormous hydroelectric reserves, one of the largest in the world, it has become evident that in the populous and developed Center-South region hydraulic potential will be exhausted by 1980 or 1985; fossil fuels for thermal power are scarce and expensive. Also by the mid-1960s attention had been drawn to the possibilities suggested by the U.S. PLOWSHARE program—the use of nuclear explosions for such peaceful purposes as large-scale excavation and canal-digging, rock fracturing applied to petroleum and natural gas recovery, and others.

Yet in the early and middle 1960s, after a fairly brisk start, the nuclear energy enterprise in Brazil was stagnating. The generalized crisis of 1962–64 affected all but the most hermetically sealed sectors of Brazilian life, and runaway inflation was especially damaging to public programs involving capital expenditures and imports requiring foreign currency. After the Revolution of 1964, despite a sympathetic stance by the Castelo Branco government toward scientific-technological advance, all public programs felt the impact of budget-trimming as a part of the effort to contain inflation. The Brazilian atomic energy program had thus experienced five sluggish years when President Costa e Silva was inaugurated in March 1967. Before his inauguration, the President-elect promised to continue the basic lines of the Revolution of 1964, but to "humanize" the austere policies of his predecessor. Many sectors of the national community hoped this policy would mean more favorable treatment of their interests; and the scientific-technical establishment was no exception.

## COSTA E SILVA'S GAMBLE

The principal factors which have worked to alter the nuclear energy picture in Brazil in 1967 have been the arrival of a new set of actors on the political stage and the linkage of nuclear energy matters to international issues. Before discussing these, let us summarize the situation prevailing at the beginning of the year.

(1) Brazil, with its continental dimensions, relatively large population, and strong natural resource base, has long aspired to the role of a major world power, and at the minimum to be a leader of the "developing" or "third" world. These aspirations, buttressed by a period of remarkable industrialization and economic growth after World War II, have not been matched by performance in important respects, especially with regard to the social infrastructure or political development adequate to the new strains of wider participation and increased state intervention. The country possesses one of the world's two largest proven deposits of thorium, a fertile element that can be transmuted in a reactor to fissionable uranium 233. It has some proven deposits of low-quality natural uranium and possible but unproved sources of higher-grade uranium. Despite a long backward tradition in general education and a slow start in science, Brazil produced in a generation Latin America's largest national grouping of research physicists, including several who attained world renown in atomic fields, and has Latin America's most advanced program of nuclear research. In that developed portion of the country where electric power needs are greatest, conventional sources would appear incapable of supplying demand about ten years hence. If and when nuclear explosions prove feasible for excavation and rock fracturing, Brazil, with its unlinked hydrographic basins and large oil shale reserves, would appear to be a prime candidate for putting them to use. Yet, in contrast to such countries as India and Spain, Brazil does not yet operate a power reactor. The gap between potential and performance in atomic energy was in a sense a miniature of that at the level of national power, each gap productive of tensions and frustrations.

(2) With regard to the making of science policy in general and nuclear policy in particular, we observe that "manifest" decision-making institutions have never dominated the process. Neither Presidents (prior to Costa e Silva) nor the national Congress have played a leading role in guiding and developing science or nuclear energy policy. From the scanty evidence available at this writing, it does not appear that the Deliberative Assembly of the National Research Council has been the most authoritative influence behind the laws, decrees, and proclamations issued in this field, although it seems to have played an important role as a kind of "communications center." The "authoritative" quality, at least in several important cases, has been imparted by the National Security Council, a predominantly military entity whose policy-making status is quasi-formal at best. The policy alternatives and inputs available to this body have been provided for the most part by a small élite of scientific and military individuals operating through informal channels outside the manifest political structure. This élite

has been pluralistic and competitive; as the issues have "migrated to the bureaucracy" the varying responses of Atomic Energy Chairmen and Presidents of the Republic to different sectors have produced plural and sometimes inconsistent policies.

The real as distinct from formal shaping of policies by a nonpolitical élite of experts was not unique to nuclear policies in the period under discussion. A strong case has been made that many fundamental and positive economic development decisions were made this way during the Kubitschek administration, not despite but because of dysfunctions and underdevelopment in the political system—the weakness, unrepresentativeness, or irrelevance of interest groups, parties, and Congress in effect insulating decision-makers from the pressures of competing claimants, in a kind of "spontaneous Technocracy." [36] But the economic-expert élite appears to have been more unified as to basic goals and means than the scientific-military élite on what could be done and how with nuclear energy. Rapid economic development as a national goal had been far more legitimized and accepted by the mid-1950s than scientific-nuclear development. In the latter process, doctrines of nationalism had already been effectively used as a mobilization device. And the restructuring of the Brazilian economy was not only linked to international issues from the beginning but was in large measure triggered by them. The important convergence of domestic nuclear policies with international issues came only in 1967.

Let us now review what happened during the first six months of the Costa e Silva administration. Even before assuming the presidency, Costa e Silva and his advisers had been searching for a theme and a symbol with which to stamp the new administration. Part of their task was to reconcile their commitment to continuity of the basic lines of the 1964 Revolution with a distinctive appearance that could be dissociated from the unpopularity and austerity of the Castelo Branco regime. The broad slogan chosen was "humanization of the Revolution," but something concrete was needed. The motif "science and technology" was especially laden with prestige connotations, and was a theme intimately associated with "development," yet one of few that was not associated (and therefore not "tarnished" in the eyes of the military) with the inflationary Kubitschek period or the populist Vargas-Goulart regimes of the previous fifteen years, when "developmentalism" had attained mystical status. By Inauguration Day in Brasília, the new commitment to push technology, science, and education was prominently inserted in the Presidential address.

Immediately developments began to converge, thrusting the domes-

[36] See Nathaniel Leff, *Economic Policy-Making and Economic Development in Brazil, 1947–1964*, New York: John Wiley & Sons, 1968.

tic science-technology policy into the arena of international relations. On February 14, fourteen Latin American nations had signed the Mexico City Treaty barring nuclear weapons from Latin America and the Caribbean, but although Brazil had previously approved the text, the Castelo Branco government did not sign the treaty, preferring to leave the final decision to the new government of Costa e Silva. In Geneva, after years of negotiation, it appeared that the Eighteen-Nation Disarmament Committee was approaching agreement on a draft treaty for the nonproliferation of nuclear weapons, and Brazil occupied a key position as one of the two Latin American nations of the Committee. Within a month after Costa e Silva's inauguration, the American chiefs of state would meet at Punta del Este, and it had long been known that a prominent place on the agenda was reserved for a declaration on the place of science and technology in hemisphere development plans. The President's appointment as Foreign Minister was José Magalhães Pinto, an astute and highly flexible politician from Minas Gerais, who as an important state governor had managed amicable coexistence with the João Goulart government, then assumed a leading part in the Goulart overthrow of 1964, then opposed the Castelo Branco government during its unpopular phase and captured a Federal Deputy's seat in the 1966 election with the largest vote in history. The new Chancellor, widely reported to have strong future presidential ambitions, embraced the science and technology theme warmly and vocally. Meanwhile, an especially able diplomat had returned from abroad to become Secretary General of the Foreign Office in the Itamaraty Palace. Ambassador Sergio Corrêa da Costa took on his new job with a decided "nuclear orientation," having served in the lengthy negotiations that preceded the Mexico City Treaty.[37] The major innovation that emerged out of this convergence of events and personalities was the assumption by the Foreign Office of a major role in science and nuclear policy-making.

Under Ambassador Corrêa da Costa, a task force of approximately twenty persons drawn from Itamaraty's departments of political affairs and international organizations matters was assembled, and in subsequent months had dealt with matters as various as the gathering of scientific information abroad, improved relations with Brazilian scientists abroad, structuring increased science collaboration with regional and international agencies, and domestic political considerations. Of course the most important task confronting the group was to develop and defend the Brazilian position on nuclear nonproliferation at Mexico City and Geneva.

[37] Ambassador Corrêa da Costa had previously been posted to Canada, where, according to a Brazilian diplomat, he took a keen interest in Canada's nuclear power program and became quite proficient in nuclear concepts and terminology.

That position is that Brazil supports disarmament, including the pro-
scription of nuclear weapons for itself and others, but reserves the
right to develop and use atomic energy for peaceful purposes, including nuclear explosions. The Mexico City Treaty forbids the manufacture, acquisition, testing or use of nuclear weapons (Articles I and V)
but permits, under certain conditions, the use of nuclear explosive devices for peaceful purposes (Article XVIII). Even with the latter pro-
viso, Brazil conditioned its signature of the Treaty on May 10th with a
note of clarification, emphasizing its understanding that Article XVIII
permits nuclear explosions for peaceful purposes even if the device
used resembles a weapon. In Geneva, however, following the announcement on August 24 of the United States-Soviet draft of the
Non-Proliferation Treaty, the Brazilian representative attacked the
Treaty vigorously. Indications from Itamaraty were that Brazil would
not be likely to sign the Treaty in its present form, although there has
been no explicit rejection, and the draft is still under negotiation. The
draft NPT, in contrast to the Mexico City Treaty, obligates nonnuclear signatory nations not to receive, manufacture, or acquire "nuclear weapons or other nuclear explosive devices." (Article II.)

There are several remarkable features about the Brazilian stand. The
Mexico City position was taken despite the views strongly expressed
by the United States, the Soviet Union, and even the Mexican government that there is no essential difference between an atomic bomb and
a nuclear "artifact" designed for peaceful purposes. The Brazilian position relies on the Roman concept of *animus* or intent, together with
the inspection system contained in the Mexico City Treaty as a way of
verifying intent, to provide both "essential" and "functional" definitions of what is a weapon and what is not. The broader Brazilian position, insistence that no rights to present or future peaceful uses of nuclear energy be waived, brings the country into direct cross-purposes
with United States policy, which strongly favors nonproliferation of
nuclear devices. As the Brazilian position became clearer, Dr. Glenn
Seaborg visited Rio in July and offered—in what was widely inter-
preted as a United States attempt to head off a confrontation with Brazil over peaceful explosions—to make nuclear explosive devices available at cost to Brazil and other nonnuclear powers, when these become
feasible and safe. Under the proposal, the device would be furnished
through an international agency but custody would be retained by the
supplier country until detonation, thus avoiding the no-transfer pro-
scription in the NPT. The Government's reaction, issued through the
CNEN, was polite and noncommittal, appreciative of Dr. Seaborg's
visit, but stating that "agreement had not been reached." [38] The reac-

38 Statement issued by General Uriel da Costa Ribeiro, President of Comissão
Nacional da Energia Nuclear, July 7, 1967.

tion of many Brazilian scientists and most of the press, however, was vigorously negative. An attempt to perpetrate "nuclear colonialism" was the charge most widely leveled. Shortly thereafter, the matter was widely discussed at the annual meeting of the Brazilian Society for the Advancement of Science. From this meeting and from the available soundings of the opinion of scientists, it became apparent that a sizable portion of the scientific-technical élite considered the Seaborg proposal—with the nondevelopment of nuclear explosives as its implicit condition—unacceptable. Now the interesting fact is that the government and the scientific élite were in substantial agreement on an important and dramatic matter of public policy, with popular opinion aroused widely and favorably, even if in a somewhat distorted and at times xenophobic fashion. Since the Brazilian government's position involved a good deal of legalistic hair-splitting, and most leading nuclear scientists believed Brazil had no interest in building the bomb, and little immediate possibility of developing peaceful explosives, what was behind their respective positions?

There were many reasons on both sides. A number of Itamaraty's concerns were those shared by other potential nuclear powers, such as India and West Germany, sensitive about the slightest possible impediment to exploitation of their own nuclear resources, particularly if there is little *quid pro quo*—not just in increased nuclear collaboration, but in terms of progress toward total and general disarmament. In the 1962 Partial Test Ban Treaty, pointed out one Itamaraty official, "There was a carrot: the nuclear as well as nonnuclear powers gave up something . . . Any sound nonproliferation treaty must reflect a balance of rights and responsibilities between nuclear and nonnuclear powers . . . but in Geneva we are getting a new Treaty of Tordesillas . . . There has been nothing like it since the eleventh century, when the Emperor and the Pope grandly drew up treaties obligating only third parties." Itamaraty's duty, the official continued, is to look ten to twenty years ahead. Particularly in Brazil, with its "national mythology about the future and the country of tomorrow," it is at best risky business to give up something whose implications for the future are not really known. "We accept being a second-rate power—but not the inevitability of it." [39] In Itamaraty and elsewhere in the government, however, many signs indicated that perhaps the most fundamental reason for a militant position is what we will term "political spin-off." A dramatic stand on this issue, apart from its objective merits, might bring the government a badly needed banner of "mobilization" with its nationalistic overtones, and at the same time repair relations with a

---

[39] The quotations are from verbatim notes taken by the writer in conversation with an Itamaraty official designated by his superiors to speak frankly, on condition that his identity be withheld.

portion of the intellectual community which might now be convinced that this was a modernizing and not obscurantist authoritarian regime.

Consultation of the public and private opinions of the scientific élite suggests three main considerations in their general, although by no means universal, support of the government's position on the treaties and the Seaborg proposal. First, many Brazilian scientists do not consider nonproliferation a viable concept with technology developing at the present rate, and against that skeptical background find resignation to the role of permanent importer of nuclear technology intolerably humiliating. Secondly, although practically all Brazilian scientists think it would be foolish to initiate an "explosive device" program in view of costs and the way it would tie up the entire nuclear establishment, some parts of such work at some point might well result in a valuable "spin-off" of technology useful in other fields. The third and probably most important is the "political spin-off" as seen from the scientists' point of view. A lesson may have been taken here from some of the Latin American economists of a few years back, the "structuralists" accused by some as defending inflation, but who maintained that a monetary approach alone would treat merely the symptoms and not the causes of inflation. A. O. Hirschman in a brilliant comment has pointed out how "structuralists" have "linked" independent problems together in order that those less privileged—or those not widely viewed as problems, or with weak backers—can ride the coattails of another problem that has somehow attained a high priority.[40] Science education, institutions, and even government programs generally receive very little money in Brazil. But nuclear programs have greater prestige than some others, and especially so when a dramatic issue laced with nationalism is attached. This issue-linking approach would appear to be directed in the present instance more toward widening the base of élite opinion support—especially military—than in any temptation toward demagoguery.

In the past we have observed instances of an impetus to Brazilian science when scientists acted as politicians (Oswaldo Cruz), or when able politicians sought out science in response to broad problems of public policy (Armando Salles). In the nuclear energy discussions of 1967 we see the political and scientific leaderships looking to each other for differing supports. This approach could have positive results, but the risks involved are also great. In its rather deliberate effort to "mobilize" élite and popular opinion on the nuclear issue, the government found in July that the response—especially by the press and lesser politicians—was more than it had bargained for. A press release issued

[40] Werner Baer and Isaac Kerstenetsky, eds., *Inflation and Growth in Latin America*, Homewood, Illinois: R. D. Irwin, 1964, p. 454.

by Itamaraty on August 4, announcing expanded nuclear collaboration offered by the United States to Brazil and minimizing policy differences between the two countries, came in response to an instruction from the pinnacle of the government to "cool it." If a compromise cannot be found to reduce the distance separating Washington and Brasília on nonproliferation, emotional escalation could conceivably ensue, with consequences disadvantageous to both countries. And on the domestic side, interest in Brazilian progress in science and technology has been raised to a point that makes it desirable for the government to point to some tangible achievements within a relatively short time, lest a new frustration set in.

There are reasons to think that the risks involved in the Costa e Silva gamble may be overcome or held within reasonable bounds. Although the London *Times* reported in October 1967 that the Brazilian position on nonproliferation was giving the Americans "many headaches," officials in Washington indicated informally that something of a reassessment was under way within both governments in an attempt to prevent the differences from hardening or assuming major proportions. In the case of the United States, this presumably meant attempts by the Department of State to temper the strongly negative reaction against the Brazilian position found within the Arms Control and Disarmament Agency, with emphasis on placing the disagreement within the broader context of long-range relationships with Brazil. The sturdy tradition of conciliating immediate Brazilian-United States differences in the interest of the larger advantages of collaboration goes back to the beginning of the century, and has survived difficult tests before, as in the administration of President João Goulart in the early 1960s. Undoubtedly Brazil is in something less than a pariah position because of the reservations on nonproliferation also expressed by countries such as West Germany, India, and Nigeria.

Within Brazil the Costa e Silva emphasis on nuclear programs was fortunate in having a second issue to be debated and to receive attention. This is the matter of a power reactor, which the administration seems fully intent on acquiring within a reasonable period. Here the decisions as to what kind of reactor technology is to be used, along with technical matters and financing, lie within a more exclusive domain, that of the Minister of Mines and Energy under whose jurisdiction the Nuclear Energy Commission is placed. Minister Costa Cavalcanti's early statements on nuclear energy matters revealed a certain difference of opinion with those expressed by Itamaraty. The working group of ten charged in mid-1967 with formulating concrete proposals on reactor acquisition was composed of ten technicians—four from the

Nuclear Energy Commission, three from Electrobrás, the government electric power autarchy; one from the Ministry of Mines and Energy, and two from the secretariat of the National Security Council. Its preliminary report was delivered to President Costa e Silva in late August, well ahead of schedule; a nuclear "shopping expedition" visited Britain in October, and there were other signs that final decisions were approaching, but no announcement had been issued by the end of 1967. The Brazilian press and outstanding political observers stressed, toward the end of the year, that differences of emphasis regarding nuclear programs previously existing between the Foreign Office and the Ministry of Mines and Energy had been resolved by President Costa e Silva, in general on the side of the more conservative and cautious approach typical of the Mines and Energy position. If this proves to be the case, there would still be good reason to believe that Brazil's entry into a modest domestic power program based on nuclear energy was speeded and supported by the raising of larger and more controversial questions in the continuing interplay of scientific and political interests.

# 5.

## SOME PROBLEMS OF SCIENCE EDUCATION IN THE DEVELOPING COUNTRIES OF AFRICA *

*BY NICHOLAS DeWITT*

*Indiana University*

The world is now well along into a stampede of the "UN development decade," the aim of which is to give a start to the multitude of newly independent and less-developed nations on the road to progress and beyond the initial "take-off stage." The drive for increasing the productivity of the low-income countries, alleviating their poverty, providing them with opportunities for political and economic development, and for reducing social inequalities—all these have become priority goals of national governments and international agencies.

In the course of this development stampede, although dissenting voices are occasionally heard that man does not live "by bread alone," the general chorus echoes P. H. Wicksteed's famous dictum: "A man can be neither a saint, nor a lover, nor a poet unless he has comparatively recently had something to eat." Progress in any sphere—political, social, or cultural—is thus viewed as contingent upon economic development in terms of some sort of temporal balance in the perpetual conflict between insatiable expectations and real resource constraints.

* Without the generous support of the Carnegie Corporation of New York, which for the last three years has assisted my research abroad—particularly in Asia and Africa—on an *International Survey of Educational Development and Planning*, this paper as a by-product of the project could not have been written.

As economists talk about the results of development and other social scientists talk about methods of effecting change, they all tend to agree that the major obstacles to development arise from the lack of education, technology, and experience adapted to development needs.

## ADAPTATION AND ASSIMILATION

"Education, technology, and experience" have their obvious origin in the high-income or so-called developed societies of the West, where they evolved and became institutionalized over long periods of gradual adaptation to the changing conditions of society and, culturally speaking, Western or European value systems. The dilemma or crisis, or whatever one wishes to call the vexing predicament of the most newly developing nations, is that this "alien" education, technology, and experience must be adapted to their specific development needs, which are obviously not the same, either in technological or cultural terms, as those in advanced industrialized countries. Such adaptation is therefore more painful and requires not theory but actual doing, not advice by foreign experts but the consent of country practitioners, not methods for planning of change but its institutional enforcement, not a nice blueprint of a national development plan but a detailed action schedule.

In reviewing the problems of science education in developing countries, we should recognize first and foremost what I consider to be the fundamental and the most difficult problem of development—namely, the process of adaptation. Scientism is not merely a method of inquiry in pursuit of knowledge, but also a cultural value system. In Africa the first attribute is readily accepted; the second is not even well understood. I would like to state without reservation that despite talk about the "Africanization" of education (which in science education has affected the terminology and examples used in biology courses) in only some countries and in only a very limited number of select schools—all African school systems continue to use course structures, syllabi, texts, laboratory equipment, examinations, and teaching practices of European design. These devices all presuppose the existing (European) cultural value system, which, to say the least, is not the case in the bush. This is simply blind borrowing, and not conscious and discriminating adaptation to local "needs." Furthermore, despite talk about the "Africanization" of staffs, most of the science instruction undertaken in secondary and higher education in Africa continues to be conducted almost exclusively by "expatriate" manpower. This practice is simply reliance upon the service of foreign technicians in transmitting knowledge and methods, and not the indigenous development of scientific attitudes and a culture of "scientism."

For most developing countries, and particularly those in Africa, C. P. Snow's ideas of the conflict of "two cultures," the literary and the scientific, must be modified by the addition of a third factor which plays havoc with "two cultures"—namely, the presence of conservative, traditional, and primitive cultures often antagonistic to both the modern literary-humanistic and the science-rationalistic value systems. It is in the context of the "cultural conflicts" and the problems of "adapting" science education to the specific conditions of Africa that our knowledge is extremely limited and development efforts exceedingly poor. I suggest that this chapter, by its design and in its intent, be viewed as merely exploratory. My general thesis is that education in general must be conceived of as a process of social assimilation, as well as an instrument for the transmission of existing knowledge. The developing countries may more readily "adapt" or "borrow" education as an instrument for transmitting "knowledge," but the concomitant of the educational process, as the assimilation of an individual to society's values and norms and its different and changing needs, more often than not simply fails.

Science education, as well as all other facets of education, plays this role of assimilation. In Western societies, science education, however limited, is essential for the assimilation of persons who will become neither practicing scientists nor technicians but who must become familiar with the rudiments of scientific and technological fundamentals in order to coexist in a modern urban and industrial state. A paradoxical situation arises in underdeveloped nations: if such an urban and industrial society does not really exist, can science education be "assimilating," and if so, to what? If it cannot perform the broad function of changing cultural values, then science education becomes the exclusive tool of professional specialization; and its general appeal and the justification for its universal introduction become seriously undermined. I am inclined to suggest that this process is exactly what is happening in most underdeveloped countries and particularly in Africa.

## EDUCATIONAL SYSTEMS—COMPLEXITY OF INTERDEPENDENCIES AND AIMS

It is idle to speak of "science education" in isolation from education in general and its role in society. Western societies are far from agreement on the function of science education in their own setting. Therefore the confusion in developing countries concerning the role of science education should not be surprising. The last two decades have produced an exceedingly voluminous flow of books, essays, studies, and reports on the role of education, science and technology in development. The proceedings of and papers submitted to the *U.N. Conference on Application of Science and Technology for Less-Developed Countries* alone occupy a five-foot shelf.[1]

Wrapped in generalities, these papers state that the "developing of human resources, training of men, training of minds has emerged as the most pivotal aspect. It is human resources, still largely untapped, which constitute man's real hope for the future."[2] There is hardly any disagreement on major postulates as they relate to the development of nations. The progress, welfare, and security of a nation depend critically on a rapid, planned, and sustained growth in the quality and extent of education, research, and application in science and technology. Science has radically transformed man's material environment. Science is universal and so should its benefits be. Science is liberating and enriching of the mind and enlarging of the human spirit. Science has added a new dimension to education, and its modernizing role in the life of a society is indispensable.

All these propositions are commonly agreed upon, and politicians in all new African states readily accept them as slogans. But as Edward Shils once tersely remarked, "The leaders of the new states of Africa and Asia are not scientists."[3] And as such, they are frequently strong on "spirit of science" slogans, but weak on the actual formulation of a "science policy" in general and policies for science education in particular. If we reach behind the façade of generalities, I think that one of the gravest problems confronting the teaching of science in Africa, as well as in many other developing countries, is not so much the deficiencies (bad as they are) of equipment and qualified staff, but rather a lack of understanding of the clear-cut purposes for which science must be taught.[4] In developing countries the fault is with the failure of their

---

[1] See, especially, "Education and Training," in *Science and Technology for Development: Report on the United Nations Conference on the Application of Science and Technology for the Benefit of the Less Developed Countries*, Vol. VI, New York: United Nations, 1963.

[2] *Ibid.*, p. 5.

[3] E. Shils, "Scientific Development in the New States," *Bulletin of the Atomic Scientists*, Vol. 17, 1961, No. 2 (reprinted in J. W. Hanson and C. S. Brembeck, eds., *Education and the Development of Nations*, New York: Holt, Rinehart and Winston, 1966, p. 210).

[4] This problem has been lucidly stated long before most African countries became independent in M. A. Faturoti, "Science in Secondary Schools," *Overseas Education*, Vol. 30, 1958, pp. 133–35.

educational systems as such to take cognizance of "science" not as a subject of instruction, but as a cultural value system permeating the whole process of teaching and learning and, in fact, life itself. There are historical reasons for this conclusion which must be briefly mentioned.

Education and society are intimately joined. The educational system viewed in its totality must in whole and in each of its parts relate specific activities to the society it is meant to serve. It is this organic concept of the functioning of educational systems that makes education the most complex of all societal institutions. The interaction of aims and social forces accounts for perennial problems of education regardless of time and place, problems highlighting what is meant by "education" and "education for what?"

"Education for what" is a major dilemma. There are many views of the functions of education in a society which, depending upon judgment and values, are selected for emphasis. However, the multiplicity of attitudes about the roles education can play may be grouped into four major areas. These are: (1) education as a human right and as an individual good *per se;* (2) education as an instrument of thought-control and mass regimentation; (3) education as a means for the creation of élites for leadership roles in society; and (4) education as a tool for developing differentiation and specialization of human inputs into the productive process. It is implicitly assumed that the process of education is based on the transmission of knowledge which is manipulated toward these ends. Some of my colleagues may quarrel with these abstract categories, but I am prepared to argue that any processes in education will fit one or more of the aforementioned "ends" of education. Most commonly, science education is thought of as serving the ends of the first and fourth categories, though it could conceivably— through its use or abuse—serve the remaining two, with the prime example being the Soviet Union, where it is consciously utilized for all four.

It appears to me that in the African setting, science education is conceived in very narrow terms, almost exclusively as a technical tool for training a limited number of specialists. Science education as an individual value and an end in itself is occasionally talked about, but there is very little in African educational practices that aids the development of an internalized scientific outlook, universal skepticism, and empiricism. Even in those countries ruled by African Marxists, there is little pressure to establish a hegemony of "scientific materialism" as an all-embracing national ideology. The technological and managerial élites are still composed largely of expatriates, and despite talk of the Africanization of the modern sectors of the economy, most qualified natives shun the scientific and technical education which would qualify them for such leadership roles.

The reasons for the limited technical role of science education must be further explained. All societies, whether primitive or civilized, carry on some kind of formal education. Education in primitive societies—crude, clumsy, unimaginative, and "unscientific" as it may appear to the Western eye—is geared to the primitive situation. But the systems of education which have come into being in Africa are of an entirely different type. Through a set of historical circumstances, all educational systems in all African countries are "Western" or "European" in design and function. They have been added on to the primitive situation and expanded by Europeans in response to the political pressure by local élites who have used education as a means of social, rather than technical, advancement.

Partaking in European education, regardless of its content and practical utility for a country's needs or performance of the individual's productive functions, has become a technique of social advancement. The "colonialists" should not be blamed for the motivations of the natives to seek education in the "humanities" and "arts" rather than in the "sciences" as a means of advancement and prestige. The distinguishing mark of the native élites in Africa is to adapt the European mode of life. The proliferating corps of bureaucrats is recruited on a competitive basis, and all the prospective candidates seek education which tends to qualify them for offices and white-collar jobs in the most expeditious manner. In the competition for entry into government service (which in most African countries offers well over half of all salaried jobs), education in the humanities, arts, and law is more valuable than that in the sciences. There is a Platonic ideal transferred to Africa by Europeans that educated leaders must be versatile generalists and that development and change irradiate from the élite to the masses.* These rationalizations reflect the convention which even in Europe and America was not modified until recently. In African attitudes, science graduates are thought of as artisans, engineers as lowly "narrow" technicians, and technological and vocational education as a pass only toward the unglamorous, undesirable, and unrewarding jobs.

Essentially, I am restating my view that in the "borrowed" systems of European education for Africa, category two—the application of education to the formation of élites—finds its expression in education with liberal and humane disciplines, literature, language, history, and philosophy. Moreover, all these disciplines are used to develop the

* See Geoffrey Oldham's chapter on science in Britain and China for further elaboration of this statement.

proper misunderstanding (I repeat—misunderstanding) of the role and function of science in society and science education as a cultural entity by continually pointing out their "limitations." These preconceptions have a direct bearing upon the deplorable status of science and technical education in Africa which has been stated on many occasions. The education ministers of the thirty-eight African countries taking part in the 1961 Addis Ababa conference on the development of education agreed that:

> One of the principal deficiencies of most educational systems is their tendency to give too little weight to studies based on the natural sciences. At the university there are usually proportionately too many students of science, engineering, agriculture or medicine. At the secondary level there is a deficiency of technical institutes and farm schools, and the great majority of secondary schools fail to make adequate provision for teaching the natural sciences. In the same way, the primary schools tend to neglect mechanical and biological studies. The chief reason for this is that the institutional patterns of education were formed many centuries before the modern technological revolution occurred, with its dependence on science. Education has therefore inherited its traditions and prejudices from a pre-scientific age. If education is to be integrated with economic development and to pay its way in purely economic terms, one of the principal changes must be a shift in curricula away from philosophic and literary studies toward natural science and its various applications. Entire substitution of one for the other is not in question; but a shift in relative proportions is of great importance.[5]

The obvious emphasis of the foregoing is on "functionality" rather than on the value of science education in its own right. Incidentally, this is the only paragraph in a report over two hundred pages long which identifies one of the major problems, but fails to spell out how solutions may be achieved.

In the several conferences that have taken place since, the recommendations were similar. In 1962 the Tananarive conference on the development of higher education recommended that some 60 per cent of the students in universities and other institutions of higher education should be trained in various branches of science, technology, agriculture, and medicine.[6] In 1962 the Rabat conference on the teaching of sciences in African universities suggested curricular revisions in line with the "Africanization" of science.[7] There are many others. In the

[5] *Conference of African States on the Development of Education in Africa: Final Report*, Addis Ababa, May 15–25, 1961, Paris: UNESCO, 1962, p. 10.
[6] *The Development of Higher Education in Africa: A Report of the Conference*, Tananarive, September 3–12, 1962, Paris: UNESCO. 1963, p. 59.
[7] *The Teaching of Sciences in African Universities*, Paris: UNESCO, 1962.

1960s every major document dealing with educational development plans and every educational or university commission has proclaimed that more science education should be given and more scientific and technical manpower should be trained. In my judgment, only very limited progress has been made in the last six years, for the real obstacles are not being willingly or seriously considered. I am inclined to attribute the shortcomings of development of science education, as well as in most other spheres of human activities in fostering development and change, not so much to the lack of "understanding" of the general problems but to a failure to adapt and implement specifically *feasible* solutions.

## PRIMARY EDUCATION—THE MISSING LINK

Every African country boasts with pride about the progress it has made in the expansion of primary education in the last ten years. I will not bore you with statistics. They are impressive indeed—two- to threefold increases in enrollment are not uncommon. The rate of primary school attendance in African countries today is anywhere from 40 to 80 per cent of the corresponding age group. While numerical gains are impressive, I was not able to observe in most of the twenty countries I visited this year (1967) any significant progress in improving the quality of primary education. There are a few government and a few mission schools which are a delight to visit, but for the most part, terribly bad buildings, overcrowded classrooms, lack of texts, lack of blackboards, lack of any school equipment and, above all, lack of qualified teachers, are most appalling. These deficiencies are most common in the overwhelming majority of African schools. The system of examinations and cramming for them affect syllabi and destroy teaching and learning initiative on the part of teachers and students. In sum, the crux of the problem is that African schools do not have those methods of schooling oriented to the individual that are essential for the development of differential abilities at an early age.

The first two or three grades are loaded with repeaters and over-aged children. After grade three, more than half of the children drop out of school before completing form five or six and without having learned either to read or to do arithmetic well. Actually, only one-fifth to one-third of the corresponding age group completes primary school. Even in quantitative terms, African primary education is an extremely wasteful undertaking. In qualitative terms it is exceedingly weak. If we assume that the early years are the most formative period of a child's life, primary schooling based on rote repetition of what the half-literate teacher reads from his text or teacher's manual must make these years that the African child is in primary school sheer frustration and a handicap for the rest of his life. There is no sense in talking about "science education" in the elementary school as an introduction to information and concepts. African primary schools do a most thorough job of not inducing the child to discover natural phenomena around him, not developing the child's natural interest and spirit of observation, not fostering curiosity about, and critical attitudes toward, problems, not leading him to generalize and somehow order his observations. There are many more "nots" in primary school practices which apply to aspects of teaching that are indispensable for rudimentary science education. The number of the "nots" is so great as to make such education virtually impossible.

In my judgment, primary education in Africa is in such a bad way that, unless it is subjected to radical surgery, it is more detrimental to further education than no education at all. Looked at critically, primary education appears to be the missing link in science education. Early science education is not to be found anywhere in Africa. A radical and yet quite feasible solution, which in most cases, however, is politically unacceptable, would be to freeze any further expansion of primary education until radically revised curricula and syllabi are developed and a substantial number of present teachers are retrained or new teachers are trained to implement these curricular reforms. Such reforms must include a provision for incorporating a certain agreed-upon minimum of scientific fundamentals, nature studies, and pupil activities related to agriculture and manual arts, in order to stimulate perception of measurement and physical phenomena. That provision should apply to all schools and all pupils, without exception.

## SECONDARY EDUCATION—SCIENCE EDUCATION AS ELECTIVE

Depending upon country and region, generally between 2 and 10 per cent of the pertinent age group of African youth are now involved in some kind of secondary schooling. Among those who do complete primary education, anywhere from one-third to two-thirds fail to gain entrance to secondary education, with the selection contingent upon examinations and primary school record. Secondary education in general and the teaching of sciences in particular are characterized by great diversity. There is a variety of administrative jurisdictions over schools—central government, local government, aided-private, unaided-private, and voluntary agency schools. Many are boarding schools;

some are day schools. The variation in size of enrollment and teaching staff by school is enormous. Differences in quality of facilities are wide. It would take many pages just to review the divisions and subdivisions and examination "certificates" of the French, British, Belgian, and Portuguese adaptations of school structures for the different countries. Briefly, it may be stated that in the total twelve to fifteen years of the primary-secondary education cycle, six to eight years are spent in primary school, and anywhere from four to seven years are devoted to secondary education, which in most cases is given in two stages—secondary or junior, and higher or senior. The sciences are taught in both stages as separate subjects of instruction. There are six science subjects (general science, physics, chemistry, biology, botany, and zoology) which are offered as separate or combination courses, with the syllabus in each subject patterned mainly upon the Cambridge or baccalaureate examination requirements. Each subject course may be repeated by students on up to three different "levels." The sequence of subjects is also variable. In addition, one of the mathematics courses (algebra, geometry, trigonometry) is also offered in different grades of the secondary school.

The secondary school student spends from twenty-six to thirty-three instruction hours per week in class. The minimum (for philosophy, language, literature students) proportion of time devoted to sciences and mathematics is about 15 per cent of the total time. The maximum (for "experimental sciences" and mathematics students) is about 60 per cent of the total instruction hours in secondary schools. It is obvious that the variation of time devoted to science education is enormous. The student who proposes to "sit" for one type of external examinations tends to cram in more courses of a desired type, or else he takes the barest minimum (general science and general mathematics). Under such circumstances, an assessment of how much science is being taught and how many students take science courses is almost a hopeless undertaking.[8] Although some countries have begun to collect statistics on the number of students taking science courses, I have difficulty in interpreting them. All that is certain is that *all* students who pass through secondary school have taken the "minimum." The proportion of secondary students who elect to take the "maximum" is exceedingly small.

The problem of teaching science in the secondary schools of Africa is not merely quantitative; it is principally qualitative. The school syl-

[8] In fact, the two extensive international surveys on science education in Africa are mute on this point. See J. Cessac, *Science Teaching in the Secondary Schools of Tropical Africa*, Paris, UNESCO, 1963; and the still unpublished report, "A Survey of Science Education in Africa," Paris: UNESCO, manuscript.

labi (either "approved" by the Ministries of Education as in most French-speaking countries, or "suggested" as in a number of English-speaking countries [note the ambivalence of this linguistic designation] —and most native populations, with the exception of the educated minority, do not have the functional command of either language!) are geared to external examinations. In fact, the topics in the "course" are often almost identical with the headings of the examination syllabus. The superimposition creates problems for changing or improving course contents. It sounds anecdotal, but it is true that when I visited one of the most progressive "comprehensive schools" in Nigeria (built with United States assistance and still largely staffed by American teachers), a chemistry teacher told me that his students simply refused to take a modified chemistry course because it did not correspond to the syllabus of the West African Examinations Council, which administers Cambridge-type examinations in the English-speaking countries of West Africa. Practically all the textbooks used in science courses are French or British in design and often even in manufacture, and most of these texts are of not very recent vintage. Teacher reliance exclusively upon textbooks is overwhelming, for the laboratory equipment is rather poor or in short supply, and frequently schools do not have sufficient allowances to purchase supplies for experiments and modern teaching aids.

The reliance upon textbooks and the traditional structure of the science courses reflect the "pressure" to pass examinations, with emphasis obviously upon memorization rather than understanding. The process of modernizing science and mathematics curricula rests not so much upon the intent of teachers, but upon the ossified system of external examinations. Presently, all these examinations are based on traditional science courses and standard Europeans texts. There is a great deal of glamorous talk about introducing "new science" and "new mathematics" in African secondary schools, but this effort must be put in the proper perspective. These programs are experimental, and at the present time there are in all of Africa only four major modernization efforts.[9] The African Mathematics Program (AMP), which is a United States-financed and United States-based activity of Educational Services, Inc., began in 1961. It is aimed at producing mathematics texts (the so-called Entebbe series) and retraining teachers in their use through workshops. This effort is gaining acceptance because at long

[9] A fifth activity, the African Primary Science Program, which is also United States-financed and conducted by ESI, was started with big publicity in Northern Nigeria in 1965, but so far has neither spread to other countries nor produced any materials. It is still in the stage of consultative "writing conferences."

last (and only in 1967) have the West African Examination Council and Cambridge agreed to permit examinations based on these materials. The second project, also started in 1961, is related to some extent to the AMP and is in a sense the British competitive effort called SMPEA (School Mathematics Project for East Africa), which is also making progress. The third effort is the UNESCO pilot project on "New Approaches and Techniques in Biology Teaching in Africa," which started in 1966. The fourth is the West African Examination Council's "A-Level Chemistry Syllabus," begun in 1964. Both projects intend to produce teaching materials and conduct teacher retraining workshops. These activities have so far affected only a few hundred teachers and schools involving several thousand students. Precisely how many students, nobody knows, for when it comes to control groups and project evaluation, these are still in the "testing stage" or else none has been undertaken so far. African ministries of education are "cooperating" by waiting to see what will become of these projects, but so far there has not been any great rush either to adopt these programs universally or to train all new teachers with an added competence in "new science" or "new mathematics." As much as their introduction might be desirable, in practice it will be a very difficult and lengthy undertaking.

## SCIENCE TEACHERS—INSOLUBLE DILEMMA

The greatest problem is the teachers themselves. In most African countries, 75 to 100 per cent of the science teachers are expatriates. Only in Ghana, Nigeria, and Sierra Leone do native science teachers account for up to a quarter of the total. Thus the dominant majority of all science teachers in all African countries are French or British. (Most of the United States Peace Corps volunteers with a science or mathematics background teach in secondary schools.) In light of a worldwide scarcity of science and mathematics teachers, Africa finds it harder than ever to get a sufficient flow, particularly of better qualified European science and mathematics teachers. The result is a very special kind of "brain drain" about which very little is being said publicly. In desperation, some East African countries are recruiting science teachers from India and Pakistan, while at the same time they are trying to repatriate or expel nationals of those countries. The status of expatriates in African education, and particularly in science and research, must be clearly understood. The world market for their services is such that they are in Africa by choice—mostly because of "topping-off" of salaries, liberal allowances, and annual home-leave arrangements. If these bonus arrangements were to be discontinued, most expatriate teachers would disappear.

The supply of native teachers lies at the very heart of Africa's educational problems. This assessment is especially true of science teachers. In any country the number and the quality of the schools are directly related to and ultimately controlled by the availability of qualified teachers. In Africa, with a rapid expansion of educational enrollments, there is a catastrophic shortage of qualified teachers and a virtual collapse in the supply of science teachers. For most African schools it is not a question of accepting or rejecting a teacher appointed to the faculty (most teachers are assigned through establishment divisions of the Ministries of Education). Regardless of that, a school is lucky to get a science or mathematics teacher—good or bad—and almost invariably he is an expatriate who will stay for a couple of years only. I actually visited some remote secondary schools where for several years there had been no science teacher, although most schools managed with one to three science and mathematics teachers, which means of course that usually each teaches more than one subject.

Most of the expatriate teachers are "experienced," but in a peculiar way. Often they have been teaching in Africa for many years, but very few have taught in the same place for more than one contract term of two or three years. The turnover of teachers is staggering. But what is more important is the corollary of this turnover, namely, that on a short-term basis these "teach-and-run" teachers do not have any vested interest in improving the "facilities for teaching"—laboratories, libraries, aids, etc. They do the job with what is available and move on to another contract.

The problem is how to create a sufficient supply of native African science teachers. Obviously, neither teacher training colleges nor other normal schools (both on the secondary level) do or can produce qualified science teachers. Science teachers must be "graduate," that is, trained in a three-year university or university college program.[10]

An educated African who has advanced that far in the educational pyramid simply does not wish to make science teaching his permanent career. Some countries, especially in East Africa, which have established the practice of "bonding" their university graduates to teach for a period of up to three years, find that they leave either as soon as their bond expires or even earlier, simply by redeeming or even forfeiting the bond. Native African science teachers leave teaching at the earliest possible opportunity either for civil service or for jobs in a private sector of the economy or through scholarships to pursue further studies. The reasons are many—low prestige; low remuneration; inadequate fringe benefits (particularly "no car" and very low housing al-

[10] Parenthetically, a number of university colleges and new universities have adopted the new policy of stipulating that 50 per cent of their students in science and mathematics must be trained as teachers for secondary schools.

lowances); limited prospects for promotion and arbitrariness in transfers (teachers are reassigned as a rule almost every other year); dissatisfaction with "conditions of work," which means that since any kind of qualified assistance in laboratory and practice classes is absent, equipment inadequate, texts in short supply, the science teacher must spend considerable time and energy out of class to attend to these chores, which he finds unrewarding.

Most of the surveys on the status of the teaching profession in Africa present elaborate rationalizations about how to induce those who were trained as teachers to remain teachers. My own feeling is that as long as the acute scarcity of indigenous technical talent continues, qualified science graduates will drift away from science teaching in secondary schools. The only way to solve this problem is to create a glut on the market by overproducing any and all kinds of science graduates. If the stock is abundant, "superior" graduates will continue to drift away and "inferior" (or more dedicated) graduates will stay on as science teachers. Some African countries are attempting to introduce higher pay scales for science teachers (in some countries they are even advocating "equalization" of pay, as was done for many civil service jobs, to the level of expatriates, which would mean that the bonus for native teachers would be equivalent to the amount of the "topping-off" for expatriates), but this would not solve the problem until the supply is greatly increased.

## VICIOUS DILEMMA—THE ABSOLUTE SCARCITY OF SCIENCE GRADUATES

It is surprising to learn that despite continuous talk that the most crucial problem of the development of high-level manpower in Africa is professional university education in the sciences, engineering, medicine, and agriculture, reasonably accurate statistics on current stocks and annual output of graduates in these fields are virtually nonexistent. UNESCO is currently (and for the first time!) attempting to collect statistics on scientific manpower in Africa.[11] Until the tabulations of country questionnaires are completed, it is a matter of educated guess as to how many professionals in tropical Africa (excluding North Africa, the Arab states, and South Africa) are currently employed in these fields. My own guess would be that the total figure could be somewhere around 20,000.[12] It must be noted, however, that the majority

[11] See UNESCO, *Symposium on Science Policy and Research Administration in Africa,* Yaounde, Cameroun, July 10–21, 1967.
[12] The eight African countries (Ghana, Kenya, Liberia, Madagascar, Mauritius, Nigeria, Tanzania, and Zambia) which have had recent manpower surveys

of these (probably over four-fifths) are still expatriates. This may be a high figure, but there are probably fewer than 4,000 native Africans in all of tropical Africa with a scientific education equivalent to university level (actually "third level," which may not be of a "degree," but "diploma" type). To state that scientific manpower is in short supply in Africa is a substantial understatement.

Every African country is aware that the number and capacity of African universities in training scientific and professional manpower are inadequate. Every manpower study for each specific African country undertaken in the last ten years has pointed out this need. Since 1961 the global target for Africa has been to bring up the output of university graduates in the natural sciences, engineering, agriculture, and medicine to about 60 per cent of total graduates.[13] However, while university enrollments have almost tripled in the last ten years, the *proportion* of students enrolled in these fields has remained basically unchanged. Only about one-quarter of all students (about 12,000) are enrolled currently in sciences and applied professional fields. The total output of graduates is therefore measured by a few hundred per year in all of these fields. An additional two hundred or so persons return each year to Africa after professional studies abroad. Although I would like to know the exact number, I think what is relevant for the purposes of this paper is the over-all dimension of effort. From a population of approximately 180 million persons, the total annual output (let us be optimistic) is somewhere around 600 to 700 graduates in scientific fields from African universities (or equivalent tertiary training institutions). Even if the output by some stroke of magic were to multiply five- or tenfold, an absolute and most critical shortage, rather than a relative one, would continue to exist.

Under such circumstances I think it idle to talk about the infusion of science into education and into the life of Africa until training in science and technology has been intensified. In the case of Africa, numbers do matter very much. The stumbling block to the intensification of training, however, is the university and higher education setup itself. In the first place, there is a vicious circle—lack of qualified applicants from secondary schools to enter new departments and professional faculties. This shortage prevents the expansion of science departments, which in turn causes shortages of teachers for secondary schools, and on and on. Remedial measures at pre-university levels do not solve the problem, for all fledgling institutions aspire to set standards which cannot be easily met. Currently in tropical Africa some

account for approximately 14,000 persons in the natural sciences, engineering, agriculture, and medicine.

[13] *The Development of Higher Education in Africa, op. cit.*, p. 59.

thirty new institutions of higher learning have either just been established or are being established or are lying on the drawing boards. The cost of creating each of these new institutions is staggering indeed, mainly for one very special reason—all institutions have aspirations to retain their degree or diploma training programs comparable with standards at an international level. What these standards are or should be is anyone's guess. In the meantime, a spirit of pretentiousness prevails. As one walks through the monumental buildings of a new African university and as one talks to the expatriate "snobs" (there is really no better word) who occupy practically every teaching position of importance in the old and new universities of Africa, one is simply shocked at the unreality and wastefulness of these ivory towers in relation to the needs of Africa. The traditional structures of universities are being transplanted by Europeans—and now Americans—to African soil without much modification. The panacea they offer is "quality" with an insistence on "standards" and "research," highbrow curriculum and top-level staffs, plush classrooms and spacious facilities, comfortable dormitories and faculty residences. All of this is so much out of line with practical needs and reality that it defies the imagination. And nobody wants to listen to the proposition that only those who are willing to become "second best" first have a chance of really becoming "first best" last.

The preoccupation with elusive standards of excellence, however, is just a veil. There is a deeper root of trouble. As stated earlier in this paper, Africans are concerned primarily with education as a tool of social and political stratification. It is in this context that

> the impact of Western education on contemporary Africa has in many cases been a source of controversy because African administrators and new nationalist leaders who as products of "academic" or general education resist proposals for introducing widespread technical and agricultural education. Because an "elitist" academic education contributed to increased aspirations for political independence, and as characteristic of developed European countries, many leaders therefore contended that a "traditional" British or French type educational system is a prerequisite for economic growth.[14]

This explanation must be qualified somewhat. Most present African leaders are not primarily concerned with establishing the preconditions of development; their basic goal is the perpetuation of their personal political power for privilege's sake. The greatest threat to the mainte-

[14] Neil J. Smelser and Seymour M. Lipset, "Social Structure, Mobility and Development" in N. J. Smelser and S. M. Lipset, eds., *Social Structure and Mobility in Economic Development*, Chicago: Aldine Publishing Company, 1966, p. 27.

nance of this power could come from the emergence of a competitive and highly functional technocratic leadership. And it is the fear of this development that constitutes the real stumbling block to the spread of science education in African universities and other institutions of higher learning.

## EPILOGUE—CONFLICT OF ASPIRATIONS AND REAL RESOURCES

The development of science education in Africa is a very difficult task. Africa is a vast but sparsely populated continent. It is rich in natural resources, but poor in their use. If the agricultural potential were to be realized, it could feed much of the world; but at present Africa can barely feed itself. Africa is great in nationalistic dreams and aspirations, but poor in operational know-how and the most rudimentary degree of human collaboration essential to realize them. The prospects for industrial and technological revolution without a unified African market and expansion of world trade are questionable. And without such revolution, training for employment in scientific and technological occupations has limited appeal.

There is a widespread belief among contemporary modernizers of Africa that a great and universal demand exists for more and better modern education in all states. This view is more an item of faith than reality. Science is an endless frontier, and education is a bottomless pit, the insatiable demands of which neither the poor nor the richest of the rich nations can ever fully meet. The race between demands and scarce resources is particularly acute in Africa. The real resources available for adapting and providing more and better science education in Africa are rather limited indeed. Most African countries already spend up to a third of their national budgets on education. The history of science and science education is that of gradual upgrading, which requires an incremental flow of resources over time. The creation of "instant" high-quality institutions for high-level university teaching and research is feasible only by bidding in presently available resources and staff. This approach is not applicable to the African setting. So far, Africa has had to buy from abroad. A large number of African countries are already bankrupt, and if it were not for foreign aid and budgetary supports of former colonial powers, many more countries would find themselves in economic straits. To Africanize science education and adapt to it Africa's specific needs in developing applied research and technological applications costs much more than the African states are presently willing or able to pay.

# 6.

# TECHNOLOGICAL GROWTH AND

# SCIENTIFIC LAG: IRAN

## BY E. A. BAYNE

### American Universities Field Staff

There is plain evidence today of a growing technological "climate" in Iran. A marked economic, industrial, and institutional development experienced during this Middle Eastern country's post-World War II period has encouragingly brought about these changes, but at the same time progress toward a broad public acceptance of the scientific outlook is less demonstrable. These preliminary stages of industrialization and the resultant wider awareness of modern technology may forecast an increasingly objective view of a Persian's relationship to his environment, but there are correspondingly negative factors, found in many developing societies, that are also apparent in Iran. A nationalism that is derived from Iran's normative tradition, at many points at variance with modern empiricism, appears to provide the societal dynamic still, only thinly veiled by material evidences of Western-type modernization. Moreover, the present centralized and quasi-authoritarian mode of government, itself an inheritance from the past, is based on a concentration of political power and decision in the individual image and reality of the monarch. Such modern absolutism may actually inhibit the free inquiry that encourages scientific development, at the same time that Iran's "white revolutionist" reformer-king encourages technological change and presses for it among the leaders of the society.

There is thus a familiar dialectic here in an apparently inexorable process of resolution. While the physical ambiance and resources of Iran provide the means and opportunity for economic development leading toward a greatly improved level of material well-being, there are cultural obstacles—traditionalisms—that inhibit the growth of modern rationalism. This is but to say again that however quickly modern communications may carry news and men, the minds of people can be changed but slowly. It also emphasizes that Iran, for all its special qualities, and an often innovative institutional history that has contributed more than once to national greatness, is in this dimension but another developing nation seeking to bring an older value system into operative balance with modernity.

Science, here meaning the application of a disciplined and testable empirical approach to change across the whole structure of social development, is new in modern Iran. Its concepts are not always friendly to the survival of the ruling powers in the country, even though many of their Westernized "scientized" scions have been among the developmental leaders of the society. To the extent that science exists in any "pure" sense, it can be typed as "colonial," derived in its outlook and measured by its rewards from outside of Iran. As the promotion of scientific research and technological change at various times in history has been a necessary prerogative of kings and nobility in their own self-defense, so it may be in modern Iran for the moment. Without constant improvement, an awakened Iranian people can become a politically restless one, and the material benefits of technology become imperative. However, the spread of a scientific outlook among all Persians would seem to involve a far deeper secularization of the culture than Iran has experienced before. Logically, this secularization would spell the end of the traditional structure.

Development thus obviously encourages revolutionary aspects in the reshaped polity it implies, as it does in reflecting a new philosophic outlook, particularly for that proportion of the population—a growing middle class—who are by their life functions committed to the constant expansion of the material basis of the society. In Iran's case, historically at a geographical and cultural frontier of East and West, it seems now that a generally capitalistic, if centralized, democracy will be the political goal of social change for the once patrimonial and hierarchical state. The early steps that have so far been accomplished to provide an enlarged frame of participation in self-government point to these ends if only for the purpose of encouraging growth greater than heretofore anticipated. In this ideological view, democratic development has grown out of needs for improved economic administration, but the Western pattern of development that Iran, in greater or lesser conscious degree, seeks to emulate may also be said to support this process. Moreover, the Western example implies that participatory democracy, by definition, is ideally secular and "future oriented"—qualities at the heart of science—and encourages an empiricism as the basis of its workability. In projecting the Iranian case, the relationship of science to a new and nonmystical national outlook upon life thus appears to have a direct bearing on the totality of social development and to be integral with it.

The Persian prospect at first sight stimulates this simplistic view of the "wholeness" of development. It begins necessarily with the contemporary social and economic gains that can be characterized as contributing to a technological "climate." There are many evidences of these advances, most of them achieved only in the recent past. An increase in per capita income from an estimated $90.00 per year to the present $248.00 per year in approximately two decades denotes a widening range of personal economic opportunity, for example.

Other post-World War II statistics add to the promise of an improved material situation. The national product has increased from $1.8 billion to $5.6 billion in roughly the same period, and has been growing at more than 10 per cent per year. Electric power capacity has increased tenfold since 1946; industrial employment has doubled at a rapidly increasing pace. The urban proportion of the population has risen from three million to five and a half million people, and now involves more than 20 per cent of the population, increasingly subject to the forms of life and the aspirations of *embourgeoisiement*. There have been radical technological modifications in production and employment patterns: while a dozen years ago, according to a recent government study, the capital investment per worker in Iranian industry was only $1,600, today it exceeds $8,000. The increase is a mark of technical sophistication, and also of development in a broader social frame.

Confidently but imprecisely, Iran is consolidating a "take-off" stage of industrialization. By these indices, it appears to be moving unevenly but indubitably from a paleotechnical agrarian age to a higher degree of technical modernity by a better organization and use of its resources and environment with increased productivity per man. Its land, the basis of life for a majority of its people, has been subject to wide reforms in ownership patterns. The old manorial system has been undermined. However, a new form of capitalistic and comparatively industrialized large-scale agriculture, operated by former landlords but applying relatively scientific methods, is developing beside the small tracts of the new peasant-farmer proprietors who have received the benefits of the land reform program. These large modern farms probably will overwhelm the small land-holder in the future, but science will have been the tool of economic change here.

In this same postwar period, progress in education has been notable, and illiteracy is being steadily reduced. In the past twenty years, elementary school students have increased from a quarter of a million to more than 1.8 million. The number of secondary school students has grown between 1946 and 1963 from a modest 26,000 to nearly 400,000 students in regular and vocational schools. University and specialized technical students studying in the country have increased ten times in approximately the same period to a total of nearly 40,000.

A critical factor in the introduction of Western scientific techniques has been the growing influence of university graduates trained abroad. Their numbers have increased from barely 1,500 at the end of World War II to more than 15,000 now studying abroad in a given year. Returned students now make up the principal technological cadres of the society, already prominent in government, education, commerce, and industry. There appears to be virtually no shortage of job opportunities for this technical élite, whose growth in numbers has been disproportionally rapid with the expansion of educational opportunity for Iranians at home and abroad. Indeed, there are those who suggest that the new increase of members in the technological élite may have exceeded the proportionate supply of infrastructural personnel such as shop foremen, mechanics, and skilled clerical staff on whom their technical effectiveness depends.

The defense budget of Iran has increased ten times in this era, although remaining at about a 40 per cent proportion of the national budget. This financial index reveals a more sophisticated Iranian military than was conceivable a generation ago, as well as demonstrating a more immediate Iranian response to the international political situation. The armed forces have become a potentially formidable regional factor in the northern tier of southwest Asia. However, here as in civilian sectors, Iran relies almost totally upon foreign suppliers for equipment and development. In practice, this dependence involves primarily the United States which has, through sales and grants-in-aid together, provided nearly $3 billion worth of military machinery and facilities for Iran since 1950, and much technical training. Nonetheless, the Iranian use of supersonic aircraft, rockets, radar defenses, mechanized cavalry —in general, a fairly complete range of modern technological weaponry—has become an accepted international strategic fact that touches, at least, nearly 200,000 Persians at a time who are connected with the military establishment, and hundreds of thousands more who have served a term of service during these years.

If a growing familiarity with modern techniques and machinery and the existence of productive functions for them in the economy is one of the prerequisites for technological development and the application of scientific ingenuity, Iran would appear to be qualifying in this area more and more. As elsewhere among the developing nations, however, this Iranian awareness of a modern technical and scientific age has inevitably been based upon importations of accumulated and applied scientific knowledge and technological development from the foreign and largely Western world. "Science," in its contemporary application, is thus a satellite or colonial enterprise, even though there has been a commendably rapid Iranian adaptation of foreign techniques and equipment to local conditions in many sectors, and government economic policy is directed toward a decreasing dependence upon foreign manufacturers for consumer durable goods.

A slowly growing acceptance of empirically based concepts of analysis in economic planning, public administration, and public health, in which the techniques of social and natural science are implicit, cannot be denied. Iranian development, more or less, is influenced by plan perhaps more negatively than positively through the manipulation of increasingly effective fiscal institutions and measures. The concept of preventive medicine in its modern institutional sense was first introduced during the Second World War. Today, government commitment to it and public acceptance of it are commonplace. The ministers of government now tend to represent technical competence, often of a high academic order, rather than Islamic piety or the prestige of "family," which were major criteria of office as late as the 1950s. Even among the less educated, there have been evidences of technical change. The use of chemical fertilizer by peasant farmers, for example, has nearly tripled in the past half-decade. Western observers point to the fact that Iranian industrialists are still imbued with very conservative price and marketing notions—relics of a bazaar psychology in a static market, perhaps—rather than by a theory of the expanding economy. There seems thus to be only a superficial intellectual quality to technological change at this stage.

Despite this over-all, if limited, progress, it still seems to be "climatically" early to expect a response in the shape of a significant native scientific establishment at this time.

However, the creative genius that Persia has demonstrated in its history suggests no unconquerable indigenous reason working against such development. Iran has produced its great mathematicians as well as its poets. Its famed architecture and crafts offer evidence of no less ingenuity as an historic people than others have possessed. Rather, the presence of scores of distinguished Iranian scholars employed at major European and North American scientific institutions reinforces the possibility of Persian scientific capability, but at this time it is an expatriate activity. It represents a loss of national talent, if to the gain of the international community, and reflects the lack, still, of a scientific "climate" in both the physical environment a modern scientist requires and the relative lack of interest in the application of scientific method to this stage of Iranian development. This "brain drain" for Iran now is estimated to involve the permanent export of more than 20,000 Iranians, but a parallel and instructive phenomenon can be observed within Iran itself. Of about 5,000 doctors in Iran, which is nearly a third the size of the continental United States, more than 4,000 are located in Teheran, the capital, where a reasonably congenial professional atmosphere involving modern facilities and higher monetary rewards is available.

The reasons behind these two factors are much the same and suggest that this may, therefore, be an appropriate moment to assess what obstacles lie within the society and its cultural predilections that inhibit a faster and more widespread national response to scientific method and outlook as Iran proceeds up the developmental grade.

Such an inquiry is also germane in view of the present Persian regime's nationalistic determination to regain a material and technological parity with Europe "within a generation." The goal is high, and probably impossible to achieve precisely, but without total social development necessarily including a modern scientific outlook that will speedily override the lingering inhibitions of traditionalism, it is obviously unapproachable. For all the nation's progress, the present reality of Iran rests with the totality of its 25,000,000 people, a majority of whom are still illiterate and for whom a religio-political ethic continues to define the natural order.

Historically, Iran has enjoyed periods of technological ascendancy in the Mediterranean area. As a settled agricultural country and a processor of raw materials on a junction point of ancient caravan routes, its medieval artisanry frequently was comparable with China's to the east and Europe's to the west in the first millennium of the Christian era, and provided economic resources for early Persian world empires. Apologists have offered various reasons for Iran's economic (and relative technological) decline in the ensuing centuries. Factors have been cited by historians that range from the disruptive twelfth century invasions of Persia by the Mongols, and the effects of Prince Henry the Navigator and the post-Renaissance Italian economic recession upon the Asian caravan trade, to a slow philosophic adaptation of Islam in Iran, and more contemporaneously to the inhibiting effects of the region's quasi-colonialization created by the out-thrust of European power. In this later context, Europe was by the end of the eighteenth century an awesomely powerful force. It had been philosophically freed centuries before by Erasmus, among others, technologically by

Galileo and Newton, for example, and administratively by the Reformation, and was already the master of the means to an industrial revolution. Iran directly experienced none of these innovative influences.

All these reasons—and more—are pertinent to an understanding of the relative Iranian decline, and may be weighed conveniently by economic measures. A superficial awareness of European technology and industrial prowess existed in Persia by the late nineteenth century, but despite the country's marginal exposure to frequently rapacious European financial promotion of industrial rights and concessions (actually, most of these were never physically developed in the mutual Iranian-western lack of interest that existed), Iran was not yet spiritually ready to respond institutionally to this era of modernization. Certainly there were individual Persian modernists among the upper classes in the nineteenth century who were conscious of the industrial development of Europe, but there were few sons of the aristocracy who became doctors, engineers, or biologists, for example.

While some Iranian military tacticians of the time were trained in Europe, there were proportionately more lawyers who studied abroad (but curiously, few humanistic scholars). As in the medieval West, scientific development in Iran was the prerogative of the ruler, largely for the defense of the realm, but in these times, burdened with rigid traditions and protective of them in an uncertain international position, defense itself lacked native resources to modernize. Progress would come by other means.

The new Constitution of 1906, which had been born of anti-imperialist sentiment rather than of any fervent desire to install a popular democracy, had leaned heavily upon a European model, and encouraged at least the study of secular law. Humanists, on the other hand, dealt with more esoteric subjects in which there was yet little pragmatic interest. There was only a handful of technologists, although concepts of modern secular education began to infiltrate Iran as a result of these individual foreign experiences by the end of the century.

It seemed, in the agrarian, God-given order that appeared immutable to most Iranians then, there was little honor and few posts promising advancement for the scientist or the scientifically minded. The relationship of class and traditional landed power to civic responsibility to bring about Iran's modernization was a concept that had not fully developed among the upper classes even by the early twentieth century. Moreover, a tired dynasty that held the throne by sufferance made few efforts to lead the country toward modernization, but rather blocked modernization in the interest of its own survival.

It was not until the end of the First World War, when Iran reached a nadir of national humiliation and dynastic disintegration, that it experienced a general awareness of the need for national technical advance. A new centralized government, personalized by a dynamic, nationalistic monarch of a new dynasty, read the signs of an inevitable future. This soldier-leader, Reza Shah, who was the father of the present king, foresaw that a modern society would be a largely secular one, and he made somewhat crude but forceful efforts to eliminate clerical influence in education and government policy. However, for all he might symbolize freedom from religious conservatism and for all his nationalistic "anticolonialism," his reign proved to be only the beginning of a transition in the society. To hold the throne, he was obliged to rely upon the traditional, hierarchical structure of political power. As a result, modifications in the pattern of society and in the value system of the leaders of Iran did not become widespread. What industrial developments were introduced were "monuments" to modernity rather than modernization itself, and were totally imported.

The discovery of oil shortly after the turn of the century, and its development particularly following World War I, presaged a revolution of means in the Iranian way of life. It would take a longer period, however, and more than the foreign concessionaire to make change effective. Nonetheless, the era of Reza Shah (1925–41) marked the first steps of a process in which domestic development, secularization, and a widening of opportunity in the country for the technically skilled were harnessed to a nationalistic spirit. Together, although frustrated by the intervention of the Second World War in Iran, these would stimulate change.

The contemporary Iranian economic renaissance may thus also be logically dated from the effective exploitation of its vast petroleum deposits. The growth to major proportions of the early British oil concessions thus assumes more specific historical importance for scientific development than might otherwise seem justified. Both by its industrial example and by the conversion of national wealth into fungible form that Iran could use for other investment, its cumulative effect has been enormous. By 1950, the size and relative importance of the functions the oil industry performed within the country caused it to be the object of a costly Iranian resentment that stopped oil production for nearly two years. Had the British entrepreneurs exhibited a greater political perspicacity, this interruption might have been avoided, but the nationalistic element in Iranian development made the resentment (and nationalization of the industry) virtually inevitable.

Even before this occurrence, however, the industry had begun to train Iranians as technicians in appreciable numbers, and later to provide for high-level training abroad. It was the first opportunity for any major demonstration of modern techniques, and it can be said to have speeded the process of technical modernization far beyond the industry itself.

Oil has now become even more central to Iranian development. The industry accounted in 1966 for 16 per cent of Iran's national product, some 50 per cent of its national income, and 75 per cent of the value of the country's exports. (Since Iran avoided involvement in the 1967 Arab-Israeli war, its oil production has increased, and an oil income of nearly $1 billion was registered in the 1967 fiscal year.)

However, the cultural effects of this invasion by a major but somewhat remotely located industry were slow to become institutionally apparent, and would not have been more than marginally effective without the modernizing dynamic of nationalism that developed simultaneously. Moreover, in the relative poverty and technical inexperience of the country in the early decades of the twentieth century, little more than random "symbols" of technical improvement could be established at first. These, more often than not, followed an ancient monarchical principle of development. They were designed to increase the stature and power of the monarchy itself as state monopolies. These symbols might be auxiliaries to state arsenals, or facilities that would insure the maintenance of food supplies, or add to improve military communications with railways or roads. The needed technicians who operated these improvements would themselves be imported, often to insure not only the technical efficiency of the project, but a political neutrality in their management. Whether or not this superficiality in approaching change suggests that Persia is any more stubbornly pragmatic than other developing societies, it implies that to produce a technologically-based effect on general social change would have required a more comprehensive stimulus than came out of the single efforts of the oil industry or the military dictatorship.

Despite a slowly growing mercantile urban middle class, which had already contributed politically to the 1906 constitutional revolt, the modern dimensions and attitudes of large-scale capitalistic enterprise were unknown. Broadly, the record seems to indicate that Iran was not then ideologically prepared to accept modern technology, or perhaps philosophically to comprehend it as anything more than an enviable but irrelevant magic, nor was Iran politically ready to encourage widespread rational foreign investment.

As the oil industry began to make its mark on the society, there were concomitant invasions of the old bazaar by British and Russian banking and commercial interests that demonstrated new functions and created a demand for new skills. The technological impact of World War II, when Iran was occupied by the Allies in major force, must also rank with these earlier influences. However, while these local physical confrontations with new techniques and machinery were undoubtedly significant in the process, and essential to it, the general opening of Iran to wider communication with the outside world was far more important. The increase of students studying abroad and returning to find uses for their skills, a post-World War II wave of Western (and a few Eastern) technicians, salesmen, and advisers into Persia, and a wider range of trade all have had significance.

The tangible factors themselves nevertheless take subsidiary roles before the harnessing of national need for social ascent. Awakened, there was an Iranian determination as a people to join the modern world, a process that can only be achieved by technological change. Without this spiritual dynamic, coupled with both direct and indirect intellectual preparation for the management of the new society, the technical achievements of the West would have been curiosities of small social or economic use. The intangible obstacles to change which Iran had to overcome by this complex interlocking of drives and tools were found chiefly in an old and cherished order.

The traditional structure of Persian society, now under attack by modernizing secularism, is normatively sanctioned by the national faith, the Shi'a branch of Islam. This belief system is committed to an eclectic cosmological code brought down through the centuries by an interdependent but fixed church-state synthesis, and kings who tampered structurally with this system risked their legitimacy, if not their heads, as absolutists and agents of the divine.

A few religious thinkers—an early nineteenth-century philosopher named Mirza Ali Muhammad, for one—had sought to find some accommodation between Western thought and Iranian Islamic thinking, but they and their followers had often found themselves cast as heretics and subject to persecution by the orthodox majority of clergy and the ruling class. An Iranian-born religious activist, Jamal al-Din al Afghani, attempted to find a new synthesis of church and state, but for most Iranians at the time it seemed that he was only seeking to enhance religious nationalism, already inherent in the Iranian faith, rather than to encourage free inquiry, or to develop a religious accord with civic secularism.

Church-state political problems aside, there would appear to be no intrinsic reason why Islamic societies should not adapt themselves to the scientific culture. They have significantly contributed to science in the past, particularly in the universalism of mathematics, and there are adequate examples of contemporary scientists of devout Islamic practice. However, the fact remains that Islamic nations have generally remained outside of the mainstream of technological development in modern times. Plainly, there are other than religious reasons for this condition, but however latent, religion would seem to be a present factor in the Iranian case.

As a church-state synthesis, and the national religious identity of most Iranians, Shi'a Islam in Persia has given a theological endorsement to the monarchy as the sole legislator of divine good on earth, under the law. The reigning king is, in an orthodox view, a trustee for a perfecting kingdom. Ultimately, the realm is to be ruled by the last Imam, a religious leader who disappeared in the ninth century, but who is expected to make a messianic return. The absolutist and quasi-divine nature of the state is thus significant, complemented by a traditional, steeply pyramidal class society maintained by the static agrarian economy. Like the society as a whole, family life has been patriarchal, legitimized by Islamic law. It seems logical to assume that such rigid institutions do not, as a rule, encourage curiosity about the environments that support them, and must themselves change if free inquiry is to be nurtured. If Iran is to have a religious Reformation, which in Western history aided greatly in stimulating scientific thought, it would seem established that intellectual "protestantism" is only developing now as a result of physical factors and post-World War II communications, and the introduction of fundamental reforms covering the status of women and the reduction of clerical influences of orthodox stamp. Altogether, however, Iran has entered the modern age without an easily discernible scientific habit.

Reforms are increasingly in process now, but the current scene in Iran reveals the paradox of history as continuity and discontinuity. While land reform or a new equal status for women make for fundamental changes in the society, the personal authority of the monarch, which is both real and symbolically mystical, has preserved an over-centralization of government, and discouraged open opposition. This statement does not deny the popularity of the present Shah, but it does suggest that if fewer matters were passed all the way up to him for decision (not all of which have come to him by his personal choice) there might be an increase in the momentum of development, and a wide application of objective governmental decision. In the past, there may have been practical reasons for such centralization in managing an extensive empire through primitive communications, while surrounded by imperialistic threats, and persistent separatisms of Iranian minorities. However, as the government has become more responsive to a developing and more highly educated people's problems, the centralized authority of the monarchy begins to seem the relic of a traditionalistic authoritarian pattern of rule. The Shah himself, aware of the transitional era in which he rules, is caught in a dilemma of power:

while he is committed to reform, his position in major part rests on the old order.

Nonetheless, there is a processional of change from old to new involving pragmatic changes of attitude. Where new agencies of the bureaucracy have been needed, at least in form, to manage the society's confrontation with technical problems, the tendency has been for these agencies to be restrictive and regulatory rather than creative. For decades, for example, the principal function of the health ministry was to licence imports of foreign medicine rather than to forward preventive care of the public. Until a few years ago, the minister of education was required personally to sign all high school diplomas for the country *in Teheran,* the capital! His professional advisory councils have functioned almost entirely as restrictive agencies, habitually committed to the preservation of educational methods learned in pre-World War II Europe. The tautness of control these examples imply has probably inhibited independent research as much as a lack of funds, but it followed the authoritarian pattern of the society in honoring the past and thus was relatively unprotested by Iranians, even though it was neglectful of the uncharted future.

Science faculties exist in Iran's higher institutions (notably at the Karaj Agricultural College, and at the Universities of Pahlavi and Teheran), but despite the frequently distinguished qualifications of individual scholars, research has been virtually nonexistent in the natural sciences, and only slightly more evident in the behavorial area. Where foreign interests have sponsored studies—the United States National Science Foundation, for example—faculties have undertaken projects willingly enough, but Iranian support has until very recently been lacking. Necessary technical research, preliminary to undertaking development projects, has largely depended upon foreign technicians and organizations, not only so that Iran might be assured of experienced judgment, but also at least partly because foreign lending institutions considered Iranian research to be suspect, or insufficiently skillful. In recent years, however, this pattern has begun to change. Most projects of importance that require preliminary surveys now will be researched by an association of Iranian and foreign technical firms, if not by Iranians alone.

Persian scientific and technical capabilities have obviously made progress, particularly in the past ten years. What were once only restrictive activities in the technical areas of government service, utilizing somewhat random, imported criteria, have improved their standards to conform to local needs. Skilled personnel is now available and an increasingly statistical basis of judgment is possible. The interior ministry recently contracted with the engineering and science faculties of Teheran University as a group to act as its research arm. Semiprivate hospitals and the Pasteur Institute have begun to sponsor research in local medicine, and units of Teheran University have undertaken social research projects of increasing complexity.

Perhaps most significant in this development of native scientific practice is the emphasis placed upon Persian scientific development under the Third Five Year Plan, which will guide the government-financed development program beginning in 1968. This plan contains, for the first time in Iranian history, an appropriately financed sponsorship of basic scientific research related to the Iranian situation and in support of Iranian institutions, including a recently established national technical university.

These signs of maturation are new and sparse in effect as yet. And when all the obstacles to the full flowering of a scientific age in Persia are summarized, they present a formidable list. Few of them are uniquely Iranian, of course, most being found in other traditional societies that seek to modernize rapidly. Moreover, it is already apparent that these same factors affect the totality of economic and social development, and cannot be separated from it. Science, today, cannot be isolated from development where resources are limited and subject to priority allocations as they are in Iran. Research must justify itself on the grounds of practical application far more stringently than in richer and less urgently developing countries. There is thus a crude process: literacy must precede a knowledge of new math; the skill needed to maintain mechanical transport comes ahead of the development of high-energy physics in the Iranian system of priorities. The limitations of the process are clear, and in part account for the loss of scientific brain power to Europe and North America. Scientists cannot be productive in an Iran where the present stage of development does not provide adequate facilities and esteem for the skills available.

The social application of Western scientific thought came about through diverse influences. Protestantism, capitalism, a greater availability of wealth, a general commitment to an elastic society—all were greater or lesser factors. Fundamentally, however, historians seem to feel that the revolutionary ideas of the sixteenth and seventeenth centuries marked the true beginning of modern society. That man could manipulate his environment became an accepted belief; the mysticisms of a divine order were cast into doubt.

While Iran is not Europe, its desire to develop under the banner of nationalism seems comparable to a modern Protestantism, and the current era may be likened, simplistically put, to the beginnings of its break with an *ancien régime*. As significant as the physical environment may be, more important are the intellectual preconditions Iran must meet before its acceptance of the empiricism of science itself, the essence of a truly modernizing break with the past. Emergence from a backward-looking national outlook, learning slowly that free inquiry and a courageous curiosity are essential to a better future and that a citizen's participation in his society is the means to make this experience effective, are not easily accomplished in a generation.

However, Iran has at least begun the process. The status of women has been legally changed, and crude patriarchism is no longer the rule. Iranian peasants are, as a group, no longer as subject to the patrimonial controls of the ages. Urbanizing citizens are finding a contractual—and freer—situation. In this generally hopeful atmosphere of political and social growth in Iran, the freedom in which the concepts of modern science can grow would appear to be in the making.

# 7

# PREREQUISITES, RECEPTIVITY, AND CHANGE: GOVERNMENT AND THE DEVELOPMENT OF SCIENCE IN JAPAN

## BY F. ROY LOCKHEIMER

American Universities Field Staff

By almost all reckoning, Japan's experience in adapting Western science and technology to its own needs in the short period of a generation is one that cries out to the underdeveloped world for attention and emulation. To be sure, especially of late, volumes of attention have been devoted to the Japanese experience, but nowhere has successful emulation occurred. Why? If a neat solution could be provided for that problem, Japan's experience, one of the apparent wonders of the modern world, could be carefully packaged and attractively presented as *the* formula for success in scientific development.

But that statement begs the very question: is Japan's experience in receiving Western science transferable? If that experience can be transferred, then there is little reason that today's underdeveloped world could not make Japan its model for scientific development. Certainly the job of gathering data ought to be easy enough—the statistics, the records, the charts, even much of the history are available for the reading. The problem of practical application and successful emulation nevertheless remains, for no matter how much information is gathered, no real progress toward the development of science can be made with the Japanese model in other countries until those countries reach the same kind of jumping-off stage that Japan had reached by the 1850s.

There is almost no end to the number of questions that could be asked about the requirements for the successful transfer of one culture's science and technology to another. Are there *prerequisites* for the transfer of science? If so, what preliminary conditions must exist within a traditional society before it is ready to turn itself to the task of adopting new knowledge and different ways of thinking? Even then, even with all or almost all the prerequisites for the adoption of Western science present, what about traditional society's ability to receive, take in, adapt, and utilize new ideas? Does *receptivity* to radically different methods of investigation and understanding of phenomena exist within traditional society, and, moreover, is that receptivity tenacious enough to withstand the great social strains and pressures that may arise because of the introduction of foreign scientific concepts?

Suppose, for example, we allow that the conditions of settled agriculture include several of the prerequisites for the successful introduction of Western science. We will for the moment consider that it is impossible for nomadic communities, whether they be largely agricultural or pastoral, or both, to take on foreign science, or even to develop a scientific tradition at all. But, even though a settled agricultural society is by our definition one that contains some of the prerequisites for the introduction of science, it will not always be able to adapt Western science to its purposes because it may be unreceptive to foreign ideas. A traditional society may, for instance, be in the strong grip of a religion that is rigidly opposed to unsettling experimentation and disturbing theories. Thus the problem of introducing foreign science is complex, for although a society may possess some of the prerequisites for the introduction of Western science, it still may prove unable to create a scientific tradition of its own, in spite of prolonged exposure to foreign scientific concepts. Such a society lacks receptivity, and, as a result, it cannot mobilize itself effectively for the difficult task of adapting foreign science to its own needs.

If, however, a traditional society, or at least one that appears to be traditional in its organization, possesses the prerequisites for science, and also shows sufficient receptivity to develop a scientific tradition of its own, then that society will necessarily be subjected to change that not only reaches into its academic and religious world of ideas, but also introduces a transformation affecting almost all aspects of national life —social, political, and economic. Once the scientific method, the inductive investigation of phenomena, is implanted within a society, the influence of that method will be widespread and permanent. Science, in fact, need not even have existed previously within traditional society for change to occur once scientific methods have been adopted. Japan was without a broad-based scientific tradition before its massive reception of Western science and technology during the last part of the nineteenth century.

## THE JAPANESE PRE-SCIENTIFIC SETTING

In nearly every aspect of its national life, Japan, even before the nineteenth century, was a well-developed society. Japan in fact was more developed two hundred years ago than some underdeveloped countries are today. Every field of endeavor that existed in the West, save one, flourished in pre-Meiji Japan (before 1868): science and its ensuing technology were the exception. Japan had art, craftsmanship, philosophy, literature, religion, centralized government, well-populated cities, developed communications, a national language, and educational institutions. But it did not have science.

A realization of the comparatively well-developed condition of pre-Meiji Japan is imperative for an understanding of the Japanese ability to receive Western science so readily. Not only was the country's level of development high, but also the singular circumstances of its national history bent Japan toward a favorable reception of Western science.

In the mid-nineteenth century, after two hundred and fifty years of almost complete seclusion under Tokugawa rule (a period, by the way, that had brought unequaled peace and security to the land), Japan was abruptly shaken out of its isolation by an expansionist West whose source of strength stemmed from a rich scientific tradition that was almost unknown in Japan. Many Japanese were quick to understand that they were doomed to foreign domination, perhaps in danger of totally losing their national independence, unless the key to Western power— science—was made available. Simultaneously, internal tension had brought the country close to dangerous domestic strife at the highest levels of government. The old Tokugawa regime was weak, near the point of collapse. Truly this was a national crisis of the first magnitude: immense foreign pressure threatened the country from without, while governmental debility mounted within.

Yet within fifteen years after the appearance of Perry's awesome "black ships" on its waters, Japan had set its house in order and had launched a spectacularly successful program of nation-building along Western lines. Japanese emphasis was placed neither on the arts, nor on philosophy and literature; rather, *fukoku kyōhei* ("rich country, strong army") became a national password, and priorities were adjusted accordingly.

Science and its application, especially in the military sphere, were seen as the sources of Western strength. Many Japanese felt that they had every moral and cultural reason to hold their heads high among the Western "barbarians"; every reason, that is, except in science, a fact that was stressed in another slogan of the period—"Western science and Eastern morals." Since Japan did not have Western science, that science had to be imported just as it was if the country was to become a Western-style power. With the thought that time was running out in the struggle to hold off the West, and with feelings of national crisis running high, the wholesale importation of foreign science was the only practical solution. Surely it was absurd to think that a handful of pioneers in the study and translation of Western scientific works, even with their disciples included, would be sufficient to build a scientific tradition in Japan, where, if any such tradition had existed at all, it was one of science as magic.

Thus, while Japan possessed an artistic and philosophical basis for exchanging ideas with the West at all levels, it had no basis for a scientific exchange. There was no possibility for adaptations and modifications to lead to new approaches, as there was, say, in the arts; Western science would have to be brought into Japan just as it existed in the West, and that was exactly what was done.

Even before the government had set its own house in order, and had begun to exercise effective leadership in the job of introducing Western science into the nation, almost a hundred Japanese had been abroad for foreign study. Although this number may not appear large, its significance becomes clearer when it is realized that as a general rule foreign travel was prohibited by the Tokugawa regime. Seen in this light, it is not unusual that the majority of this early group of Japanese foreign explorers, some of whom traveled in secret, came from the *han* (feudal domains), especially from those *han* that tended to resist the central authority of Tokugawa rule. The Tokugawa regime itself, not to be outdone, sponsored study abroad for the first time in 1862, and before its demise in 1868, it had sent forty-seven students abroad for study, all of them going to France, Great Britain, The Netherlands, Russia, or the United States, in that order.

From the outset, time was not wasted on "frills." Whatever was needed to make the nation (or, in some instances in late Tokugawa times, the *han*) prosperous and strong received emphasis: medicine, gunnery, engineering, science, agriculture, manufacturing, and commerce. By the end of the Meiji period (1912), more than 65 per cent of all the students who had gone abroad for study under the sponsorship of the Ministry of Education had specialized in the "hard" areas of the basic and applied sciences, especially in the latter. The only major exception was law; but legal studies can hardly be called a special case.

Meiji oligarchs, in a dedicated effort to demonstrate national equality with the West, were determined that the country be provided with Western-style, or at least Western-appearing, law and government. Legal studies, as well as scientific and technological ones, would help to make Japan strong and independent. Unlike some of today's underdeveloped countries, Japan channeled its intellectual resources into areas that would bring the greatest immediate returns to the state.

If the government could not afford to send sufficient numbers of students abroad, or, in consideration of national requirements, if that method proved impractical, then the foreigner could be brought to Japan to teach and to advise. If incentives were needed, then the government would provide them: both high salaries (usually several times greater than the income of cabinet-rank ministers) and careful attention were paid to foreign instructors.

The government was dedicated to strengthening the country as rapidly as possible. If desired results could not be obtained at home with native talent, or if study abroad proved inadequate, then what was needed could be imported—not only foreign teachers, but foreign technology, patents, licenses, and publications. All this was done at great expense, but with spectacular results. A fantastic foreign boom was generated within the country in the early days of the Meiji era, not to be exceeded in intensity until the post-1945 foreign craze. Alas, as some Japanese have come to realize of late, no matter how much foreign science and technology are imported, there is no substitute for a solid national basis for creative scientific research. There comes a time when the price of foreign technology becomes too high. Japan today, aiming to become the third greatest economic power in the world, has found that the price of foreign-developed scientific innovations is very high indeed. In 1868 and immediately after, however, the importation of foreign science filled a preciously important need in Japanese national life. Why foreign science was successfully transferred from the West and grafted onto Japanese society through wholesale importation under government leadership is a subject deserving a deeper investigation than it has yet received. Companion studies should be made of contemporary problems in the development of a creative scientific tradition in today's Japan.

## PREREQUISITES

Japan was able to receive Western science, and adapt it to its purposes, because by the mid-nineteenth century it was well endowed with the prerequisites for science. Not only did Japan have a flourishing culture based on a settled agricultural economy, with educational institutions, communications, a bureaucracy, a tradition of scholarly discourse, as well as some preliminary accumulation of scientific knowledge by individual scholars who had limited contact with Western scientific publications, but it also had many of the aspects of a modern nation-state. As an organized national entity, Japan possessed large cities and a developing national economy, all of which were supported by a heavily agricultural population. The country was not divided by differences in language or in culture; on the contrary, the insularity of the Japanese islands had engendered strong feelings of unique identity among the people.

In sum, pre-Meiji Japan had the most crucial of all the basic prerequisites for facilitating the reception of foreign science—an organized national statehood with a common national language and culture. The Tokugawa tradition of centralized government and bureaucracy was tremendously valuable as a legacy that could be modified, improved, and transferred to Meiji Japan. Although pre-Meiji power was shared by the Tokugawa government with several hundred more or less autonomous feudal domains, the control of the central government was great enough to require the feudal lords and many of their retainers to spend alternate years in the Tokugawa capital of Edo, present-day Tokyo. This custom allowed ideas and opinions to be exchanged not only in Edo but also along the routes to the capital; it was in fact a source of a centralized system of national communications. Tokugawa samurai, who in total probably did not number more than 6 per cent of the population, became the source of the Meiji oligarchy, and the backbone of the new bureaucracy. The crisis of the last days of pre-Meiji Japan—foreign pressure and internal dissension—evoked an active response from the nation's only source of trained talent, the samurai élite. For results a national science program, like any other national policy, needs national direction, open channels of communication, and competent administrators.

The Meiji oligarchy clearly saw the need for a national system of education to provide a foundation for the development of national science; it did so, however, not from scratch but with the benefit of Tokugawa educational institutions. In 1868, Meiji Japan inherited the Tokugawa educational legacy of several thousand schools of various kinds, ranging from centers of Confucian studies for the ruling classes to local parish schools where the commoners were taught the "three R's." There are no generally accepted figures for the amount of literacy in Tokugawa Japan; estimates range from 30 to 70 per cent of the adult male population. Perhaps, however, if put more crudely, figures for the amount of literacy among the people are not of immediate importance; what matters is that in mid-nineteenth century Japan, those who counted in positions of leadership and authority, including of course the administrative class of samurai, were usually literate. For many others not of the ruling classes, Tokugawa parish schools and private academies provided educational opportunities which, although varying considerably in quality, offered everything from simple instruction in reading, writing, and abacus to, in some cases, detailed examinations of foreign works on science and technology.

Broadly speaking, science in Japan, especially its speculative and creative aspects, has not been part of a deep, national historical tradition. During Japan's early history what science and technology existed were borrowings from the overwhelmingly flourishing culture of neighboring China. Later on, in the sixteenth century, when Portuguese ships ventured into Japanese waters, a revolution in native military technology was initiated with the introduction of firearms. Military men, however, were not the only ones who were impressed with Western technology. Japanese enthusiasm for Portuguese rifles was to have implications that would extend beyond the martial arts, and mark an important advance in the development of native science and technology. Aspects of Western technology, therefore, were favorably introduced in Japan several hundred years before the Japanese themselves began in earnest to make that technology, and its parent science, their own.

Thus a small but significant foundation for the building of a scientific tradition was laid in sixteenth-century Japan. Although there were serious interruptions in the process of enlarging that foundation, enlarged it was, slowly, over the centuries, through limited contact with the "barbarians" from Portugal and Holland. This is not to say that a viable scientific tradition in the Western sense existed in pre-Meiji Japan. It did not. For the majority of the population, natural phenomena were "understood" only through superstition and magic. What is more, Japanese master technicians, some of whose studies approached the scientific manner as they dealt with natural phenomena, tended to be highly protective of their observations, revealing them only to their most trusted disciples. Even though it would be excessive to suggest that Tokugawa scholars possessed a general understanding of Western scientific concepts, some pre-Meiji scholars did have sufficient contact with Western studies to have had a grasp of those concepts that are prerequisite for the creation of a scientific tradition based on Western principles. Nineteenth-century Japan, therefore, also possessed two further prerequisites for the introduction of Western science: a native scholarly tradition which concerned itself with speculation on natural phenomena, and some contact with Western scientific concepts.

Crisis, social tension, and nationalism make up the last group of my hypothesized prerequisites for science, and, here again, Japan was fortunate in having had all three at the same time. From the beginning of the last half of the nineteenth century, Japan experienced a crisis in its relations with the outside world; simultaneously its society was under pressure from within, and its government was weakening, soon to topple. New attitudes and fresh thinking were critically needed. An intensely patriotic yet socially insecure group—the samurai—were available and came forth to fill many important positions of leadership in the Meiji oligarchy. Forming the administrative backbone of that oligarchy in the new bureaucracy, the samurai élite sensed the proportions of the national crisis caused by the appearance of the West, and, once they had placed internal governmental affairs in order, they concerned themselves with the task of making Japan the equal of the West. The oligarchy, with deep feelings of national crisis, recognized that the country needed to establish as rapidly as possible those elements that constituted the basis for the superior strength of the West. Among those elements, science and technology, especially the latter, were emphasized above all else.

## RECEPTIVITY, CHANGE, AND GOVERNMENT LEADERSHIP

Even though its geographical insularity, its distinctive language, and its own form of social organization had created a pride that amounted to nascent nationalism in pre-modern Japan, that nationalism, in other circumstances, could have acted as a barrier to the introduction of alien concepts. But Japan's natural insularity had a twin effect: it made the Japanese suspicious of foreigners, but it also made them curious about the outside world. As I have already mentioned, the Japanese showed enthusiasm for Western technology as early as the sixteenth century. Long before that time, they had shown great interest in Chinese cultural achievements, many of which they adapted to their own use. Acceptance of foreign ideas, therefore, when those ideas appeared to offer decided advantages, was hardly a new aspect of Japanese history by the nineteenth century. When Perry's ships steamed up Edo Bay in 1853, there was already a small group of men in the land who had some familiarity with Western scientific principles through contact with the Dutch at Nagasaki. Informed Japanese, moreover, could understand, and they soon became aware, that their country did not have all the answers, that there was much to be learned from the outside world.

No observer who has ever lived among the Japanese would deny that they are a keenly competitive, success-minded, goal-oriented people. They are so now, and they were so during the Meiji period. Causes, conditions, and circumstances change, and when they do, Japanese values change with them. If most Japanese were antiforeign when Perry attempted to end their isolation, in less than fifteen years, when it became clear to all but the most rigid that resistance to foreign demands was futile, many of those same Japanese were reaching with enthusiasm for Western ways, and the country experienced a foreign boom. Three generations later, most Japanese were convinced that their nation was invincible, and that they would fight to the last rather than surrender. But after a few short and painful years had passed, they surrendered in all meekness, submitting to defeat and occupation. Part of the explanation in both cases for these sharp changes in national attitudes is that national circumstances had changed; therefore, so did national goals. Regardless of change in national circumstances, however, the Japanese did not lose their drive for success; they simply adjusted themselves to new goals, which now seemed proper against the background of their new environment. The leaders of the Meiji period saw science and technology as the source of Western strength; new challenges require new responses, and Meiji Japan acted accordingly. Japan's value system, with its situational ethic and goal orientation, allowed the nation an extraordinary receptivity to science, much in the same way as it later allowed the population to behave with dignity and cooperation while under the occupation of a formerly detested enemy. The same astonishing response to national goals was seen again recently in the way the whole country vicariously participated in the huge preparations for the Tokyo Olympics in 1964. Today (1968), throughout the country, large clocks, which count down the day, hour, minute, and second remaining before the opening celebrations for the Japan World Exposition, EXPO '70, in 1970, indicate once more Japanese goal and success orientation.

The Japanese are a pragmatic people. Their history is rich in examples of their interest in the practical and, comparatively speaking, their disregard of philosophical idealism and a search for universals. Japanese pragmatism has allowed a great diversity of thought to coexist peacefully without contradictions arising, or at least without being felt. In pre-Meiji Japan, Shintoism, Buddhism, and Confucianism were major influences, as indeed they are today. Confucianism more or less provided the philosophical framework for Tokugawa society, but it was not without internal division. Rivalry and diversity of thought over Confucian teachings became in fact so rampant during Tokugawa times that the central feudal government felt compelled to reimpose its brand of Confucian orthodoxy throughout the land. Pragmatism and diversity of thought, as well as the flexibility that these two character-istics provide, were important assets, which helped to facilitate Japan's reception of Western science.

In addition to being a prerequisite for science, the factor of tension also has a bearing on a society's receptivity to science. In Japan's case the drive for success in dealing with the West—to beat it at its own game—undoubtedly increased social tensions, which had existed even before Perry's appearance, because intercourse with the West implied change, and change threatened vested interests. Japan, then, at the be-ginning of the Meiji period, was in crisis. Its leaders reacted by com-mitting the nation to a course of modernization with Western-style window-dressing in hopes of dealing with the West on equal terms. What is striking in the Japanese experience is the early recognition given to the role of science and technology as key elements in the pro-cess of national development. But it is one thing to recognize national needs, and quite another to respond quickly to fulfill those needs, even with a high degree of national receptivity to foreign concepts. Leader-ship is required.

Leadership for the introduction of science and technology in Japan was undertaken by the government from the outset of the Meiji pe-riod, beginning a tradition of governmental initiative and bureaucratic influence in the sciences that has continued down to the present. The oligarchy, as swiftly as possible, wished to create a strong country built on Western scientific principles, and working with Western technology. At huge costs to the national treasury, foreign teachers, specialists, and technology were imported, students sent abroad, for-eign books translated. The goal of developing Japanese science was certainly a long-range one, but, in a sense, for reasons of expediency, rather short-range measures were adopted in favor of the rapid devel-opment of native technology, with the result that even today Japanese science is without a strong creative tradition in basic research.

Although later on special problems became manifest because of the way science was introduced under government leadership, change did occur, results were forthcoming, and the pace was a fast one. A broad view of the development of science and technology in Japan over the past century shows three main periods of growth: (1) the beginning of the Meiji period (1868) to the outbreak of World War I (1914); (2) the Japanese interwar period (1918–37); (3) the period after World War II (1945 to the present).

The Meiji period saw the establishment of many of the basic educa-tional institutions that had the responsibility for training native scien-tists. The University of Tokyo was founded in 1877, then reorganized and combined with the College of Technology in 1886 as Tokyo Imperial University. The government-sponsored ordinance that defined the character of the Imperial University stated the school's purpose clearly: "The aim of the Imperial University shall be to teach and study such sciences and practical arts as meet the demands of the State." Before the Meiji Emperor's death in 1912 other imperial universities were established in Kyoto, Sendai, and Fukuoka. As early as 1884, an astronomical observatory was established at the University of Tokyo.

The first steps taken by the Meiji government toward the development of native science and technology were, however, more internal ones. A Ministry of Engineering was established in 1870, and under its aegis railways and lighthouses were built, telegraphic services provided, and modern techniques in mine and factory management developed. It was during this period that foreign advisers were most important to the new government. In addition to about a hundred foreigners teaching in the sciences, the government at the same time also employed some 560 foreign experts in the Ministry of Engineering. At one time when the pay of the Japanese Minister of Engineering was about $500.00 a month, more than two hundred of his foreign engineers were receiving $2,000.00 a month for their technological skill. By 1893, when the lecture system was started in the national universities, almost all foreign teachers were replaced by Japanese instructors, a fact which testifies not only to the rapid advance of native scholars, but also to the high cost of foreign instructors.

The Tokyo Mathematical Society was founded in 1877, and two years later the Ministry of Education established the Tokyo Academy as the first government-sponsored academic society. As scientific societies increased in number (there were about twenty by 1900), and as scientific principles were increasingly discussed openly, the old practice of keeping techniques secret and knowledge confidential swiftly disappeared. Research institutes were also established through government leadership; significantly, the first so established was a military agency, the Naval Hydrographic Division in 1871. By 1900, the government had established twelve other research institutes. Furthermore, by 1883, when the government was able to enforce a nationwide examination system for medical practitioners, the prestige of Chinese medicine was given a heavy blow.

It should not be forgotten that Japan's aim in developing science was to build a "rich country and a strong army." Japanese military victories over China (1895) and Russia (1905) indicate a considerable strengthening of military technology. It is typical of the early development of science in Japan that the government sought immediate results from scientific research for the building of a powerful industrial basis to sustain the country's growing military capacity. Theoretical developments in creative science were given a secondary emphasis. Before the end of the Meiji period, Japan had established an important capacity in heavy industry, with obvious military implications. Facilities for shipbuilding, iron and steel production, coal mining, machine production, and electric power were all given government support for the development of military and industrial power.

During the second major period of Japan's development of science, from the outbreak of World War I to the Japanese attack on China in 1937, significant advances were made in heavy industry and its supporting technology, again with the building of national power receiving first priority. Electricity, gas, chemicals, ceramics, metals, machinery, all employing the most recent improvements in technology and in methods of mass production, made large strides forward. But, faced with the prime responsibility of maximizing national power, Japanese science during the interwar years did not have time to think; in fact, it barely had time to keep up with foreign scientific developments.

To some extent, however, the interruption in scientific communication caused by the outbreak of World War I made the Japanese realize how dependent their science was on foreign sources of information. As a consequence of this experience of wartime deprivation, Japanese attention was drawn to the task of creating an independent foundation for scientific research, again largely under government initiative and direction. Starting in 1917, and continuing on until the mid-1920s, the following scientific institutes were founded, one after another: the Physical and Chemical Research Institute; the Research Laboratory of the Tokyo Shibaura Electric Company; the Metal Materials Research Institute of Tohoku Imperial University; the Japan Scientific Research Council; the Aeronautical Research Institute; and the Seismological Research Institute. Although there was concern expressed at the time about the need to develop a better foundation for basic science, it is probably fair to say that without exception the new research institutes were primarily designed to serve Japanese industrial and military technology; nevertheless, the new institutes did help to strengthen the bond between Japanese science and technology.

Almost simultaneously with the launching of its program of aggression on China in 1937, Japan's science and technology were mobilized for war. Basic science, the investigation of phenomena for the advancement of knowledge without necessarily seeking practical applications, never was given a chance to take root in Japanese soil. The brief period of promise that appeared after World War I, when there was a slight opportunity for the development of independent science in Japan, went unfulfilled. Within three generations science in Japan had progressed from magic to a foundation for national development—only to suffer an almost disastrous blow from the distorted influence and increasing isolation brought on by the military adventures that eventually led to defeat in the Pacific War.

## A WORD ON JAPANESE SCIENCE IN THE POSTWAR PERIOD

Japanese science did not grow during World War II. True, some important technological innovations were made to meet wartime requirements, but, duplicating the experience of World War I (only this time with very much greater gravity), Japan was cut off from worldwide scientific developments. Pasteur once claimed that science knows no boundaries, that only scientists do; however, Japan's isolation during the Pacific War, which caused serious retardation in the development of that country's science, indicates that without open channels of communication, science as well as scientists can be subjected to the limits of national boundaries.

Defeat in war brought Japan under military occupation for almost seven years, during which time significant change was wrought in the organization of national science and technology. Demilitarization was one of the goals of the Allied Powers, and since the National General Mobilization Law had put all national life on a wartime footing in 1938, during the occupation science and technology in Japan became prime targets for reorganization.

In the early days of the occupation scientific research in Japan came almost to a halt. Any investigation with military implications was naturally prohibited, especially studies concerning atomic energy. Naturally enough, however, Japanese investigations of the effects of atomic bombing were not entirely prohibited. Gradually, as the occupation developed more confidence in itself and in the Japanese, the resumption of research was permitted, and in some cases even encouraged. Research in aeronautical science, for example, was at first all but eliminated, but as early as 1946 modifications in policy allowed the resumption of research on aircraft fuels and tires. It was not, however, until the very end of the occupation that the resumption of aircraft manufacture was allowed.

American scientific advisory missions often emphasized the following points in their reports to occupation authorities concerning the organization of science in Japan: (1) a reluctance of scholars to seek direct industrial application of their research; (2) a tendency of scientists in the academic world to ignore their counterparts in industrial laboratories; (3) an overly strong tradition of government initiative in the sciences; (4) a reluctance on the part of senior scientists to encourage a development of independent research by their younger colleagues; (5) a tendency to avoid priorities and to treat all research activity equally; (6) a lack of attention to the maintenance of private research organizations; and (7) a tendency to organize science and scientists on a hierarchical basis. In reaction to this final point, the occupation, in one of its most noble experiments, encouraged the "democratization" of the Japanese scientific world on all fronts.

The establishment of the Science Council of Japan (SCJ) in 1949 was a direct result of occupation policy for introducing democracy into the Japanese world of science. The primary aim of the SCJ was to mobilize professional talent in all fields to advise the government in the following areas: (1) the development of science and technology; (2) research utilization; (3) research training; (4) scientific administration; and (5) the infusion of science into industrial and national life. Unfortunately drastic changes occurred in the Asian political setting in 1949 and, as a consequence, relations between the government and the occupation authorities on one side, and the SCJ on the other, became increasingly strained. Especially after the outbreak of war in Korea in 1950, left-wing forces sought to use the newly created body as a political sounding board for charges that the occupation authorities were attempting to use Japan as a pawn in a scheme of anti-Communist encirclement.

These were the days of the so-called "reverse course," when occupation policy tried to counterbalance the powerful influence of left-wing groups, which had sprung up unopposed in Japan during the early postwar period. Japanese science since that time has been heavily politicized through the efforts of various groups, not all of which are on the left. The shibboleth of politically oriented Japanese scientists is peace, and, consequently, all research becomes divided into two categories: peace and war. This extreme sensitivity to possible military applications of scientific research—both a legacy from wartime experience and a requirement of postwar conformity to an antimilitary posture—has caused, for example, serious delays in the development of Japanese space science. Research in rocketry may be permissible, the reasoning goes, but since guidance systems help to turn observation rockets into war missiles, guidance systems had better be avoided. Research on guidance systems was neglected for a long time at the University of Tokyo, and perhaps as a consequence, the University has yet to achieve success in its attempts to orbit a scientific satellite.

If the politicizing of science and the hypersensitivity of some scientists to alleged schemes of the military to control research activity are unhappy conditions that evolved out of the period of postwar occupation, the increased participation and greater mobility of Japanese scientists are decidedly happy results. Although the occupation wrought these changes in attitudes, as well as others in scientific education, in the organization of research institutes and scientific societies and in the direction of international scientific exchange, the foundation of science in Japan went unaltered.

Government initiative and the importation of foreign technology remain—as they have since the nation first adopted Western science during the Meiji period—basic to science in Japan. Creative science has yet to come to full bloom. Like any other nation, Japan cannot escape the influence of its history. The old master-apprentice relationships, the custom of secret techniques, the prestige of the national over the private universities, the tendency to departmentalize and equalize research, the consciousness of hierarchy and mutual exclusiveness among researchers in the university and in industry, the fear of military applications—all these factors have worked both to impair scientific cooperation and to hinder the development of a creative scientific tradition.

Instead of ideas, personnel, and funds moving easily from government to industry and to the universities, there are only minimal links of exchange. In recent years the transfer of government funds to industry for contract research and subsidies has amounted to less than five per cent annually of all government funds allocated for research. Moreover, research done in the universities on contract from industry is equal to a mere one per cent of the total annual industrial expenditure for research. Broadly speaking, postwar Japanese industry, in a search for immediate application and profit, has concentrated on the improvement and refinement of foreign technology. For the most part, basic science has been left to the universities, even though only 25 per cent of the total amount of Japanese research expenditure in 1963 was devoted to university-directed research.

Today the problems of science and the development of its creative aspects are beginning to be given national recognition. The country is already groping for the establishment of a national science policy. Hopefully such a program would go a long way in replacing jealousy, suspicion, rivalry, and shortsightedness with scientific cooperation and coordination.

In a final word on the implication of the Japanese experience for the creation of a scientific tradition in the developing countries, I should remind those who would seek to use the Japanese model that as amazing as the growth of science in Japan has been, the Japanese jumping-off point was an extremely high and favorable one. The prerequisites I have listed earlier must be present in a developing society if the Japanese experience is to be useful, not only as a method for the introduction of a scientific tradition, but also for the inducement of social change. Where the Japanese experience with foreign science can be instructive, however, is in the teaching that it offers the underdeveloped world once the prerequisites for science have been established. The most important lesson that can be drawn from the Japanese experience is that no matter how much effort is spent on building scientific traditions swiftly, there is neither a shortcut nor a substitute for the development of a nationally based, cooperatively organized, research foundation for the stimulation of creative, basic science. Science through governmental initiative and foreign technology, and science for national power, may offer significant encouragement for the growth of some native scientific traditions, but, in the light of the history of Japanese development, creative science does not appear to flourish until scientific research is nationally supported for its own sake, without any immediate thought of practical applications. Creative science, of course, may well be a luxury that the underdeveloped world should forgo in favor of encouraging the growth of native scientific and technological traditions. If such a decision is made, and creative science is left to a time of affluence, then the developing countries will find much of the Japanese experience instructive, provided that some of the prerequisites and a measure of receptivity for science are present.

## SOME RECENT SUGGESTED REFERENCES ON JAPANESE SCIENCE

Slowly and painfully a body of literature on the development of science in Japan is becoming available in English. Most treatments of the subject, however, are limited in scope, specialized in nature, and more concerned with description than analysis.

The books and articles listed below, although varying considerably in quality, offer different viewpoints, or deal with different aspects of science in Japan not otherwise readily available in English. The OECD survey of Japanese science policy is the only thorough and objective treatment of that subject in English; it should be read with Professor Tuge's more subjective historical study of the development of science and technology in Japan. Three Japanese works are listed because each one makes a significant contribution: the *White Paper* for its statistics; Professor Yoshida's little book for his provocative and stimulating analysis; and Professor Hoshino's study for his pioneering work on the history of technology in Japan.

# ARTICLES

Albert Craig, "Science and Confucianism in Tokugawa Japan," in Marius B. Jansen, ed., *Changing Japanese Attitudes Toward Modernization*, Princeton: Princeton University Press, 1965, pp. 133–160.

Yoshirō Hoshino, "Science and Technology," *Japan Quarterly*, Vol. XIV, No. 1, January–March 1967, pp. 45–52.

F. Roy Lockheimer, "The Rising Sun in Space, Part I: The University of Tokyo," American Universities Field Staff Reports, East Asia Series, Volume XIV, No. 1, January 1967; and "The Rising Sun in Space, Part II: International Co-operation, Organization and the Future," American Universities Field Staff Reports, East Asia Series, Volume XIV, No. 2, February 1967.

Theodore Dixon Long, "Science and Government in Japan," *Särtryck ur Svensk Naturvetenskap 1967*, Stockholm: Statens Naturvetenskapliga Forskningsrad, 1967, pp. 296–315.

Shigeru Nakayama, "The Role Played by Universities in Scientific and Technological Development in Japan," *Journal of World History*, Volume IX, No. 2, 1965, pp. 340–362.

Masayoshi Sugimoto and David L. Swain, "Science and the Intellectual History of Japan," in *Japan Studies*, No. 10, Nishinomiya, Japan: International Institute for Japan Studies, 1966.

# BOOKS

Tetsuya Kobayashi, *General Education for Scientists and Engineers in the United States of America and Japan*, Ann Arbor: University of Michigan, Comparative Education Dissertation Series, No. 6, 1965.

Nippon Kagaku-shi Gakkai [The History of Science Society of Japan]. *Japanese Studies in the History of Science*. Annual journal of the History of Science Society, Tokyo, Japan, published regularly since 1962.

Organization for Economic Co-operation and Development (OECD), *Reviews of National Science Policy: Japan*, Paris: OECD, 1967.

Science and Technology Board of the Japanese Government, *Foreign Technology Introduction White Paper*, Japan Industry Series, Volume XII, Tokyo: Trade Bulletin Corporation, 1967.

Hideomi Tuge, *Historical Development of Science and Technology in Japan*, Tokyo: Kokusai Bunka Shinkokai, 1961.

# BOOKS IN JAPANESE

Yoshirō Hoshino, *Nihon no Gijutsu Kakushin* [*Japanese Technological Innovation*], Tokyo: Keisō Shobō, 1966.

Kagaku Gijutsu-chō [Science and Technology Board], *Kagaku Gijutsu Hakusho* [*White Paper on Science and Technology*], Tokyo: Science and Technology Board, 1966.

Mitsukuni Yoshida, *Nihon o Kizuita Kagaku* [*The Science That Built Japan*], Tokyo: Kodansha, 1966.

# 8.

# THE POLITY OF RUSSIAN AND SOVIET SCIENCE: A CENTURY OF CONTINUITY AND CHANGE

## BY NICHOLAS DeWITT *

Indiana University

The word "science" is commonly used with reassuring definiteness despite the fact that from the Middle Ages to the present it has consisted of many distinct activities, diverse contributions, and different results attained under varying material and intellectual conditions of the developing societies of the West. However, throughout the ages sciences as a process of the development of knowledge has usually been confused with its products, namely the utilization of science for the solution of problems in industry and the arts. If any valid generalization is in order, it would be that science is a systematized body of knowledge and is thus an "idea" or a "thought"; technology is the apparatus through which this knowledge is put to practical use and is thus an action. It is mainly the technology which profoundly affects the shape of society, for in order to put any idea into action, institutions must be created for channeling human effort. In turn, however, it is society which allows the individual to develop his "thoughts," to pursue his creative efforts in search of abstract ideas.

* Without the generous support of the Carnegie Corporation of New York, which for the last three years has assisted my research on an *International Survey of Educational Development and Planning*, this paper as a by-product of the project could not have been written.

Historically, a great deal of confusion has prevailed in Russia about what science is and this ambiguity has been significantly accentuated during the Soviet era. The Russian word *nauka*, commonly and conveniently mistranslated as "science," is an all-embracing term. *Nauka* really means that kind of knowledge which is acquired through some sort of research activity. But since the words "science" and "scientific" have been elevated in the Marxist epistemology to the symbolic status of positive value, they have been usurped by well-nigh anyone having the slightest pretense of engaging in any kind of study-research activity. Homer and Pythagoras, Shakespeare and Newton, Marx and Darwin, Weber and Einstein—all fit into the unified conceptual basket which the Soviets call "science." The design of a power dam on the Volga or a sewage system on a collective farm, together with research on Rubens' paintings or the music of Khachaturian are also found within the jurisdiction of Soviet *nauka*. The Academy of Sciences of the USSR engages in a variety of activities which have only a remote relationship to "science" as conceptualized in the West.

But even if we were to take a more limited definition of "science" as research in the natural sciences, the seemingly precise term "natural sciences" is also like a rubber band which may be contracted or stretched at will. It can be all-embracing—as broad as the German *Naturwissenschaft* or its Russian counterpart *yestestvoznanie* can make it; or very narrow, limited to physics and chemistry as is sometimes done. If the broad definition is accepted, then it has to be stretched even further so as to include mathematics ("the logic and the symbolic language of science"), and the applied natural sciences, such as engineering, medicine, and the like. The problem still remains when we speak of research in the natural sciences, or in any other field, as to whether we are concerned with the product or the process, and how we can make a meaningful separation in order to distinguish the two.

D. I. Mendeleyev's system of periodic elements or N. I. Lobachevskii's non-Euclidian geometry, V. I. Veksler's autophasing (for cyclotrons) or the BESM digital computer, are all "products," though quite distinct in their substance. There are many other "products" of this type, and all of them in combination represent a specific item in our applied and theoretical knowledge. Each one of these "products" was obtained through a certain creative process, which in turn had been conditioned by social, political, and economic factors. The essential point is that while the individual steps in the methods and epistemology of the creative process (particularly those of abstraction, analysis, and synthesis) may be the same for different individuals in diverse localities and at distinct points in time, because of the impact of external factors these products may be of better or worse quality or may even not emerge at all. It is like baking a loaf of bread—the ingredients and process are the same, and yet the oven temperature may burn it to a frazzle.

In general terms the nature of the problem with which this paper is designed to deal is extremely complex. Which is it going to be: the product, the process, or the factors which condition the process and in this way affect the product? At times scientific activity is viewed as an ivory tower created by man for its own sake, isolated from the rest of society by the very nature of its self-sustained creative activity. Scientists know what science is and science is what scientists do. Just as the poet or painter allegedly couldn't care less what society thinks of his sonnets or paintings, so the scientist, as the producer of ideas about the universe which surrounds him, is not susceptible to anything else but the logical truth of his hypotheses about the nature and laws of that universe.

Although we should grant the point that science exists and proceeds in the minds of men, it is by no means an isolated phenomenon. It is not a self-sufficient system of knowledge which can exist in abstraction. It is a social activity, firmly rooted to social environment. The individual scientist is not a king, but a pawn, and the rules of the game do matter. Therefore, one cannot understand the role of science or of the scientist outside the social system in which it or he functions. Most factors influencing the relationship between science and society are in the domain of the "polity of science."

## IS SCIENCE A PRODUCTIVE RESOURCE?

The main topic in studying the historical trends accounting for the transformation of Russian society in the last hundred years can be most meaningfully approached by studying the process of scientific research and particularly the factors which condition it, rather than the products. It should be added hastily, however, that if we were concerned not with the interrelations of science and society but rather with the substantive indices of science or the qualitative evaluations of a certain level of accomplishment at some specific point in time or with the dynamics of the accumulation of theoretical and applied knowledge, then for all this we would have to turn to products. Furthermore, the products of scientific research, through their embodiment in technologically determined means of production, affect the social structures. It is true that it is indeed in this sequence, as Bertrand Russell has postulated, that the natural sciences exercise a powerful impact upon social organization, which in turn causes political change.[1] However, if for analytical convenience, we are to break the chain of interrelationships and dependencies, this break should come at the level of factors affecting the process of scholarship or research rather than at any other place. In examining trends in scientific research in Russia and the USSR during the last hundred years, this paper will be concerned primarily with those factors which may conceivably have their impact upon the process of creative scholarship in the fields of the natural sciences.

In following this approach, we should not, however, inadvertently open a Pandora's box, namely the disquisitions of Marxism on science. What Marx and Engels did or did not say about the philosophy of science is not very relevant. Stripped bare, Marxian analytical categories of "the superstructure" and "the base" do not offer much help in explaining the processes of creative scientific research and the development of technology as an extension of scientific advances. Investigations in the natural sciences are indeed by and large manifestations of intellectual activity. Marxist definitions regard "all intellectual activity as a part of a superstructure of social development taken as a whole." [2] Thus scholarship in the natural sciences belongs there too, but at the same time the natural sciences are an indispensable tool in the creation of the technical means of production and therefore must be regarded as a part of the "base." In order to get out of this muddle, the Soviet academician S. G. Strumilin, the "Great White Father" of Soviet economic thought, proposed "not to assign all that science deals with to the category of superstructure." [3] Since science plays the role of a productive force (technology), it should be viewed as a "natural resource" and thus one of the primary factors in production or the "base."

These statements were an obvious heresy and the party theologians immediately condemned such an interpretation. Shortly thereafter Mr. Strumilin had to reverse his position and to recognize sheepishly that "it would be totally erroneous to recognize scientific thought as a primary source of technical progress," that science was *not* a productive

[1] Bertrand Russell, *The Impact of Science on Society*, New York: Columbia University Press, 1951, p. 3.
[2] P. E. Mosely, "Freedom of Artistic Expression and Scientific Inquiry in Russia," reprinted from *Annals of the American Academy of Political and Social Science*, Nov. 1938, Vol. 200:254-74, p. 1.
[3] S. G. Strumilin, presentation at "Nauka v svete ucheniya I. V. Stalina o bazise i nadstroike" [Science in the Light of the Teachings of I. V. Stalin about the Base and the Superstructure], *Izvestiya Akademii Nauk: Otdeleniye Ekonomiki i Prava* [Proceedings of the Academy of Science: Division of Economics and Jurisprudence], Moscow, 1951, No. 4, pp. 287-88.

force, etc., etc.[4] Many other examples of such theological discussions can be found in the Soviet press, and the ideological debate continues. It is very doubtful that much insight can be gained by following Soviet "theoretical" arguments as to the "causal factors," namely the deterministic assertions about the relationship of the "base" to the "superstructure" as explaining the level of scientific research activity in Russia or anywhere else. In the Soviet Union today it is a politically expedient assertion to state that achievements of Soviet science and technology are not a part of, though attributable to, the proper "base," namely the "superiority of a socialist society." [5] In retrospect, as will become apparent below, in the nineteenth century the meager Russian "base" was out of kilter with the flourishing intellectual "superstructure."

## HISTORIOGRAPHY OF RUSSIAN SCIENCE

The natural sciences and technology in Russia, their development and interrelationship with the world's scientific and technological progress, and their interdependence with the social and political institutions of Russia are vast and important, though highly neglected subjects. These subjects must be approached with great humility for the evaluation of science in any country. In particular, the assessment of the contribution of "X"-institution, "Y"-scientist, and "Z"-field to the universal pool of scientific knowledge is not only beyond any one researcher's capability, but is in any event a most hazardous undertaking. The interaction of ideas, theories, and their empirical verification are so complex that even if we could neatly isolate the individual variables, any attempt to draw causal relationships among them in order to indicate the progression of scientific development is a well-nigh impossible undertaking. Such an exercise is doubly hazardous for the Soviet Union, since although we are familiar with generalities and are able to trace some details, we still know precious little about the inner workings and interactions of the Soviet science organization.

Although some work has been done in regard to the substantive aspects of science and its interrelations with communist ideology and politics during the Soviet era,[6] no integrated studies with historical

---

[4] S. G. Strumilin, "Nauka i razvitiye proizvoditel'nykh sil" [Science and Development of Productive Resources], *Voprosy Filosofii* [Problems of Philosophy], Vol. 3, 1954, pp. 46–61 (esp. pp. 46, 51–52).
[5] *Pravda*, October 19, 1967. Statement of the Central Committee of the CPSU concerning Venus-IV probe.
[6] E. Ashby, *A Scientist in Russia*, Harmondsworth: Penguin Books, 1947; C. Zirkle, ed., *Soviet Science*, Washington: AAAS, 1952 (evaluation of contemporary

retrospect have as yet appeared. The difficulties in handling this pre-plexing subject are not indigenous to Western scholars of Soviet Russia. Even in the Soviet Union itself integrated surveys of the development of the natural sciences and technology do not exist, although there has been enormous activity in the field of the history of Russian science. Prior to the mid-1930s a number of descriptive histories of the Academy of Sciences appeared, but the Academy's own effort to do research on the history of the Academy was reconstituted so as to give it the broader task of investigating the role of the Academy in developing Russian science.[7]

During World War II in 1942–44, half a dozen commissions emerged, each of which dealt separately with the history of a given field of science (such as commissions on biological, engineering, physical-mathematical, chemical science, etc.). In addition, in 1944 under the Division of History of the Academy of Sciences of the USSR an Institute of the History of Natural Sciences of the USSR under the direction of Kh. S. Koshtoyants was formed. The mushrooming activity in this field by the Academy in the 1940s was promoted to a great extent by political motivation and party edicts designed to prove the superiority of Russian and Soviet science.

In the fall of 1953 the Institute of the History of Natural Sciences was transferred directly under the jurisdiction of the Presidium (governing board) of the Academy of Sciences, and all commissions were incorporated into its structure, including the renowned Lomonosov Museum (formerly Kunstkamera) and another natural history museum. This newly reconstituted establishment was named the Institute for History of Natural Science and Technology, at first headed by A. M. Samarin and since early 1957 by N. A. Figurovskii.[8] These original commissions and the Institute were designated to study the history of science in Russia from the point of view of demonstrating the gains of "native science" (*otechestvennoi nauki*). The strength of this expression, *scientia patriae*, has no English equivalent. Their activi-

Soviet science by 9 authorities); A. Vuchinich, *The Soviet Academy of Sciences,* Stanford: Stanford University Press, 1956 (institutional research activities); Arnold Buchholtz, *Ideologie und Forschung in der Sowjetschen Naturwissenschaft,* Stuggart: 1953; B. Moore, Jr., *Terror and Progress: USSR,* Cambridge: Harvard University Press, 1954.

[7] For a discussion of the role of the Academy as a *leader,* see, for example: Akademiya Nauk SSSR, *Ocherki po istorii Akademii Nauk* [Survey of History of the Academy of Sciences], Moscow: 1945, in five parts (biological, chemical, linguistic, historical, and physical-mathematical sciences).

[8] For more details, see Akademiya Nauk SSSR, *220 Let Akademii Nauk SSSR* [220 Years of the Academy of Sciences of the USSR], Moscow: 1945, *passim; Vestnik Akademii Nauk* (to be referred to hereafter as *VAN*) 1954, No. 4, p. 88; 1953, No. 10, p. 109; 1957, No. 3, p. 18; and, in English, A. Vuchinich, *The Soviet Academy of Sciences,* Stanford: Stanford University Press, 1956, *passim.*

ties resulted in a veritable outpouring of publications—all of which had one major bias: nationalistic and chauvinistic defense of the priority of Russian science.

During the decade 1941–51 alone it was reported that some 800 books and 3,500 articles appeared concerning the history of science in Russia, the majority with distinct emphasis on achievements (*dostizheniya*) of native scientists.[9] Significant portions of the annual general assemblies of the Academy in the 1940s, as well as special conferences, were devoted to the history of Russian science. The famous general assembly in January 1949 was devoted exclusively to *Problems of the History of Native Science*.[10] As a result of this mushrooming activity, a large number of pamphlets, books, and articles appeared.[11] This work ultimately culminated in the publication of the first volume of *History of the Natural Sciences in Russia*.[12]

## NATIONALISM

What kind of information do they present? The majority of these publications deal with the biographies of outstanding Russian scientists,[13] or certain discoveries or detailed surveys of the development of narrow specific branches of science and technology.[14] Essentially they are a description of who did what and where. What are the trends that these Soviet studies of the "native science" are trying to ascertain?

[9] *VAN*, 1953, No. 5, p. 12.

[10] Akademiya Nauk, *Voprosy Istorii Otechestvennoi Nauki* [Problems of the History of Native Science], Moscow: 1949 (a volume on the proceedings of the general assembly).

[11] Perhaps the most complete (though a bit out-of-date) bibliography can be found in *Akademiya Nauk SSSR*, S. I. Vavilov, ed., *Trudy Instituta Istorii Yestestvoznaniya* [Proceedings of the Institute of History of Natural Sciences], Vol. I, Moscow: 1947, pp. 457–535 (summary bibliography).

[12] Akademiya Nauk SSSR, Institut Istorii Yestestvoznaniya i Tekhniki, N. A. Figurovskii, ed., *Istoriya Yestestvoznaniya v Rossii* [History of Natural Sciences in Russia], Moscow: 1957, Vol. I, parts 1 and 2. Volume I covers the period until 1860. (Volume II has not yet appeared.)

[13] A useful shortcut can be found in dealing with brief biographical data by consulting the two-volume reference: S. I. Vavilov, ed., *Liudi Russkoi Nauki* [Russian Scientists], Moscow: 1948. Otherwise, there are several hundred books dealing with biographies of individual scientists.

[14] The interested reader should start exploring this vast material by consulting first the three main sources: (1) Akademiya Nauk, *Trudy Instituta Istorii Yestestvoznaniya* [Works of the Institute of History of Natural Sciences], 5 volumes, Moscow: 1947–51; (2) Akademiya Nauk, *Trudy Instituta Istorii Yestestvoznaniya i Tekhniki* [Works of the Institute of History of Natural Sciences and Technology], Moscow: 1953–current (to date 15 vols.); (3) *Uchenyye Zapiski Moshkovskogo Gosudarstvennogo Universiteta* [Digest of the Moscow State University], (various issues, especially during the years 1947–49).

Several are in evidence in all these studies, including the magnum opus, *History of the Natural Sciences in Russia*. First, they perpetrate and promote the view of unadulterated nationalism and chauvinism as far as scientific discoveries and theories are concerned. It is indigenous science first and foremost. Occasional lip service is paid to Western science, but the tune of "prioritet" (priority) of Russian science is ubiquitous. The trend which is artifically constructed is that any Russian scientist, past or present, had also a Russian precursor.

It would be easy to shrug this off if it were not relevant as a factor influencing research. Throughout the centuries many scientific theories and discoveries were made because people who made them were skeptics and did not accept as "truth" the postulates of their predecessors. The Russian and Soviet scientific discoveries were made by skeptics. The search for "native ancestry" in scientific theories, discoveries, and technological inventions, when it enters into the mental process in the course of creative research and when it is institutionalized as a credo, may result in very unfortunate effects upon current scholarship in the natural sciences. Using Whitehead's apothegm, "A science which hesitates to forget its founders is lost," the search for continuity of Russian and Soviet science, particularly in isolation from international science, has imposed severe limitations in many fields of Soviet scholarship over the last three decades. The adverse impact in some fields of chemistry, biology, and mathematics are attributable to this day to the "Russian" tradition.

## IDEOLOGY

The second trend which the Soviet studies of the history of the natural sciences in Russia were trying to prove is the ideological thesis that the process of scientific inquiry progresses to higher levels in successive stages, from "primitive materialism" to "chaotic" and "non-systematic" "natural-historical materialism" (*yestestvenno-istoricheskii materializm*), on to organized, conscious, and orderly philosophical "dialectical materialism." [15] Archives and the writings of most pre-revolutionary scientists are gone over with a fine comb in order to find even the vaguest hints of "materialism" as a belief. In its dogmatic essence it

---

[15] Among a number of works on this topic, see the outstanding example: A. A. Maksimov (corresponding member of the Academy of Sciences), *Ocherki po istorii bor'by za materializm v Russkom yestestvoznanii* [Survey of the History of Struggle for Materialist Outlook in the Russian Natural Sciences], Moscow: 1947. (Volume imprimatur of the Institute of Philosophy of the Academy of Sciences of the USSR.)

is related to an "ancestry search" though it is carried out with far greater vigor. The pilot light, of course, is Lenin's quote of 1911 that physics is undergoing labor pains for "dialectical materialism" as the sole philosophical foundation of modern physics (and science at large) is being born.[16] This "official ideology" may be even more constrictive to the process of scientific inquiry and organized skepticism than the "ancestry" search. The indoctrination of Russian science with "dialectical materialism" as a method of scientific inquiry has been under way with great intensity for about four decades (since the late 1920s). It represents a reversal of the real trend which prevailed in the prerevolutionary period and which is characterized by complete lack of any unifying ideological orthodoxy among Russian scientists.

The impact of ideology upon the Soviet scientist varies. One variation is by field of knowledge, with physical sciences the least vulnerable, social sciences the most vulnerable, and the life sciences somewhere in the middle. The impact of ideology upon an individual scientist also shows marked differences. To some extent scientists may internalize ideological tenets, and yet for many they may remain outside. For each individual, ideology is a matter of conviction and/or convenience. The relative proportion of each is wholly unpredictable. There is also a variation of the ideological impact in accordance with the cycle of international or domestic difficulties. The ideological pressure and demands on scientists for practical results relax in periods of quiescence and usually intensify in periods of crisis.

Aside from these variations and the degree to which they may affect scientific inquiry, with the existence of tight controls and centralization the ideology can have a very negative impact upon scientific inquiry, for one scientific school attempts to secure a monopoly by using ideological weapons to discredit and to impede the activities of other scientists. Detrimental effects may also be felt in the political arena, where there is a tendency by one school to force its conclusions upon all scientists and to require their unanimous support.

The capacity of self-delusion in scientific research is a well-known phenomenon throughout history. Many a fraudulent scientific claim has been advanced not necessarily in bad conscience but as the result of the self-delusion that a scientist's own pet theory is the "true" one, and mountains of experimental data are marshalled to prove its empirical validity. The problem is more complex in the Soviet setting, where numerous cases are known of deliberate fabrication of research results in order to substantiate "theories" in the social sciences, biology, and

[16] V. Lenin, *Sochineniya* [Works], 4th ed., Vol. 14, Moscow: State Publishing House of Political Literature (OGIZ), 1947, p. 299.

other life sciences, and even in certain branches of physics. "Ideology" used by some unscrupulous political charlatans (such as Lysenko) certainly helps to stimulate self-deception.

Finally, communist ideology has a tendency to isolate scientists from their colleagues, both in the Soviet Union and abroad. Mainly because of ideological pressures Soviet science was, and will continue to remain, uneven in quality, with the best minds staying away from those science fields which are most vulnerable to ideologically motivated controls. In areas of research susceptible to dogma, hacks and crackpots of the Lysenko type were, and will continue to find their way, in positions of leadership.

The bias expressed in the two aforementioned trends leads to a common joke that the Academy was so much involved in the ideology search and in ancestral research that only two major prizes for scholarly books were to be offered—"Classics of Marxism-Leninism on the Origins of Elephants" and "Russia is the Fatherland of Elephants." All these trends—the attempts to reorient science along national lines, the forceful persuasion to accept dialectical materialism as the method of science, and the use of ideology as a weapon—are different in the USSR from those in pre-revolutionary Russia. The over-all ideological creed and the political conformity promoted by the Soviet regime were really not fostered by the pre-revolutionary government in Russia. They represent a new departure in the Soviet period. While there are undoubtedly conflicts on a philosophical plane which may be resolved (or at times neglected), it is essential to realize the fact that since the mid-1930s, and especially in the 1940s, ideological and political factors had their impact also upon institutional arrangements. Professor Mosely observed almost twenty years ago that "politicians, but slightly acquainted with complex problems which are being worked out along the frontiers of knowledge, attempt crudely and arbitrarily to define the channels and goals of human thought." [17] It was not only the philosophical plane but the substantive part of research which was affected.

## SECRECY

As is the case with most booms, the rapidly expanding Soviet research and development establishment is suffering growing pains. These pains encompass the entire gamut of Soviet science policy, institutional arrangements, management problems, and the functions of individual sci-

[17] P. E. Mosely, *op. cit.*, p. 20.

entists. They are likewise responsible for the lively debate concerning the role of science and scientists in Soviet society, a debate which has raged since the 1950s in the Soviet press and which has often been carried on with an unusual frankness almost entirely absent during the two Stalinist decades.

But despite the greater "openness" in Soviet discussions of their own problems, and despite the increased flow of information both through the press and exchanges of persons concerning the USSR's scientific activities, we must recognize that the most effective secret weapon of a totalitarian society is still secrecy itself. It is this secrecy which creates a great handicap for those who set out to assess the substantive dimensions of the Soviet research and development effort in many strategic fields, and also the factors influencing the process of research. In the realm of the politics of Soviet science we really know very few of the specifics relevant to an accurate judgment of how the system actually works. Thus, instead of basing our generalizations on specific case studies, we must usually be content with the observation of general factors relating to the organization of scientific activity in the Soviet Union. To use a figure of speech, we are pecking at the surface of the iceberg without really knowing how deep or how well held together it is.

## INSTITUTIONAL IMPACT

In science the substantive parts of research were effected via institutional channels. In a number of instances arbitrariness was introduced because scientific charlatans had the political power to manipulate the direction of research. This did not happen in all areas of research, but there are a number of well-publicized instances (notably Lysenko's genetics) which reveal the possible extent of damage to scholarly pursuits resulting from this politically oriented arbitrariness. Consequently, it was, and still is, feared that:

> . . . such a hamstrung species of science is not likely to advance the frontier of general knowledge very far. Over a short period of time, extreme specialization, based on intensive work and also on the general advances borrowed from countries with a relatively broad scientific freedom may give striking and valuable results. In the long run, and especially if cut off from like activities in other countries by deliberate self-isolation, this policy is likely to result in intellectual sterility. Such restriction of freedom in abstract science will ultimately affect unfavorably the development of practical knowledge.[18]

[18] *Ibid.*, p. 20.

Furthermore, it is being argued (despite the demonstrations of some recent Soviet advances in science and technology, from atomic energy developments to space technology) that we are now still dealing with short-run developments, and as far as the long-run impact is concerned, only time will tell.

Western analysts of Soviet affairs hold two divergent views concerning the evolution of Soviet society. Reduced to fundamentals, one group's position is that whatever tactical shifts may occur from time to time, the ultimate goals and the operational mode of the communist dictatorship remain unaltered. The Soviet Union is a totalitarian society where power is concentrated in the hands of a dictator who, with the aid of the party élite, controls all aspects of the political, economic, social, and cultural activities of the nation. Soviet scientists are either willing members of this élite or simply obedient tools of it. The revisionism in ideology, moderation of terror, and greater compassion for the consumer which have occurred since Stalin's death have not changed significantly the nature of the totalitarian dictatorship.

At the opposite pole are observers who contend that the Soviet Union is rapidly becoming an industrialized society, where technocracy seeks greater rationality of social organization and thus political pluralism, with the result that the absolute dictatorship is withering away and totalitarianism is "mellowing." The post-Stalin reforms were but the initial manifestation of the "inevitable" process of liberalization and democratization of Soviet society with its concomitant diminution of the drive for world power and expansionism, the desire for "coexistence," and so forth. The Soviet scientist may be instrumental in fostering the political and social development of the Soviet Union in the desired direction of a "more rational" (though not necessarily more liberal) society.

While it is essential to keep these trends in mind as the guide rails of the evolution of scholarship in the natural sciences in Russia and the Soviet Union, the question which still remains unanswered is how an individual Soviet scientist feels about them. We have very meager clues, but during the brief period of the thaw in 1956 some tell-tale stories came out. One of them, told by a well-known Soviet writer, Valentine Kaverin, in his novel *Search and Hope*, makes most worthwhile and revealing reading:

> In the post-war years we were posed before the strange task of proving that our medical science [the story specifically deals with the invention of penicillin] was developing with unusual speed, or at least with a faster rate than the developing of science in other countries and in the world at large. It has been asserted in books and articles, in movies and plays, that all the major discoveries of

the 19th and 20th centuries were made by us. Yes, by us alone and nobody else. And in making this claim, while defending this invented, imaginary priority, it has gone unnoticed that we are losing the real advances obtained through agonizingly hard work and search. There are dozens of reasons why we were losing this real priority, but the main one among them was that no one of us had the right to share his discoveries even with the neighboring laboratory.

Oh, this secrecy and gloom which prevented us from seeing one another! Even now as I write these lines in 1956, we still have not called it quits to this ignorant nonsense, mysterious rubbish around which we have built barbed-wire fences and which was stored after hours in sealed-for-security safes. There were many "wise guys" who had absolutely no place in medical science, who received high titles under the protective cover of this artificial secrecy, without which—strangely enough—we could neither work nor live.

This imaginary, artificially invented science required artificial invigoration as well, and to accomplish this, wide debates were organized in order to show off to the entire world the sparkle of our creativity, the clash of our creative minds. But even under this most artificial light, there appeared in full view only the shabby decorations of dogmatism, ready-made concepts and prompted thoughts.

Of course this was the victory of Kramov [a Soviet scientist-bureaucrat with party affiliation and baking]. It was a victory, the evil consequences of which he himself could not have foreseen.[19]

Perhaps the chains on the process of creative scholarship stemming from national-traditional, ideological, and political pressures and secrecy only look strong, but underneath them there may be an undercurrent of healthy organized skepticism. When Soviet intellectuals and scientists are told that "whatever cult there may be . . . , wherever there is a cult, scientific thought must retreat before blind faith, creativity must submit to dogma and popular opinion to the rule of arbitrariness,"[20] there is at least the realization of the predicament that confronts creative activity in the Soviet Union.

This discussion may be summed up as follows. In pre-revolutionary Russia creative intellectual activity and scholarship in the natural sciences were not subjected to the influences of one unifying ideology. The attitude of the state was one of indifference or, at times, of suspicious hostility. The concept of "native ancestry" was not held in a po-

[19] V. Kaverin, "Poiski i nadezhdy" (a novel, a third part of the trilogy *Open Book*), in M. I. Aliger *et al.*, eds., *Literaturnaya Moskva: Sbornik Vtoroi* [Literary Moscow: Second Collection], Moscow: 1956, pp. 277–278.
[20] A. Kron, "Zametki pisatelya" [Notes of a Writer] in *Literaturnaya Moskva*, Moscow: 1956, p. 780.

sition of authority. During the period of the 1920s, which can be characterized by the so-called "proletarization" scheme (namely, trying to point out the proletarian origins of intellectual activity and its participants) and a campaign of "withering away of the differences between mental and physical labor," Russian science and scientists occupied an ambiguous and uncertain position. This period of the 1920s might be called a transitional one, during which the natural sciences gained some recognition and state support but still retained freedom in the sense of neutrality and noninterference. Since about the mid-1930s, the period of active conversion begins to take place. For two decades there is a period of heavy intrusion of ideological dogmatisms, nationalism, and secrecy. Their pressure subsides somewhat in the mid-1950s, but the problems posed by their presence remain.

## THEORETICAL SCIENCE VERSUS APPLIED RESEARCH

Another trend in the development of science and technology in Russia which ought to be singled out is the interaction of applied and theoretical science. It appears to be of primary significance that Russian scientific development proceeded largely without the blend of pure and applied research. It appears characteristic for the Russian and Soviet scientific and research effort that there have been and still are different and conflicting levels of pure and applied knowledge.

It is a well-recognized fact that continuous interdependence of abstract (theoretical) and applied knowledge (inventions and technology) is essential for the progress of both in the natural science fields. They are but two manifestations of the unified human effort to reach higher levels of understanding and the mastery of nature. To divorce one from the other, to explain or justify one at the expense of the other, or to promote one while neglecting the other, is bound to result in conflict. This conflict manifests itself first in the lags which accompany the process of introducing inventions and innovations and, second, particularly in the ways in which a body of applied knowledge is advanced and modified by internal, indigenous theoretical research, rather than by external, imported inventions, equipment, and techniques. Conflicting levels of theoretical and applied advances or states of knowledge result in gaps and particularly in qualitative unevenness. Obviously, these problems are universal in nature, but the enormous differential which is observable in the state of pure (theoretical) knowledge and applied research, in the body of theoretical knowledge and its application to industry and technology in pre-revolutionary

Russia and still present in the Soviet Union, represents a striking and unique historical trend.

The crucial factor indispensable for the understanding of the nature of this paradox of flourishing theoretical science versus the lack of its application is that in the second half of the nineteenth century in Russia there was hardly anything to which to apply the rich theoretical findings of natural science. In Russia at that time there was a virtual lack of what the Soviet historians now commonly call "broad material and technical base." This term, as already mentioned, orginates in Marxist analysis, but in this case it simply meant that Russian industry was very weak. Technologically, it was uniquely static and backward as compared with the rapidly developing industry and technology in the West. Furthermore, there was for the most part an ominous lack of contact (and at times even antagonism) between those who were in theoretical research and those who had anything to do with entrepreneurial and innovative activity. In short, the flourishing of the natural sciences in the second half of the nineteenth century in Russia was not paralleled by a technological and industrial upswing.

During the period of industrial expansion of the 1890s and the 1900s the technology introduced into Russian industry came, by and large, from the West; and again native scientific research played a relatively minor role in the solution of applied problems of technology. For about twelve years after the Revolution of 1917 the Soviet Union's stagnant industry, like the economy at large, was not receptive to any technological change. In the 1930s the advent of the era of forced industrialization opened up a new chapter in the interrelation of applied and theoretical pursuits.

Now science was being compelled to become applied. New institutional arrangements were rapidly shaped to foster these applied pursuits. But again the applied research pursuits were still largely oriented toward the modification and adaptation of technology, processes, models, specifications, etc., which again were not of domestic, but of foreign origin, American and continental. The older generation of Russian scientists, although paying increasing lip service to applied needs, remained largely outside this process of integration and continued with some difficulties the abstract theoretical orientation of past decades. It is only since the late 1940s, when the new generation of Soviet-educated scientists began to come to the fore, that we began to observe a more genuine and natural blending of applied and thoretical research. This blending, now just beginning to emerge, has many signs of carrying applied research pursuits into a dominant position, but it is too early to tell whether it will turn to the opposite extreme where applied tasks completely overshadow theory.

Perhaps several examples will help in illustrating these tendencies. First and very obvious are the role played by and the accomplishments of mathematics in Russia. Euler and Lobachevskii are long-revered ancestors in this field. Chebyshev, Markov, Lyapunov, Khinchin, Kholmogorov, and many others are world-renowned for their contributions in theoretical and applied mathematics. The reliance on mathematics in the applied sciences in Russia is enormous, which in effect gives the applied sciences an added theoretical slant. And yet after A. N. Krylov invented a simple model of analogue computer for solving differential equations in 1911, it was four decades before analogue computers (of S. I. Bruk) appeared in Russia after World War II. Despite a score of excellent mathematicians in the field, the digital computer technology in the Soviet Union is still very weak.

In aerodynamics and related fields the work of N. E. Zhukovskii, the father of Russian aviation, and S. A. Chaplygin before the revolution was carried out exclusively in theoretical terms. In fact until the 1930s we cannot even speak of an aircraft industry in Russia. The indigenous aircraft industry simply did not exist until about 1932.

A similar situation is true in regard to S. V. Lebedev's discoveries in the polymerization process in 1910. The theory of synthetic chemistry emerged in the next two decades, but it was not until the mid-1930s, with the aid of A. E. Favorskii's work and further research by Lebedev, and with the further aid of equipment purchased from Germany, that synthetic rubber production was begun in the USSR.

Another striking historical example will illustrate the point. M. O. Danilovo-Dobrovol'skii was indeed the inventor of an asychronous motor and originator of AC (alternating current) three-phase electric power technology in 1888–91. However, because the world was them mostly concerned with direct current (in fact the great Thomas Edison was at first radically opposed to AC technology, erroneously fearing its inefficiency), Russian administrators and industrialists were not impressed. Danilovo-Dobrovol'skii, after demonstration exhibits in Germany, sold some of his inventions and patents there. The advantages of AC technology were recognized and conversion to it proceeded rapidly. Meanwhile, in Russia proper industry in the 1890s was largely geared to DC technology with equipment purchased from French firms and most of the power stations (primarily local) used imported DC equipment. Thus they were "stuck with it," and wide reliance on DC technology continued into the 1920s, subsequently causing severe handicaps to industrialization and the program of GOELRO, State Plan for Electrification of Russia for a rural electrification network calling for the use of AC technology.

A similar situation prevailed in electronics. A. A Eikhenval'd's theoretical investigations in 1901–05 laid the foundation of modern electronics. A. G. Stoletov discovered photoeffect in 1889. I. E. Tamm and S. P. Shubin were the first to work out the quantum theory of photoeffects (in 1931). And yet in the mid-1930s, Soviet industry was importing, and then finally buying patents, plant, and equipment, for simple electron tubes from RCA.

It might be convenient to conclude these examples by mentioning the fact that the foundations of space technology were mathematically derived by K. E. Tsialkovskii in 1903. And yet it was not until the post-World War II period, after the capture of German scientists and equipment, that Soviet space technology began to gain momentum. There is still substantial disagreement in the West as to the quality of Soviet space research, particularly as far as instrumentation technology is concerned.

Related to this problem of applied versus theoretical research is the trend of descriptive studies in Russian science which has been very prominent in the last hundred years. K. A. Timiryazev once stated that, "it is not the accumulation of an endless series of numbers from meteorological bulletins, but the discovery of the laws of mathematical thought; it is not the description of fauna and flora, but the discovery of the laws of the evolution of organisms; it is not the description of the many riches of our country, but the formulation of the laws of chemistry—these are the principles which guided the historical development of Russian science and offered it equality with and at times supremacy over World Science." [21]

We may qualify what the Russian natural sciences are noted for, but it is indisputable that in this passage Timiryazev touches upon one of the fundamental trends in Russian research during the last hundred years. There are the so-called "group research projects" such as are found in astronomy (for example, V. Y. Struve's star catalogues), in geology, meteorology, geo-botanics, plant and animal ecology, etc. Ever since K. M. Bear's *History of the Animal World* (1828–37) to the current 15-volume set of *Flora of the USSR*, the Russians have been keen on meticulous, detailed, and descriptive surveys of nature, from stars to seaweed. These systematic survey projects were conducted by a large number of scientists, and at times individual projects span decades. These projects were especially prominent between 1850 and 1880 and throughout the Soviet era. (Actually, the formation of KEPS—Commission on Productive Resources of Russia—in 1915 gave renewed stimulus to this activity, especially in geology.) Whether these activities are to be considered as "creative research" can be openly disputed, but the fact remains that they provide an indispensa-

[21] K. A. Timiryazev, *Sochineniya* [Works], Vol. 5, Moscow: 1938, p. 142.

ble foundation for the general development of scientific research in many fields of the natural sciences.

## MODERN SCIENCE AND THE INDIVIDUAL SCIENTISTS

Man entered the age of science and technology just about a century ago. Most modern conveniences, almost every device or gadget, tool, or medium of communication and transportation are products of these last one hundred years. Reinforced concrete, which made the modern construction industry possible, or the Bessemer process, which created the modern steel industry, are slightly more than a century old. Lenoir's combustion engine is not even a hundred years of age. Thomas Davenport's invention of the electric generator was made just about one hundred years ago. And when we look at a radio, an airplane, or a plastic pen, we see only products of this century. It was in 1869 that Mendeleyev formulated his periodic law of elements, and we are still adding elements to the empty spaces in the periodic table. It is the relative youth of modern science and technology which has to be remembered in speaking about "trends." The end of the nineteenth and first half of the twentieth centuries brought about the development of science in breadth and in depth.

It is characteristic of scientific research during this period that on the one hand there is a continuing process of differentiation of fields and differentiation within each field, and on the other, the interpenetration of distinct disciplines which results in the establishment of interdisciplinary fields. The process of differentiation resulted in a greater need for coordination of and cooperation in research. In order to solve a problem, diverse groups of research scientists are brought together and consequently scientific experimentation has lost its individual orientation and has begun to require the participation of large numbers of scientists and of complex supporting staffs. The process of experimentation is being applied more frequently and with the wider utilization of various technical means of increasing complexity and precision. In order to process a wide range of experimental data, greater reliance is placed on mathematical and statistical generalizations. And in order to facilitate the recording and processing of data, automatization (from automatic measuring and registering devices to computing technology) of research is gradually being introduced and perfected.

These are the general trends in scientific research over the last hundred years and particularly since the turn of the century. They are evident in all countries and are universally recognized, and the developments in Russia do not represent an exception. What is different and distinct, however, is the role of institutional arrangements.

In the second half of the nineteenth century, research in the natural sciences was centered around individual scholars and a small group of immediate associates or aides. By the mid-1930s in Russia we begin to deal mainly with institutions of research, which begin to employ hundreds of research scientists grouped under or aligned with some "name" scientist. The "depersonalization" of research effort, particularly the experimental part of it, does not, however, replace the individual's research ideas or scientific theories.

Directly related to the problem of "schools" is the problem of group-work of scientists who are doing research in the same field and following the direction of research originating in a given institution. In tracing scientific schools, it is sufficient to point out two schools, the Moscow and the St. Petersburg-Leningrad schools in mathematics (especially the theory of probability).[22] In organic chemistry there was and continues to be the Kazan University school, the Vernadskii school of geochemistry, etc.

Also related to the problem of individual versus organized research is the trend in international contacts on the part of Russian scientists. It is very important that in the pre-revolutionary period, promising university graduates were given *komandirovka* (assignments) to study abroad. Soviet historians of science try to belittle the importance of these studies by stating that their contribution should be disregarded since people who went abroad "went there not necessarily for study." [23] It is said that assigning significance to foreign studies of Russian scientists leads to the "malicious lie" that there are "foreign roots" in Russian science spread by "bourgeois historians." It is not the problem of "foreign roots," but the stimulus caused to scholarly pursuits through these foreign contacts.

It is true that Heidelberg University, Berlin, and Paris were common meeting places of Russian natural-science scholars in the second half of the nineteenth century. D. I. Mendeleyev, K. A. Timiryazev, and Sofia Kovalevskaya (mathematician, inventor of the gyroscope), among many others, studied at Heidelberg. I. I. Mechnikov spent many years in Rome and Paris (in fact, the Nobel Prize for bacteriological re-

[22] A detailed discussion may be found in: B. V. Gnedenko, "Rezvitiye teorii veroyatnosti v Rossii" [Development of Theories of Probability in Russia], *Trudy Instituta Istorii Yestestvoznaniya*, Moscow: 1948, Vol. II, pp. 390–425.
[23] N. A. Figurovskii (presently the director of the Institute of History of Natural Sciences and Technology), "Zadachi sovetskikh istorikov khimii" [Tasks of Soviet Historians of Chemistry] in *Trudy Instituta Istorii Yestestvoznaniya*, Moscow: 1949, Vol. III, p. 42.

search was awarded not for his work in Russia, but for that done at the Pasteur Institute in Paris). I. P. Pavlov spent two years abroad. A. G. Stoletov, the "father of Russian physics" (discoverer of electrical discharge and photoelectricity), was Kirchhoff's pupil in Heidelberg, and later studied in Berlin and Paris. P. N. Lebedev was August Kund's pupil in Strasbourg and later did research in Berlin. N. S. Kurnakov (who established the school of physical-chemical analysis) spent years in Freiburg. Zhukovskii, Chaplygin, Umov, Williams, Vvedenskii and many others also studied abroad. In addition to actual studies abroad, it is important to mention that there were frequent contacts by Russian researchers and inventors with foreign firms, especially because many patents were filed abroad, particularly in Paris.

After the revolution, during the 1920s, there were still opportunities, though greatly restricted, for foreign study and travel, but the Kapitsa incident marked the terminal point of these practices. Dr. Petr L. Kapitsa, having been sent abroad in 1930 for the third time, and having in 1931 been named director of a low-temperature research laboratory in Cambridge, England, had to be forcibly repatriated to the Soviet Union. For some twenty years thereafter, foreign study was absolutely taboo. Presently, there are very timid steps to resume such foreign study and travel abroad, but the path of their development still remains uncertain.

Partly in order to substitute for the lack of personal opportunities for foreign study, but largely because of the necessity to provide a flow of increasing information required in day-to-day research, in the last two decades, particularly in the postwar period, the Soviet Union has embarked upon information-processing and dissemination programs on a grandiose scale. The State Scientific Library and the Academy's Institute of Scientific Information are rendering many services to the community of Soviet research scientists. This information-processing and the reference services provided by separate bodies represent a new departure in the research sitting.

## INSTITUTIONAL FRAMEWORK

Education and science in Russia from their very institutional inception (let us say from the time of the opening of the Academy of Sciences under Catherine I in 1725) have been the business of the state. Originally teaching and research were blended together, but even after they were divorced (at the Academy in 1747) and universities began to emerge (particularly in the early nineteenth century), it was the state which operated them, and the academicians, adjuncts, professors, and researchers were all civil servants confirmed, if in most instances not actually chosen, in their positions by imperial administrators. For more than two centuries, teaching in higher education and research were carried on by civil servants; the changes in employment arrangements in the sphere of education and research which have occurred during the Soviet era are a continuation of the existing trend and not an entirely new departure.

The growth in complexity, specialization, and coordination of research functions resulted in an enormous expansion of research personnel and institutions. In terms of research and teaching personnel, Russia had perhaps several hundred people in 1861 and certainly less than a thousand. In 1913 there were about 10,000 teachers and researchers in higher education, in various institutions of research and industrial laboratories, of whom about 4,200 were classified as research personnel.[24] In 1940 there were already 98,000 in higher education teaching and research, and in research alone 26,000. And in 1956 there were 240,000 in teaching and research, of whom 106,000 were performing research only.[25] These figures refer to all fields of research, among which all natural science and applied science fields account for about one-half to two-thirds of the total personnel. In terms of institutions performing research functions during the last fifty years in Russia and the Soviet Union, their number has grown from several dozen to 2,800. This formidable numerical growth was accompanied by institutional rearrangements which resulted in the emergence of hierarchical pyramids of control and subordination over individual institutions and the personnel within them.

In the Soviet Union today the "industry of invention" is experiencing the biggest boom in its history. During the last five years alone the numbers of employees, professionals, and research scientists engaged in the sprawling research establishment of the Soviet Union have doubled. The Soviet research and development organization employs an estimated 2,000,000 persons, 600,000 of whom were professional higher education graduates (including 370,000 engineers). Among the latter, 240,000 are classified as researchers or research scientists. In addition Soviet institutions of higher learning employ some 600,000 persons, of whom 200,000 are professional graduates, and of these 160,000 were classified as senior academic rank holders. This unprecedented employment boom has been accompanied by enormous increases in the allocation of physical resources to sustain the research and development effort. The annual outlays for this effort have skyrocketed to some 4

[24] A. Beilin, *Kadry spetsialistov SSSR*, Moscow, 1935, p. 388.
[25] TsSU, *Narodnoye Khozyaistvo SSSR: 1956* (National Economy of the USSR: 1956), Moscow, 1957, p. 257.

billion (new) rubles, or a little over 2 per cent of the Soviet gross national product. It is not difficult to surmise that this boom will doubtless gain even further momentum.

Contrary to some Western interpretations that the Soviet scientific organization represents a rational and streamlined administrative pyramid with a well-developed decision-making mechanism, Soviet science in reality has been an unwieldy maze of haphazardly thrown-together institutions with different lines of administrative subordination, parochial interests, and widespread duplication. In the last decades "institutional research" has mushroomed in the USSR along functional lines. Whenever the need arose to design steam turbines, a research institute was formed by the appropriate ministry for this purpose. The same was true of coal mining or school construction or welding technology or chemistry.

Three pyramids came into existence: higher educational establishments (*vysshie uchebnye zavedeniia*), institutes of the academies of science (*akademicheskie instituty*), and ministerial-departmental research institutes (*otraslevye instituty*). The growth was most extensive in the latter two pyramids, with functional institutes formed at the academies and under ministerial-departmental auspices. The enormous proliferation of functions and unwieldy fragmentation of research tasks brought to the fore the recent institutional reorganization of Soviet science.

The debate concerning the Soviet science and research setup originated in July 1955. In February 1956 at the 20th Communist Party Congress, Khrushchev declared, "The separation of research activity of the Academy of Sciences, departmental research institutes, and higher educational establishments can no longer be tolerated. This separation and lack of coordination prevent the concentration of research activity on the solution of major scientific and engineering problems, lead to duplication of effort and waste of resources, and retard the introduction of research and engineering achievements into production." [26]

## LEADERSHIP ROLE OF THE ACADEMY

Traditionally the Academy of Sciences was the leader of research in Russia. In the eighteenth and early nineteenth centuries the Academy of Sciences in fact can be thought of as the seat of Russian science and research. During the first quarter of the nineteenth century the universities began to assume a growing role as seats of learning and at times

[26] *Pravda*, February 15, 1956.

even research. The emergence of learned societies (such as the Moscow Society of Natural Experimentators—MOIP since 1803) also contributed to diversification, and they began to play an important role. Indeed, the MOIP contrasted itself to St. Petersburg's Imperial Academy as being the "Moscow Academy." In the eighteenth century the Academy was dominated by foreigners who were brought by the Crown from abroad to serve there. Discontent with such a situation was voiced quite frequently. But it was not until the 1860s, however, and particularly during the 1870s, and 1880s and the "revolt" of the Russians against foreign-born members of the Academy (particularly Germans), that the discontent reached its climax. The clashes often centered around elections and appointments, eventually resulting in the easing out of the "foreigners," and by the late 1890s there we find a pronounced "Russification" of the Academy. This occurrence is background for the following general trends in institutional arrangements.

During the last half of the nineteenth century the Academy lost its footing as the seat of learning and research, and the majority of scientific discoveries were made in the universities. In physics, mathematics, and chemistry, the array of world-renowned Russian theoretical scientists and experimenters were associated with the universities. The end of the nineteenth century, and until the time of the Revolution, is the period of shift of research (particularly in physics) to Russian universities. It was at the end of this period that large-scale experimental research (such as in Lebedev's physical institute) began to be established.

In describing these developments, it is important to note that the shift of the research burden and theoretical investigations from the Academy to the universities in the late nineteenth and early twentieth centuries happens to coincide with the "Golden Age" of Russian science. The resurgence of the Academy to a position of leadership, coordination, and planning in the Soviet era took place at a time when organized massive research began to supplant individual effort, and technical means became paramount attributes of the research effort. It must also be emphasized that in the last two decades the Academy has been operating in the new circumstances, caused by the function of research proper, namely the need for information and activity as a main and gigantic clearing-house of research outside its auspices. The new function was assigned to it by the Soviet government, but its actual need came from the changing nature of the process of research. This fact is often overlooked.

It is also important to recognize that the emergence of the Academy as a global clearing-house and coordinator of research has created new problems. The Academy is run largely by scientists themselves, but their political orientation and lack of autonomy have in a number of instances caused arbitrariness in decision-making on the avenues of research to be followed, thus playing havoc with its function. The setting of priorities is made not on scientific grounds exclusively. Granted that the advantages of a research establishment such as an Academy in applied research fields and such theoretical mass experimentation as nuclear research is obvious (the United States has also set up "agencies" such as NASA or AEC to cope with similar problems), the agency which is a performer of research as well as a decision-maker about priorities for research has a great many bureaucratic problems. One involves internal politics and inbreeding which may conflict in decisions about research priorities. In view of the complexity of contemporary research, even greater effort of coordination is essential with outside institutions and particularly the separation of decision-making from actual performance of research tasks.

On April 12, 1961, *Pravda* published a major decree of the Central Committee of the Communist Party of the Soviet Union and the Council of Ministers of the USSR entitled "Concerning Measures to Improve the Coordination of Research and Development Work in the Country and the Activities of the Academy of Sciences of the USSR." This decree resolved, finally, the protracted institutional debate which had raged since the mid-1950s concerning the management of the Soviet Union's burgeoning research and development effort.

## CENTRALIZATION OF DECISIONS ABOUT RESEARCH

The new decree established for the first time in Soviet history a central coordinating agency for research and development for the country at large. It also in a sense created an independent board to make decisions about research priorities. This board acts through "expert commissions" consisting of individual scientists drawn from diverse institutional networks. The State Committee on the Coodination of Research and Development is to supervise the work of research and development establishments in fulfilling the most important scientific research and engineering objectives in accordance with the directives of the party and the government. It coordinates the work of the Academy of Sciences of the USSR, of the academies of science of the union republics, and of ministries and departments in fulfilling research objectives of an interdepartmental or interdisciplinary nature, and guides the direction of research and development work up to the point of its integration in the national economy.

On the recommendation of the Council of Ministers of the USSR, the councils of ministers of the union republics, and ministries and de-partments, the State Committee on the Coordination of Research and Development, together with the State Economic Council and the State Planning Committee, is responsible for developing plans for research and development work in the country at large and for the introduction of scientific and engineering accomplishments in production. The task of the new committee is to propose these plans for approval to the Council of Ministers of the USSR.

Although this account of recent institutional developments in the Soviet research establishment is not complete, it provides the necessary background for understanding the interrelationship between individual scientists and the organization of scientific activity in the USSR. In the Soviet case, the scientific organization is characterized by a high degree of centralization with decisions often made as to research priorities by those far removed from the scientist's place of work. Each Soviet research institute belongs in a clearly designated institutional hierarchy with specific designations of functions, tasks, missions, and so forth.

Soviet scientists do not really "manage" their research budgets in a business sense, as commonly understood in Western market economies. To be the deputy director of a research institute in charge of adminis-tration is really to be an accountant-clerk who supervises the book-keeping, the flow of funds, materials, employment records, and the like. All these resources are allocated by the government for a given purpose. There are two basic types of resource allocation schemes—ordinary and extraordinary (or top-priority). Once the government singles out the top-priority allocation, the "storming of targets" is greatly facilitated, which accounts for the lavishness of funds in one field of research (usually related to the military effort) as compared to the poverty in others (biology, for example).

Although scientists may propose that certain research ought to be undertaken, there is no guarantee under such a bureaucratic structure that such preferences will be considered. The scientist's task, however, is not by any means a hopeless one, for most administrative jobs in So-viet research and development organizations are held by scientists themselves, some of whom are of high repute and some of whom con-tinue research activities in addition to their administrative responsibili-ties. On the one hand, this organization is an advantage, for a scientist is subordinate to other scientists who are qualified to judge him and his work, and are often able to reach important decisions about the desired lines of research and development. On the negative side, however, there is the real danger of having a man in a decision-making position who, for reasons of personal likes or dislikes, vested interests in advanc-ing his pet projects, or similar personal factors, can stifle research which he does not deem desirable or even considers detrimental to his scientific reputation.

The trouble is that in such a highly centralized and bureaucratic structure, an individual scientist's lines of communication tend to be intra-organizational and vertical ones, in which loyalty to superiors and the organization very often supersedes even the commitment to the scientific tasks at hand. There is no doubt in my mind that horizontal communication by a Soviet scientist with his colleagues in another institution in the Soviet Union or with his fellow scientists abroad is substantially more handicapped than we can imagine from our experience with corporate or interagency rivalries. In this connection, of course, the problem of secrecy is an extremely important political factor with which the Soviet scientist must cope. There is a sharp separation (much more pronounced than anywhere in Western pluralistic societies) between those "who know and who have a right to know" and the average scientist.

The centralization of coordination and planning of research have their pronounced negative effect, for though widening the base (in terms of facilities and personnel) in one organization, the pyramidal institutional structure stifles individual initiative and independence of thought and research action. All this, it seems to me, has resulted in the trend of having a smaller number of outstanding researchers at the top than would be the case without centralization. It seems that in the second half of the nineteenth century Russia had larger numbers of outstanding scholars in the natural sciences in relation to the over-all base than it has today—but let us underscore the relativeness of that statement. This is true, of course, in general for all countries, but the "first echelon" or "name" scientists seem to be rarer in the Soviet Union in relation to the over-all number engaged in research than is the case in the West. The fundamental problem of the relation of individual effort within the framework of organized research is a general one in modern science, and the Soviet Union does not seem to have any specific solutions of its own.

The distinguishing mark of the Soviet era as compared with the nineteenth century is the planning aspect of scientific research. This Soviet planning of science is said to be currently guided by its task-orientedness (*tselenstremlennoye planirovaniye*).[27] It is often said that the absence of competition and pressure of vested interests is the main advantage of Soviet advances in developing science and technology. Soviet leaders are invariably saying that Soviet science has an "inherent

[27] A. Blagonravov (academician), "Plan i nauka" [Plan and Science], *Izvestiya*, Feb. 7, 1958.

superiority because of the Socialist system and will be in the lead in times to come." [28] This will take place because of the planning of the socialist system and of the method of dialectical materialism which is the most progressive force propelling socialist science forward. Some would quarrel with this view by stating that the achievements of Soviet science and technology have occurred "not because of the alliance between Soviet physical science and dialectical materialism, but in spite of the entanglement of science with ideology." [29]

## IMPACT FACTORS

The accomplishments of science in the Soviet Union are highly uneven. Although the Soviet government somehow attempts to regulate the creative activities of Soviet scientists, the progress of science in the USSR during the last fifty years has been achieved by some probabilistic or even chance factors of development: namely, the unknown, undefined and unidentified causes of events, which were beyond the calculations of Stalin and his successors, the plans of the USSR Academy of Sciences and other bureaucratic directives, and decisions in allocating resources to certain priority fields of research and development. Under such assumptions it would appear that Soviet scientists excelled in many fields because they were just like creative painters obsessed by the product of their creation, and thus succeeded not because of some highly organized and directed effort but in spite of it. This interpretation is highly fallacious if we do not take into account some of the environmental factors and influences upon the development of Soviet science in the last five decades. The balance sheet of some of these factors, stating summarily what their positive and negative influences were, is as follows:

PLANNING On the positive side, the centralization in decisions about the allocation of resources has resulted in most generous support of the science establishment in general, and made all—good, bad, and indifferent—results possible. On the negative side, within the science establishment itself, centralized control over the allocation of priorities led to differential support for different fields of scientific research so that some fields received lavish funding, and others were starved. The

[28] *Pravda*, Oct. 25, 1967 (M. Keldysh, President of the Academy of Sciences, Speech to the Academy).
[29] G. Wetter, "Dialectical Materialism and Natural Science," in *Soviet Survey*, London: Jan.–March, 1958, No. 23, p. 59.

identification of priorities themselves was made at times on highly realistic, pragmatic, and rational grounds, and at other times it was based on phantom political justification.

IDEOLOGY On the positive side, embracing Marxist and communist ideology, the scientific and technical outlook was introduced into education and the daily life of Soviet society. Scientism became a positive cultural value and a world outlook, if you please. On the negative side, ideology was used as a device in the political struggle among different cliques of science bureaucrats who used it as a shield to silence their critics and to block competitive research ventures. Ideology was used by competing bureaucratic power structures to destroy institutions and individuals with dissenting views thus leading to purges and consequently resulting in an enormous loss of creative talent.

POPULARIZATION The role of the scientist in society is of crucial importance in creating an understanding of his activity. During the last century and a half one of the fundamental links with society which Russian scientists have tried to develop was their mission to popularize science. This task is explicit in the edicts of the Academy since the beginning of the nineteenth century. And when Lenin in 1920 called on the Academy to broaden this task, he was merely reaffirming the traditional orientation. Today these activities are conducted on a scale unmatched by any other country, and they are responsible to a great degree for preserving the prestige of scientists and in mobilizing public support. Of course the circumstances and the causal factors have altered, but the missionizing function of the Russian popularizers of knowledge in general and science in particular has paid dividends. On the negative side it drained many energies of scientists from creative to pedestrian pursuits.

BUREAUCRATIZATION On the positive side, very extensive and diverse functional hierarchies developed parochial interests in conducting research and forced the establishment of a highly proliferated network of scientific research institutions. This immensely increased employment and research opportunities for hundreds of thousands of science graduates, and helped to create new institutions and centers of learning and research. On the negative side, the bureaucratization of research created enormous red tape, hampering the completion of research projects and bringing about great duplication of effort.

EDUCATION On the positive side, the Soviet Union did in fact introduce universal and compulsory science education, which in addition

198

to molding a scientific outlook and developing the productive skills of millions of Soviet citizens created a large base for recruitment of potentially creative talent for advanced study. On the negative side, the formalistic and authoritarian system of education placed the burden of proof about learning capacity upon examinations and certifications, which often resulted in nominal rather than actual attainment and performance.

RECRUITMENT On the positive side, the output of secondary and tertiary educational institutions, with two-thirds to four-fifths of all graduates produced with science or applied scientific specialties, created a favorable selection base for channeling human talent into science and technology. On the negative side, the influx of large numbers seeking specialized training for the sake of future employment opportunities created a large army of "status seekers" who were mediocre doers and performers. Only because of the random probability of abilities was the truly exceptional talent channeled into science fields. The majority who were recruited into scientific and technological fields through training ended up performing job functions which did not necessarily require scientific or technological skills.

INCENTIVES On the positive side, the favorable differential salary and other compensatory benefits, including honorific rewards given to persons employed in scientific research, developed a strong motivational pattern to enter these fields. On the negative side, like honey which attracts hard-working bees, excessive incentives for scientific careers brought about the influx of many flies. The Soviet research establishment is infested by these flies doing little creative or meritorious work, and the burden of performance rests with the few working bees.

MOBILITY On the positive side, the increased training and employment opportunities in science fields fostered social as well as geographic mobility. On the negative side, attractions of older cities, location of specialized training institutions and research establishments around them, and particularly the higher quality of urban-type schooling, all resulted in the perpetuation of status and training and employment advantages to the former advantaged groups of society—the descendants of the old pre-revolutionary and new post-revolutionary Soviet intelligentsia.

MILITARY On the positive side, the establishment of powerful military forces resulted in the creation of a research and development organization to serve their specific needs. The performance of high-caliber research for strategic reasons created a degree of excellence in these institutions. On the negative side, because of security requirements and resulting secrecy, a wall of separation came into being between military and civilian research institutions, with severe restrictions upon the transfer of applied as well as theoretical knowledge from the former to the latter. This created further imbalances in the quality of research performed in the two systems.

COMMUNICATIONS On the positive side, the Soviet Union has established a massive publication effort in the popularization of science, scholarly books, and periodical literature, and created extensive translation and documentation services. All this kept Soviet researchers informed and Soviet libraries burdened with a flow of publications. On the negative side, the pressure to publish some information about some research, however mediocre, led to the deterioration of standards in the information flow. Censorship and security restrictions banned the release and publication of significant domestic research results, thus hampering internal comparison and validation of research findings.

EFFICIENCY On the positive side, the input of resources both physical and human toward the attainment of certain scientific and technological goals always produces some results. Efficiency in their use is often not the question when confronted with the political demands of achieving those ends at all possible costs and by all possible means. All of this fostered huge investments in the Soviet research establishment, which were often wasted. On the negative side, once some results were obtained what was to be done next has been a vexing problem, which when faced with cost-benefit analysis has already resulted and might further lead to the curtailment of resource inputs. The problem is whether the Soviet Union will devise some sort of pluarlistic decision-making mechanism to enable it to define goals correctly in the future. There are many social needs which remain unsatisfied after fifty years of forced industrial and technological development. If resources are to be devoted to them, it may well lead to cutbacks in the support of science and research.

The Soviet regime, through fostering scientific and technological development, has succeeded in making Russia the world's second strongest power. From a stage of relative insignificance over the last half century, Soviet science has emerged as one of the world's largest research enterprises. The issue is not what happened in the past, but what are the prospects for the future. What is the main moving force of scientific inquiry? Perhaps it is the same Russian intellectual, who at all costs dedicates his life to scholarship, in the tradition of the nineteenth century. This is perhaps the real source of vitality in Soviet science today. "I will not tell the long story, which is one of many stories about Great Science, in which those who are generous win and those who are niggardly lose, for in Great Science nothing can be accomplished with less than the work of an entire life." [30] To this Valentine Kaverin adds—"even if the cost one pays is his own life."

[30] Kaverin, *op. cit.*, p. 284.

# 9

# SCIENCE AND SOCIAL CHANGE:

# POLITICS AND THE ORGANIZATION

# OF SCIENCE

## BY C. H. G. OLDHAM

*Science Policy Research Unit*
*University of Sussex*

This essay is composed of four parts with little or no connection among them. These parts are chosen to illustrate different aspects of a very wide-ranging topic. The relationships between politics on the one hand and science and social change on the other are frequently complex and usually involve a consideration of other activities. An integrated paper would also have demanded my taking economic, religious, and military factors into account. I have excluded these other factors, partly because my terms of reference limited the paper to a consideration only of the political factors, but also because to have included them would have required much research and a book-length presentation.

I start with the contention that "science and social change" is a two-way interaction. Science plays an important part in causing social change, and social change has a profound effect on the development of science itself. No one is likely to doubt the validity of the first part of the contention. That science has brought about vast changes in society is evident to all, although most of the obvious changes can more appropriately be ascribed to technology. The organizational framework which promotes the interaction between science and society, and the roles of scientist and politician in defining and implementing the social functions of science, will be one of the topics of this paper.

But society, and social attitudes, have also played an important role in the growth of science itself. Political decisions have greatly influenced the availability of money for certain branches of scientific research, and in some countries politics have seriously affected the growth of science. It will be the second major concern of this paper to analyze selected aspects of this problem.

It is important to recognize that the definitions of science are somewhat different for the two interactions. The first interaction—that of science on society—concerns the role of science in policy (economic, social, foreign, military, etc.). It embraces the whole spectrum of scientific activities from basic research, through applied research, development, information, and diffusion, to the popularization of science on a massive scale. The second interaction, that of society on science, concerns a policy *for* science. In this context a much narrower definition of science is relevant, since we will be concerned primarily with man's search for truth about nature.

## SCIENCE IN POLICY

In the first part of the paper the political response of two societies, the British and the Chinese, as each was confronted with modern science, will be analyzed. The historical starting point will be just before the scientific revolution which began in Britain about three hundred and fifty years ago.

Prior to this landmark each society had developed its own highly individualistic science, which only rarely had much impact on state affairs. It seems there was no great difference in standards of living between the two societies.

## BRITAIN

In Britain at the beginning of the seventeenth century, as Merton [1] has shown, about half of the men of science came from the upper classes (peers and landed gentry), and a further 41 per cent were from the middle classes (clergy, professions, merchants, and civil servants).

---

[1] Cited by Everett Mendelsohn, "The Emergence of Science as a Profession in Nineteenth-Century Europe," *The Management of Scientists*, Boston: Beacon Press, 1964, p. 5.

There was no organized scientific profession and research was either self-financed, or carried out with the help of a wealthy patron.

Then, roughly dating from the time of Galileo to a little after Newton, there occurred in Britain a profound transformation in men's understanding about nature. Why this scientific revolution should have first occurred in Europe rather than in China, India, or one of the other great civilizations is still debated. But the combination of theory and experiment using mathematics as a link gave much more to British society than just the "scientific method" which it gave to her scientists. It led to a new world view and brought the realization that man could not only understand the laws of nature, but could use his knowledge for his own practical ends.

Some historians consider the social changes which orginated in the scientific revolution to have been the most profound in the history of mankind. Caryl Haskins has pointed out its possible relevance to those societies which never experienced the scientific revolution and which now constitute the less developed parts of the world. He points out that the transformation in world view actually took place in Britain before the industrial revolution and states:

> But it was not only the careers of a few great individual scientific explorers that lived independently of an industrial environment. The major steps in the transformation of world view in British society as a whole from an essentially Ptolemaic concept of the Universe to a Newtonian one came, in the main, during the feverish period between 1660 and 1700—approximately 80 years before the start of the great period of British industrial growth. And it is hard, at this remove, to fully comprehend how consuming was its effect on society as a whole. Not only did the outlook of an entire nation during no more than forty years suddenly undergo a transformation more profound than any wars or drastic political changes might have wrought. Even more prodigiously—and in the context of the new nations perhaps even more significantly—the fever and excitement of the change were truly universal in the society, reaching far out beyond its rare leaders of Newtonian stamp. This astonishing movement opened windows for the intellect so universal and compelling that in less than a generation the vision of a whole people was intellectually transformed.[2]

This is a sweeping statement, and it raises many questions about how specifically the transformation occurred. One would like to know, for example, what levels of society were affected. Was the "message" passed by word of mouth, or in printed form? Were there public lectures or small discussion groups?

[2] Caryl P. Haskins, *The Scientific Revolution and World Politics*, New York: Harper & Row, 1964.

If the scientific revolution was as significant a cause of social change as Haskins would have us believe, and if most of the underdeveloped countries are still in a pre-scientific revolution phase, then it is clearly of paramount importance that further research be carried out— research both to try to understand better the processes of the scientific revolution in Britain, and research to learn how to bring about such a revolution in developing countries. I shall have further comments on the significance of the scientific revolution for China later on, but first the political significance of the growth of science in Britain will be considered.

There were few immediate political consequences of the scientific revolution in Britain. But gradually a number of trends both in the organization of science and the social implications of science began to emerge. First of all, during the eighteenth and more especially during the nineteenth centuries there was a growing specialization of science. It became more difficult for the men of science to be truly men of science. They became instead men of geology, or men of astronomy, etc. It also became increasingly apparent that science could no longer be the preserve of amateurs—it was a full-time job.

These trends were accompanied by a change in the social origins of scientists. By the end of the eighteenth century only 18 per cent were from the upper classes and 82 per cent from the middle and lower classes.[3] Even more significant than the social origins was the educational background of the late eighteenth-century men of science.

In the early seventeenth century, 58 per cent of the men of science had been to one of the famous public schools or had been privately tutored, and 67 per cent were graduates of Oxford and Cambridge Universities. By the end of the eighteenth century, only 18 per cent were from the public schools and 20 per cent graduates from Oxford and Cambridge. A common feature of both the public schools and Oxbridge was their scorn of science, and in fact the public schools openly rejected the sciences as valid subjects for serious study. They continued to hold this attitude until the latter part of the nineteenth century and even into the twentieth century. The significance of this rejection for the discussion on science and government is apparent when the dominance of public school and Oxbridge classical scholars in the civil service is realized.

Other trends which were to have significance in the nineteenth-century science-government confrontation were [4] (a) the fall in importance of the Royal Society—which by 1830 had only a third of the members of the council who were scientists; (b) the move of the cen-

[3] Everett Mendelsohn, *op. cit.*, p. 5.
[4] For further discussion of the impact of these trends see E. Mendelsohn, *op. cit.*

ters of scientific activity to the new industrial cities in the Midlands, especially Leeds, Birmingham, Manchester, Bristol, and Newcastle; (c) the establishment of new specialized scientific societies, such as the Geological Society (1807), and the Astronomical Society (1820); (d) the establishment in 1831 of the British Association for the Advancement of Science—which in many ways took over the role of the Royal Society as the mouthpiece of British science.

It was against this background that the series of confrontations between science and government got under way. In a complex society the details of any political confrontation are difficult to decipher. This is certainly true of science-government relations in Britain, and it must be frankly admitted that it is a hazardous task to draw conclusions.

On the one hand the scientists themselves were deeply divided about science-government relations. Some, using the British Association as a platform, pleaded eloquently for greater support of scientific research, and pointed out the many contributions which science could make to the attainment of national goals. Other scientists were extremely worried about the state intervention. There was, for example, considerable reluctance on the part of some members of the Royal Society to accept the £1,000 which Parliament began to award annually for the support of scientific research in 1849. But for the majority of scientists there was little contact, either social or professional, with civil servants and politicians, and little apparent interest in the problems of government or the contributions which science could make to the solution of these problems.

Similarly in government, a few members of the civil service made excellent use of scientific advice in the work of their departments, whereas the majority were unmoved by the pleas of the scientist and many were disinterested.[5] Most was accomplished when an official had a close friend who was a high-ranking scientist. But even here this traditional "old school tie" approach was made less effective than it might have been by the reluctance of the public schools to teach science. There were few scientists with the "right" tie.

The principal platform for the scientists to air their views was the annual meeting of the British Association. And in 1859 the Prince Consort summed up the prevailing sentiments when he said in his presidential address to the Association:

> We may be justified in hoping that the Legislature and the State will more and more recognize the claims of science to their attention, so that it may no longer require the begging box, but

[5] British government views in the nineteenth century about science have only recently begun to be available due to research by Dr. R. MacLeod and his colleagues at the University of Sussex. I am grateful to them for permission to use some of the results of their research prior to publication.

speak to the State like a favoured child to its parent, sure of his paternal solicitude for its welfare; that the State will recognize in science one of its elements of strength and prosperity, to foster which the clearest dictates of self interest demand.[6]

Twelve years later a survey officer of the Royal Engineers was even more prophetic; in a paper to the Royal United Services Institution in 1871, Colonel Alexander Strange said:

> The duty of the government with respect to science is one of the questions of the day. No question of equal importance has, perhaps, been more carelessly considered and more heedlessly postponed than this. And now that a hearing has been obtained for it neither the governing class, nor the masses, are qualified to discuss it intelligently; the governing class, because it is for the most part composed of men in whose education, as even the highest education was conducted 30 to 50 years ago, science occupied an insignificant place; and the masses, because they may be taken to be almost destitute of scientific knowledge. Those who wield, and those who confer, the powers of government being alike incapable of dealing with this question, it devolves on another section of the community to urge its claims to attention.

> . . . I must guard myself against the supposition that the proposal I have here advocated comprises all that is necessary for the efficient administration of scientific State affairs. It is only one part of a great system that has to be created. Other parts of the system will, no doubt, receive due attention from the Royal Commission now considering them. But there is one part so important that I feel called on to name it—I mean the appointment of a Minister for Science . . . .

> When we have all scientific national institutions under one Minister of State, advised by a permanent, independent, and highly qualified consultative body; when we have a similar body to advise the Ministers of War and Marines in strategical science, then the fact that, in accordance with our marvellous constitution, these ministers must almost necessarily be men without pretension to a knowledge of the affairs which they administer need cause us no alarm. When these combinations have been, as they assuredly will be, sooner or later, effected; the wealth, resources, and the intelligence of the nation, having due scope, will render us unapproachable in the arts of peace, and unconquerable in war, but not until then.[7]

Another British scientist to speak critically of State support for science was Lyon Playfair, and he played a large part in helping to persuade the government in 1872 to appoint a Royal Commission on Scientific Instruction, under the Duke of Devonshire. In fact it seemed to

---

[6] Cited by R. V. Jones, "Science and the State," *Nature*, Vol. 200, 1963, pp. 7–14.
[7] *Loc. cit*

be a favorite government ploy that when the pressures for action became sufficiently strong the issue would be conveniently shelved for several years by appointing a Royal Commission to investigate the matter.

Playfair shared Strange's view that the neglect of science in British education was appalling, and this view was echoed by the Devonshire report which stated: [8] "Considering the increasing importance of science to the material interest of this country, we cannot but regard its almost total exclusion from the training of the upper and middle classes as little less than a national misfortune."

But the public schools were not easily persuaded to change their habits. The headmaster of one of the most famous of the schools—Winchester—told the Commission: "I will give prizes for collections of wild flowers, but as for including science in the curriculum—we have no time." [9] Even early in the twentieth century, the prospectus for the same school said: "For the boys who have no ability in classics or modern languages there is a science side." [10] It was Lord James of Rusholme who provided these quotations in a speech to the Royal Society in 1962. He went on to say "Even today, of course, we are all of us prepared to send our children to schools where eleven hours a week of Latin is thought to be the basis for a broad and humane culture, and two hours a week of science is called premature specialization."

The Devonshire Commission was followed in 1881 by another Royal Commission on technical education. But the influence of the Commission's reports on the public schools, Oxford and Cambridge Universities, the civil service examinations and hence the type of person who entered government service, was marginal.

The scientists' view about science-government relations are relatively well known, thanks to the papers which they wrote for the British Association and the editorials of the journal *Nature*. It is only recently, however, that MacLeod and his colleagues at the University of Sussex have begun to decipher the attitudes of the British Civil Servants during the period 1830 to 1914 toward the question of science. The picture is, of course, exceedingly complex with individuals reacting in different ways. In general, however, his work shows, perhap surprisingly, that many of the Treasury officials were sympathetic to the demands for money from the scientists, especially if the request was couched in terms of bringing national prestige.

MacLeod's work confirms that the number of scientists who were

---

[8] *Loc. cit.*
[9] Lord James of Rusholme, *Notes and Records of the Royal Society,* Vol. 17, No. 1, May 1962, pp. 1–5.
[10] *Loc. cit.*

articulately conscious of the social implications of science were very few. He believes that by far the most effective way of affecting government policy was by the personal influence of one of the small band of scientific élite upon the top civil servants. The reasons the government failed to take a more dynamic role in utilizing science were largely legalistic and traditional. The civil service was a highly conservative organization with watertight compartments. With such a structure, it was exceedingly difficult to innovate.

Two areas where the government of mid-nineteenth-century Britain were especially reluctant to take initiative were in education and industry. These areas were considered to be the domain of either the local authorities or of private enterprise, and it was considered politically and constitutionally wrong to interfere. Yet it was education which most of all needed reform.

The further institutionalization of science and especially the organization of research were issues which caused as much difference of opinion among the nineteenth-century British scientists as they still do among scientific advisers today. Should the government support scientific research in universities, or should specialized government laboratories be established? On this issue, too, the British Association became a platform where the scientists aired their views. For example, Sir Oliver Lodge made a strong plea for a government physical laboratory in his presidential address to the Association in 1891. Nine years later the government established the National Physical Laboratory.

Although science was used much more effectively by the government in the second half of the First World War, by the 1920s the science-government relationship had slipped back to its prewar condition. Money for university research was difficult to obtain. The government laboratories were not particularly effective or productive, either as a means for relating science to national goals or as a source of new additions to scientific knowledge. And although science was now established as a profession, the salaries were low and there was little social prestige attached to a scientific career.[11]

World War II changed the entire picture. Britain now had, in Churchill, a Prime Minister who actively sought out advice on how to use science as a tool to achieve national goals. Lord Snow [12] has described in black and white terms the now famous Lindeman-Tizard controversy. This story has frequently been used to illustrate the prob-

---

[11] One of Britain's scientific knights, and a Fellow of the Royal Society, once told me that when he was a boy, his father had discouraged him from becoming a scientist, on the grounds that if he did, he would never earn sufficient money to afford a car.

[12] C. P. Snow, *Science and Government*, Oxford: Oxford University Press, 1961.

lems, and dangers, of the scientific adviser who is called on to advise on matters outside the area of his scientific expertise. It is a fact that although the scientists had been the principal agitators for a more dynamic government role in the use of science in policy, many were ill-prepared for the task of providing advice when the government finally responded to this agitation.

Now, in 1968, all the political parties in Britain accept the view that a prosperous and thriving science and technology are essential for the national well-being, and in the 1964 elections the precise way in which science should be used for social purposes was a party political issue. The present Labour government has separated science from technology and has separate advisory councils to advise the two government departments concerned. A new science advisory committee under the chairmanship of Sir Solly Zuckerman was formed in October 1966 as part of the Cabinet Office. There is now an opportunity for a confrontation between scientist and politician at the highest government level.

I have tried in the above discussion to sketch some of the highlights in the development of science and government relations in Britain from the seventeenth century to the present. There are still many gaps in our knowledge, and the more detailed evidence for many of the conclusions has yet to be published by MacLeod and his colleagues. Nevertheless, certain general trends can be discerned.

The first general observation is that it has almost always been a handful of scientists who have seen the longer-range social implications of their work, and who have urged the government of the day to take action. Other scientists have taken a contrary view and felt it wrong that government should concern itself with science. The scientists used their scientific societies and especially the British Association for Advancement of Science as a platform to air their views, but until quite recently, there has been a lack of an official forum where scientist, politician, and civil servant could discuss science in policy. In the nineteenth century, the Royal Society, because of its desire to remain outside controversy, failed to serve as a focus for policy discussions.

The government response to the scientists' initiatives has been mixed. There seems to have been reasonably generous Treasury support in the mid to late nineteenth century for individuals to pursue their own research, especially if the research could be justified in terms of national prestige. But throughout the nineteenth and early twentieth centuries the government took little initiative to use science in a deliberate way as a tool for causing social change, or as a means of achieving national goals. The reasons are not entirely clear. Undoubtedly the influence of *laissez-faire* political doctrine was partly the reason. The classical, nonscientific educational background of the politicians and civil servants was also relevant, as was the traditional, legalist, and constitutional difficulty of changing the system of government to enable science to contribute in a more direct way to policy. Furthermore, the difference in class origin between most men of science and civil servants inhibited (although did not exclude) the formation of close personal friendships between politicians and scientists in nineteenth-century Britain. This also retarded the development of a policy for science.

# CHINA

The influence of politics on the use of science to promote social change has followed a very different path in China. Science never developed indigenously as a profession in eighteenth- and nineteenth-century China, and despite valiant efforts on the part of the Jesuits in the seventeenth century there was little progress made in assimilating the new world science from the West.

Nor would we have expected there to be much progress in adopting modern science. China in the seventeenth, eighteenth, and much of the nineteenth centuries was rigidly Confucian in its outlook. Confucianism is a very conservative force dedicated to the maintenance of the status quo. It venerates tradition and eschews change. The world view provided by science is the opposite. It stresses the impermanence of the present and seeks always for change. It questions hierarchical authority, whereas an hierarchical society is at the very basis of the Confucian social order.

After the crushing defeats imposed by the vastly superior military technology of the British at the time of the Opium War in 1839–42, cracks began to appear in the Confucian conservatism. Some Chinese saw the need for reform and realized that it could only be achieved by the systematic acceptance of modern science and technology. Others thought it might be possible to adopt the technology without the science, and yet other scholars continued to reject both.

Certain milestones in the long process of modernization can be charted: the establishment of military arsenals; the work of a few dedicated missionaries to translate scientific books into Chinese; the inclusion of physics and mathematics into the civil service examination system in 1887 (several years before science was included in the British civil service examinations); the establishment of the Tung wen Kuan, the interpreters' college of the Foreign Ministry, which included science in its curricula; the establishment of science courses at the University of Peking; and the establishment of a few centers of scientific activity (such as the Geological Survey) in the government.

Foreigners played a leading role in many of these developments, and there is little evidence of any major commitment to science on the part of the Chinese themselves. China lacked the pressure group of articulate scientists who could provide the sort of confrontation between scientist and politician that was taking place in Britain at this time.

In fact, it took a series of political events to provide the environment which finally enabled a confrontation to take place. And when it did come, the scientists played a relatively minor role. In 1911 the Manchu dynasty was overthrown. The ensuing post-revolutionary period was a time of domestic chaos and increasing disillusionment with Western democracy. The disillusionment reached its peak at the time of the Treaty of Versailles in 1919, when the Chinese felt that the Western Powers had betrayed them and had unfairly allowed the Japanese to remain in control of the former German concessions in Shantung province. This event, and the May 4th student movement which followed, marked the beginning of a major reappraisal by the Chinese intellectuals of China's place in the world, her international philosophy, and her future goals. Confucianism had been rejected, but what should replace it?

It was in this political setting that the great debates of the 1920s took place. To a considerable extent the debates, many of which took place at the University of Peking, centered on the place of science and the world view implied by science in Chinese life. The protagonists were all men who had received their early education in the classical schools, but several had been abroad for their higher education. Some, such as Hu-shih, were philosophers; others, such as V. K. Ting, the geologist, were scientists in their own right. Yet others, such as Chen Tu-shiu who went on to found the Chinese Communist Party, were educators and journalists.[13]

The debate about science was long and exceedingly wordy. There were fierce differences of opinion as to the philosophical implications of science. But the variety of opinions and the validity of the philosophical arguments used are not as important as the fact that a debate about science took place and that many people were involved. The debates on science were only a part, although a very important part, of a genuine cultural revolution sweeping through Chinese intellectual circles at that time.

Out of these discussions emerged a commitment to change such as

[13] A valuable summary of the debates is contained in D. W. Y. Kwok, *Scientism in Chinese Thought, 1900–1950*, New Haven: Yale University Press, 1965.

had been unknown in China for centuries. A new world view was emerging which for both Nationalists and Communists alike was to be based on science. In some ways the 1920s in China might be likened to the period 1660–1700 in Britain. The discussions helped to create a climate of opinion favorable for the growth of genuine scientific activities. Afterwards the Nationalist government began to institutionalize science on a much more systematic basis. Research laboratories and academies of science were founded, graduate studies introduced into universities, and a number of scientific societies came into operation. By the mid-1930s many of the features of a well-integrated science system existed in China.

It is tempting to speculate on whether such debates on scientism are a necessary prelude to the acceptance by a traditional society of the new world view which science implies and demands. Individuals can undoubtedly carry out scientific work in a traditional society, but it is doubtful that science can be effectively used as a tool in national policy unless an extensive debate takes place. For this to happen in a democracy it is likely that some aspect of science must become a major political issue.

Although the debates of the 1920s involved a few hundred or perhaps a thousand intellectuals, and undoubtedly had an influence on government policy, they had little impact on the vast majority of the Chinese people. Their world view changed little, and it was not until the Communist government's efforts of the 1950s and 1960s that a serious attempt was made to alter this situation.

The question of peasant attitude to change lies at the very heart of the development problem, and yet it seems to be a topic on which many social scientists disagree. One view maintains that peasants in traditional societies are superstitious, accept an hierarchical ordering of society, and often act in irrational ways. If they are to modernize, then it is argued that their world view must change. The other opinion holds that peasants act in a perfectly rational manner, and that their reluctance to innovate and change is dictated primarily by economic considerations. Life is so close to minimum subsistence that if the peasants were to innovate, and the innovation failed, they would starve.

A study which has a bearing on this problem was published recently by Francis Dart and P. L. Pradhan.[14] They made a study of a group of Nepalese children's attitudes on how new knowledge about nature is obtained. The children believed that all new knowledge was obtained from teachers or books. It did not occur to them, nor would they believe when it was explained to them, that fundamentally new knowl-

---

[14] Francis E. Dart and P.L. Pradhan, "Cross-cultural Teaching of Science," *Science*, February 10, 1967, V. 155, No. 3763, pp. 649–56.

edge could be discovered by scientific experiments and research. For them all knowledge was revealed.

Chinese cadres claimed that a similar attitude existed among Chinese peasants. On my trips to China in 1964 and 1965, I heard repeatedly that superstition and belief in revealed knowledge were some of the biggest barriers to change in China. A tremendous drive was under way to break down these barriers, and an enormous effort was being made to replace the old attitudes with a combination of science and Communist ideology.

Part of the campaign was reflected in conventional educational programs, but in addition to these there was a massive effort to indoctrinate the Chinese people with a scientific attitude. "Support the three great revolutionary movements" says one of the ubiquitous slogans— one of the revolutionary movements being scientific experimentation. Peasant scientists and model workers who had shown an ability to innovate were given great publicity and praise.

Large numbers of experimental fields were established in the communes, and school children with only a minimum of scientific instruction were sent to work in them. The campaign to generate a complete scientific revolution in China must be reckoned as one of the most important ever to have been consciously attempted by any government at any time. It is an attempt to extend the debates of the 1920s to 700 million people in all walks of life, and is without doubt the most massive campaign to mobilize science as a tool to bring about social change that has ever been undertaken.

Unfortunately the effects are unknown. There has been little systematic study of the phenomenon, and what impact the campaign has had in affecting attitudes in the Cultural Revolution can only be speculated upon. There is no doubt that the efforts to indoctrinate the Chinese people with science are accompanied by equally massive efforts to indoctrinate them with a political ideology. In fact it is the combination of science and politics that makes the Chinese campaign so intriguing. It is difficult to understand how the campaign to encourage innovation, to break conventions, to "dare to do and dare to think," and to adopt a scientific attitude to life can be reconciled in a peasant's mind with the insistence on the rightness and correctness of one political viewpoint.

In this discussion of science in China, I have not considered the present organization of science. This is deliberate since we have so very little information about the way scientists are able to influence policy in China. It is, however, noteworthy that the foremost policy-making group for science, the State Scientific and Technological Commission, contains several nonscientists.

There is some evidence that the views of the scientists are suspect, and when their advice is contrary to existing government policy they are ignored or, worse, are accused of opposing government policy on political grounds. This was brought home to me in Shanghai in 1964 in a conversation with the secretary of China International Travel Service. I queried him concerning the illogicality and danger of assuming that the party line was always correct, and cited the case of the sparrows. In 1958, it had been decided that since sparrows ate grain they should be exterminated. A massive campaign was mounted, apparently designed to prevent the sparrows from resting. Drums were beaten and the noise continued unabated for three days—at the end of which hundreds of thousands of sparrows were reputed to have died from exhaustion. Later it was found that insect pests which the sparrows would otherwise have eaten were causing a greater loss to the crops than the volume of grain which the birds would have eaten. The sparrows were posthumously reinstated.

I suggested to the Chinese cadre that there must have been some scientists, experts on sparrows, who must have known about their propensity for eating insects and pointed out the folly of a mass extermination campaign. I asked why their advice (if given) was not heeded. He admitted that some scientists had protested—"But," he said, "it is because they were rightists—they wanted the sparrows to eat the people's grain."

Thus, the science-politics interaction has developed in Britain and China in quite different ways. In Britain, it has largely been the scientists, albeit only a few of them, who have taken the initiative in urging government to make greater use of science in policy.

In China, there was no similar professionalization of science during the nineteenth century, no scientific societies, and no confrontation. It was not until the twentieth century that a series of political events led to a situation conducive to extensive debates about science and society. These discussions in turn led to a deliberate government policy to encourage the professionalization of science in China. And when the Communist government came to power in 1949, the new rulers had very definite ideas about the role of science in policy.

## POLITICS AND A POLICY FOR SCIENCE

In this second part of the paper I will discuss some examples of the impact of politics on the growth of science. It is important to stress again the very considerable difference between the role of science in policy —with its consequent effect on social change—and the effect of politics on a policy for science. The discussion will be limited to basic or fundamental research.

Although it is frequently acknowledged that fundamental research is exciting and worthwhile for its own cultural value, it is also true that out of basic research come the ideas and knowledge that lead to developments in military techniques and industrial processes. Indeed, it has always been necessary for scientists in all countries to argue their case for government support for their basic research largely on utilitarian grounds. Thus, in the United States, only 10 per cent of all federal funds for basic research originate from the National Science Foundation, the only federal agency which has the freedom to provide research funds for cultural purposes.[15] The remaining 90 per cent comes from mission-oriented agencies.

It is the significance of this method of funding which I now propose to consider. The statistics relate to the United States because it is only in this country that such complete information is available, and also because the amount of basic research carried out in the United States plays an important part in determining world scientific fashions.

In 1964, the federal government of the United States spent $1.9 billion on basic research. This sum accounted for 12 per cent of total federal research and development expenditures. The funding agencies for this research are shown in Table 1.

TABLE 1

FUNDING AGENCY FOR FEDERALLY SUPPORTED BASIC RESEARCH

| Agency | Per cent of total federally supported basic research |
|---|---|
| NASA | 37 |
| Health, Education, Welfare | 17 |
| Atomic Energy Commission | 15 |
| Department of Defense | 13 |
| National Science Foundation | 10 |
| Other | 8 |

Thus, NASA, AEC, and DOD collectively funded 65 per cent of all the basic research sponsored by the federal government in the United States. The nature of the interests of these three agencies in turn means an overwhelming commitment to support research in the physical sciences. This conclusion is borne out by Table 2, which shows the portion of federal basic research funds spent in a variety of disciplines, again for the year 1964.

[15] Statistics in this section of the paper are from *Federal Funds for Research and Development and other Scientific Activities,* National Science Foundation, NSF 65-19, Vol. XIV. More recent statistics change the figures slightly, but do not affect the main argument.

### TABLE 2
#### BREAKDOWN OF EXPENDITURES ON BASIC RESEARCH BY SCIENTIFIC DISCIPLINE

| Discipline | Per cent of basic research budget |
|---|---|
| Physical Sciences | 58 |
| Mathematics | 3 |
| Engineering | 8 |
| Medical Sciences | 16 |
| Biological Sciences | 8 |
| Psychological Sciences | 3 |
| Agricultural Sciences | 2 |
| Social Sciences | 2 |

The percentage breakdown within the physical sciences is also of interest and is shown in Table 3.

### TABLE 3
#### BREAKDOWN OF EXPENDITURES IN THE PHYSICAL SCIENCES

| Discipline | Per cent of total federal basic research for physical sciences |
|---|---|
| Physics | 30 |
| Astronomy | 21 |
| Solid Earth Sciences | 21 |
| Atmospheric Sciences | 13 |
| Chemistry | 10 |
| Oceanography | 3 |

Thus, more federal money was spent on basic research in astronomy in 1964 than in the whole of the biological sciences, and twice as much as on chemistry. It is true that some sciences are more expensive than others, and it is not immediately obvious that by spending more on the neglected subjects there would be commensurate returns to the advancement of knowledge. Nevertheless, once such a lopsided effort is launched, there is a built-in amplification factor that tends to cause further distortion of effort.

The basic research effort is only the tip of the iceberg as far as total research and development funding of the mission-oriented agencies, as demonstrated in Table 4.

### TABLE 4
#### PROPORTION OF BASIC RESEARCH TO TOTAL RESEARCH AND DEVELOPMENT EXPENDITURES

| Agency | Approximate percentage |
|---|---|
| NASA | 18 |
| HEW | 35 |
| AEC | 22 |
| DOD | 3 |
| NSF | 98 |

Thus, the total manpower required for all the research and development activities will also be heavily biased in favor of the physical sciences. In turn, the relevant university departments will tend to expand to meet the demand, requiring yet more physical scientists to staff the expanded departments, and because of the inseparability of teaching and research, there will be even more research in the physical sciences. The sum effect is to make certain areas of scientific inquiry fashionable.

The argument can be extended to consider the influence on other countries. Scientists, more than most professionals, tend to be internationally minded and want to work at the forefront of knowledge in the currently fashionable areas. If they are to be able to stay in these fields, then they must either emigrate to the United States or persuade their own governments to fund their research on a scale that enables them to keep up with the efforts in the United States.

Many governments in Europe are now faced with a dilemma— should they continue to provide financial support to their scientists in certain expensive areas of basic research, or does the high cost of keeping in a competitive position vis-à-vis American research mean that the European country should opt out of this field and allow their scientists to join the brain-drain?

The dilemma for developing countries is even greater since their resources are so much smaller. Yet their scientists also wish to work in the fashionable areas—and this is usually true whether they were trained abroad or at home. The matter is complicated even more because if the university scientist in a developing country does obtain financial support for his research, then the next generation of research scientists will also be trained in this same branch of science, the relevance of which for the developing countries is likely to be remote. Thus, in an indirect way, political decisions in the United States are influencing the development of fashions in science—which themselves have serious political, economic, and social implications in other countries throughout the world.

It is not my intention to put value judgments on this state of affairs. Similar arguments could be made for Soviet science funding, and to a lesser extent for that of Britain and other European countries. It is, however, important that the full implications of such political decisions be appreciated.

It would be useful to consider the political activity that would be necessary to establish different goals that would result in the emphasis of different branches of science. How, for example, could the American people be persuaded to support the sort of schemes which American scientists Alvin Weinberg and Rodger Revelle proposed at the recent Pugwash Conference [16] in Sweden? Weinberg suggested the development of nuclear agro-industrial complexes in such coastal desert regions as the Gaza Strip, and Revelle discussed the challenge posed by the development of the Brahmaputra-Ganges basin. Such projects call for massive research and development efforts, and emphasis would be given to quite different branches of science from those now supported by the space program. Not only would the over-all goal be more worthwhile (admittedly a value judgment!) but the new areas of science which would probably become fashionable would be of much greater relevance to the needs of the developing countries.

CHINA Even more dramatic than the impact of American political decisions on world science is the effect of politics on science in China. In the final part of this paper three aspects of politics and science in China will be discussed.

(1) *The effect of politics on the level of support for basic research.* The key slogan in any decision-making about science in China is, "Science must serve the people." Science for its own sake is not acceptable. This being the case it comes as something of a surprise to visit Chinese research laboratories and to see the extent of the long-range research programs in basic research. Unfortunately no statistics are available which enable us to determine the percentage of the Chinese research and development expenditures which do contribute to the advancement of knowledge—but judging from the evidence available it is by no means negligible.

There are probably two principal reasons why this amount of effort is devoted to basic research. The first is that the scientists wish to work on interesting new problems, which they attempt to justify (as do scientists everywhere) on economic grounds. Secondly, and I think more importantly, is the political decision that China should aspire to Great Power status. One activity which the Chinese believe will contribute to the acknowledgment of China as a Great Power is excellence in science. It has been stated as a national goal that China will catch up and surpass the advanced nations of the world in science within twenty to thirty years. To do so means excelling in contributions to new knowledge across a broad scientific front. It also means devoting resources to basic research. This, of course, is not the only reason—there are compelling economic arguments, too, for supporting basic research. But the amount of political capital made of successful synthesis of insulin is indicative of motivations.

(2) *The effect of the "Thoughts of Mao Tse-tung."* Each research institute in China has a political appointee who usually acts as vice-

16 *Pugwash Newsletter,* Vol. 5, Nos. 2 & 3, October 1967—January 1968, p. 86.

director or secretary of the institute. It is his job to ensure that the scientists are both "Red and expert." On my visit to several of the Academy institutes in 1964 and 1965, I asked some members of the political cadres to explain what their cliché meant. Briefly their answers amounted to saying that a scientist might be technically excellent, but he would be unlikely to orient his work in the way most beneficial to China unless he accepted the political viewpoint of the Communist Party and wholeheartedly supported this view. On the other hand, they said it is also important that a political cadre improve his technical knowledge. It is not enough to be either Red or expert—one must be both at the same time. The debate on "redness and expertise" has waged for a long time in China, and entered a new phase when the redness meant accepting the "Thoughts of Mao Tse-tung" as a basis for all activities—even scientific research.

The campaign to deify Mao was already under way in 1964, and I was told of several technical innovations made as a result of studying Mao's works. At one factory it was the speed of rotation of a spinning machine which had been increased from 9,000 revolutions per minute to 13,000 revolutions per minute, and at a school it was the eyesight of school children which had been improved. I always asked for a chapter and verse and requested to be taken step by step from Mao's writing to the implementation of the technical innovation. There are, of course, no direct links, but merely an attitude of mind is created which suggests that problems *can* be solved.

Nevertheless, the extent of the Mao campaign is so great, the time devoted to reading his works so enormous, that one is forced to question the impact his writings have had on the conduct of research. Are they likely to hinder research, have little impact, or is there anything which might have a positive value?

The official line is revealed in a *Peoples Daily* editorial published on 24th January 1966.

> Sixteen important achievements in science and technology have been reported in China's chemical industry. Most of them have been applied in production. Some of these achievements have caught up with, while others have surpassed, the world's advanced levels. It took only a few years, and only five months in some cases, from starting research work to wide scale application, to make these achievements which, in other countries, would have taken a dozen years at least, and possibly, several decades. This is really a high-speed, big leap forward, and a great victory in catching up with and surpassing the world's advanced levels in the chemical industry.
>
> These sixteen achievements in science and technology are of great significance not only materially, but also spiritually. They have once again provided eloquent proof of China's capacity to trans-

form thoroughly the backward state of her science and technology and to catch up with and surpass the world's advanced levels within not too long a period to come.

Why? Because we possess the ever-victorious and all-conquering thought of Mao Tse-tung.

Scientists and technicians taking part in these sixteen items of research said: "Formerly we consulted Chairman Mao's works only when we encountered ideological problems. We referred exclusively to foreign books when we met technical problems. However, after repeated failure and after taking tortuous paths many times in practical scientific research, we finally realized that the thought of Mao Tse-tung was not only the best weapon for transforming society and man's thinking, but also the best guide to disclose the secrets of science and technology. We succeeded quickly in making these sixteen important, new achievements in science and technology because we were enlightened and guided by *On Practice, On Contradiction* and other works by Chairman Mao." This experience derived from practice is very impressive and enlightening.

Some people may be curious as to how the thought of Mao Tse-tung can solve technical problems. It is true that the thought of Mao Tse-tung cannot solve concrete technical problems. However, by revolutionizing the people's thinking, it first gives them courage and awakens their intelligence, leads them to change their attitude toward technical innovations, and encourages them to carry out technical innovations for the sake of the people and the revolution. This releases a force of incomparable potency. The thought of Mao Tse-tung is thus well able to solve the problem of the direction for technical development. This is the key problem for our technical development. If this problem is solved, if the right direction is followed, and if the objective laws are determined, what difficulty can there be in solving the concrete technical problems?

A paper which was presented at the 1966 Peking Physics Colloquium gave a more explicit explanation of how Mao study helped scientific research. The Colloquium was an international scientific congress limited to delegates from the Afro-Asian-Latin American countries. In addition to several papers on particle physics which were contributed by the Chinese delegation, was one called "Making Lamps for the Revolution." This paper attempted to show how Mao's writings had contributed to the solution of technical problems in the design and manufacture of new types of light sources. When removed of jargon the particular "Maoisms" used by the scientists are mostly rather obvious truisms. Typical are the following:

If you don't at first succeed try, try, and try again.

In solving a complex problem, break it down into its component parts. There will usually be one part more significant than the rest.

If this can be identified and solved, the other parts will fall into place and will be easy to solve.

Science progresses by a combination of theory and experiment.

Do not be overawed by what "authorities" in science say, be willing to challenge their beliefs.

Sometimes progress is made by going from the general to the particular, and sometimes by going from the particular to the general.[17]

There is nothing inherently wrong with these maxims; many will be recognized as standard procedure by all research workers. But neither is there anything very profound about them. It is conceivable that relatively ill-educated peasants and workers might be encouraged to innovate by such statements. It is exceedingly difficult to see how well-trained scientists could benefit. On the contrary, the frustrations and waste of research time required by Mao study on the part of scientists must be considerable.

(3) *The effect of the Cultural Revolution on Chinese science.* When the Central Committee of the Chinese Communist Party laid down the ground rules for the Cultural Revolution in August 1966, they deliberately excluded scientists from its effects. Scientists and technologists, and especially those who had made contributions and who had not had illicit contact with foreign powers, were to be allowed to change their world view gradually.

It is still too early to make any final assessment, but from the evidence available it now appears that this ground rule has not been adhered to. Chinese scientific journals have not been received in Britain since October 1966. Reports appearing in the Chinese press indicate a major disruption of work in the research institutes of the Academy of Sciences. The *Peoples Daily* of 19 April 1967 revealed that clashes had occurred between the revolutionary cadres at the Oceanographic Institute of the Chinese Academy of Sciences in Tsinan and those "taking the bourgeois reactionary line" who supported the "top party person in authority taking the capitalist road." The *Peoples Daily* report says that "White terror reigned in the Oceanographic Institute. According to statistics, 25% of the ordinary cadres, 60% of the intermediate level cadres, and 50% of the leading cadres in all the Oceanographic Institutes were hit and persecuted and labelled with different political terms." [18]

The 14 July 1967 issue of the *Peoples Daily* said that more than 20,000 proletarian revolutionaries of the fifty or so units of the Acad-

[17] Tsai Tsu-chuan, "Making Lamps for the Revolution," *China Reconstructs*, Vol. 15, No. 12, Dec. 1966, pp. 28–33.
[18] *Survey China Mainland Press*, No. 3930, May 2, 1967, pp. 18–19.

emy of Sciences in Peking had been involved in a struggle for control of the Academy Institutes. The paper claims that the revolutionaries have fought the "white terror" created by supporters of Liu Shao-chi (referred to as the top party person in authority taking the capitalist road), and seized power from their hands.

It seems that there were rival factions among the revolutionaries and "civil war" broke out among the two most powerful groups. One side accused the other of "rightist tendencies," and the other side said the first were Trotskyites and "left opportunists." The civil war lasted twenty days, after which the protagonists read Mao Tse-tung's *On the Correct Handling of Contradictions Among the People* and engaged in self-criticism. The *Peoples Daily* article claimed that although there are still differences of opinion at the Academy of Sciences, everyone is now more "sophisticated" and "civil wars are not allowed." [19]

Regardless of the disruption which the Cultural Revolution appears to be causing in the laboratories, it has already seriously interfered with the scientific and technological manpower program. Schools and universities have only recently been reopened after having been closed for a year. Furthermore, new regulations make it more difficult for children from families with other than peasant and worker backgrounds to gain entrance to higher education. Both of these steps must inevitably delay China in her ambition to be a great world power; certainly they will delay the speed with which China will be able to catch up with science in the more advanced countries.

Thus, the social changes which are taking place in a country that contains a quarter of mankind, through political intervention at both laboratory and university levels, appear to be having a profoundly disrupting effect on the progress of science in that country.

This essay shows that politics plays an important part in determining the precise ways in which science contributes to causing social change. However, as already noted in the introduction, politics are only one of many factors involved, and it remains to write a more integrated account. The urgent problems of the developing countries make it imperative to understand the complex process of social change. Science is only one ingredient, but it seems to be an important one. Further research on this topic should be a matter of high priority.

[19] *Survey of China Mainland Press*, No. 3990, July 28, 1967, p. 6.

# III *Conclusions*

Science, both in the sense of accumulated scientific knowledge and in the sense of a way of going to work on problems (that is, scientific method), is not concerned with metaphysics. *As science* it provides neither a cosmology nor an ontology, nor a full teleology. Science *as science* makes no attempt to answer—does not even ask—the Big Questions of human destiny, of God's ways to man, of Right and Wrong and Good and Bad. Some scientists as individuals come near not asking any of the Big Questions, come near guiding themselves in daily life by custom and authority, as do most of us most of the time. Some scientists, that is, may be without metaphysical curiosity, or metaphysical anxiety—as may be many of the human race. (This is a point about which even professional psychologists seem to know little—the writer's guess is that very few human beings indeed are altogether free of metaphysical anxiety, or at any rate, metaphysical concern.) As soon as the scientist asks and tries to answer any of the Big Questions, however, he is ceasing to behave as a scientist. He is at the very least doing something *additional;* he is probably doing something *different.*

Crane Brinton

*The Shaping of Modern Thought,* Englewood Cliffs, Prentice-Hall, p. 83.

# CONCLUSIONS

## BY KALMAN H. SILVERT

*American Universities Field Staff*

Men proud of human progress tell us that we live in a scientific age. Proof is said to be in the artifacts that surround us, move us, amuse us, and even teach us, and in the esteem accorded to scientists in high places. Still, it is no passing mood of pessimism, induced by a violent death here, a political breakdown there, or a loss of freedom elsewhere, that lets us doubt that the existence of a scientific age is truly evidenced by the prevalence of technology or the prestige of scientists. The subject of this book, *science* and social change, was chosen to underscore the possible divisibility of science and technology, a discrimination which, if fruitful, can clarify thought about social change in the developed as well as the emergent worlds. If no such distinction is useful, whether for historical explanation or prediction, then we will have learned that a "scientific-technological age" is compatible with such a wide range of political and social happenings that we must look elsewhere for guides to the achievement of public decency, however defined.

The contributors to this volume, however, suggest that science and technology can indeed be thought of as separable in human affairs and that to separate them rigorously assists in the development of strategies of human change. The purpose of this concluding chapter is to examine how that conclusion has been given form and content by the body of this book. Thus we are dealing with no such simple assertions as that science produces technology for human consumption, or that the prime causal element in social change is the development of a new tool.

227

To the contrary, we have been given evidence that technology can exist without science, although science cannot be imagined in the absence of technology; and that science seems to demand particular environments if it is to flourish, but that technology is a human universal to be found under any social conditions. Let us synthesize the way in which these statements flow from the supporting studies.

For the purposes of this set of conclusions, the contents of all the chapters can be reduced to the following three major subject areas: concepts and definitions; models of relations between science and the social order; and strategies of scientific development and social change, including much of the case material in which theoretical and empirical questions merge. Put in another way, we have followed a scientific course by defining terms and establishing hypotheses, constructing generalizable patterns of relationships, and then empirically testing the validity of our sets of postulations. Let us trace this line in the following discussion.

The definitions of science by the writers of this book have been various, falling into the following categories: science as an activity, or the doing of science; science as ideology, or "scientism"; science as a social value, bearing such labels as the idea of science, the posture of science, the scientific attitude or stance, and so forth; and, lastly, science as an institution or an institutionally situated procedure, with particular reference to universities and institutes as well as scientific "establishments." A closer look at these four categories suggests that they may well be collapsed into only two: science as an activity, and science as an attitude. The "doing" of science thus includes the work of the individual scientists, as well as the ordered and routinized social behavior in identifiable constellations that we call "institutions." The "thinking of science" may then embrace at one extreme ideological pleas that all of life be reduced to scientific principles and apposite behavior patterns. Against that invitation to put science completely in charge, is the other extreme, which thinks of science as simply an experimental cast of mind functioning only in a limited environment of controlled speculation and testing. This confrontation of two complexes of behavior and attitudes suggests that just as technology and science should be thought of as being separate and standing in different relationships in different situations, so should scientific behavior and scientific attitudes be recognized as not necessarily correlational partners. They, too, can exist at given times, either separately, or in many differing relationships.

Professor Morton, writing of the development of military technology, showed clearly how the development of military implements can be said to be related to "science" only if we presume that any speculative act is a scientific one. If, on the other hand, we take the more standard view that science as a procedure and a cast of mind dates only from the seventeenth century, then we are drawn to an appreciation of the universal and independent importance of technology, and the different significance of science as defining a particular set of historical occurrences. Flint arrowheads and fire-hardened pointed sticks are as much technological innovations as are steam engines and airplanes. Trial-and-error discovery and the cultural spread of innovation may well have characterized even prehistorical man in his slow technological evolution. But such procedures should not be confused with science; it is in their organization and their control mechanisms that they differ. The search for scientific truth is based on disciplined thought and experiment, the conscious arrangement for replication, and the acceptance of the idea that knowledge is cumulative and never absolute. To say that science cannot exist without technology (because it is imperative that science have technological means for testing hypotheses) but that the converse is not true, has relevance not only for historical analysis, but also for the developing countries.

The way that this view of the science-technology relation applies to problems of social change is reflected in two differing approaches to the development process. Proponents of what may be called an immediacy view of modernization argue for the rapid transplantation of technology to the underdeveloped world, in the expectation that desirable qualities will then develop in the society. An opposite view is that the attitudes of modernism, including the scientific stance, should be a first order of developmental business, so that resultant changes in social organization and behavior will then become the prime movers of modernization. As is usual in such disagreements, there is likely to be a blending of the two approaches in developmental practice. In any event, it seems that it is possible for a society to experience technological innovation without a subsequent creation either of scientific behavior or scientific attitudes. An important variation on the debate between those who want to export technology and those who want to cultivate the scientific attitude, however, is clearly suggested by some of the case studies. That is, it is certainly possible for persons and groups to engage in the scientific use of imported or preexisting technology without themselves possessing the culture of science. The analogue of "doing" technology without science is that some societies also manage to "do" science without "thinking" science. Thus, we have the instances in which technicians and scientists deliver themselves into the service of the kind of regimes whose ideologies will, in the long term, destroy science by negating the conditions of freedom needed by science for controlled experimental validation and replication. Professor DeWitt chronicles the problems of Soviet science in this very dimension; the science of Nazi Germany also leaps to mind, as do such other cases of stunted growth as Spain, Portugal, and some

Latin American nations. Consequently, a time dimension is of critical importance in discussing the disjunction between scientific behavior and scientific culture. A short-term curtailment of the libertarian requirements of science may still permit scientific activity to proceed on the legacy of the past or the work of others in more propitious societies. However, the long-term effect of a lack of scientific freedom appears to be one of stultification. Even so, one would presume that technological elaboration in authoritarian surroundings could proceed longer and more effectively than scientific innovation.

In sum, then, one may postulate that the doing of science is semi-independent of the idea of science in short and intermediate runs. In the long run the two are mutually dependent. The idea of science, in addition, must have a social base outside the scientific community: enough agreement must exist to make possible the maintenance of the institutions within which science proceeds, and the freedom of experimentation and communication the scientific endeavor demands. If the positive conditions exist (the actual successful practice, the institutions, and the required social agreement), then science can promote the technology that in turn repays the social investment in the total process and, further, makes future scientific advances possible. Pre-scientific societies may choose to import technology without supporting either scientific practice or values. In any event technology, as has always been true, can be made compatible with social systems that may be either increasingly repressive, increasingly libertarian, or even relatively unchanging. Although this set of conclusions is not the place for the introduction of new evidence, Israel, Egypt, Argentina, India, Ghana, and many other developing countries demonstrate the wide array of possible adjustments to technological change with and without scientific development.

The postulates mentioned above served some of the authors of this book as elements in the building of models to explain what may give a society the ability to make the changes required for scientific endeavor. Although no agreement could have been reached within this format on any given set of conditions and the relations among them that we can dignify with the word "model," certainly the major elements have been clarified. First is the existence of an appropriate value structure, the recognition of what science and its necessary environment are. Second, we have those procedures, devices, and behavior patterns needed to make the values effective. And, lastly, the model should describe procedures by which individuals are related to the ideas and the practices of science.

No author has specifically described the value structure supportive of scientific endeavor. Probably none would dispute the statement, however, that the value posture hospitable to scientific endeavor is rationalistic in the choice of alternatives, relativistic in judgment and expectation, and anticipatory of change. A pragmatic rationalism may be contrasted with a ritualistic motivation for action. A relativistic stance may be differentiated from an organic one; the relativist presumes that the effect of his actions will be something less than absolute, and thus he does not call into play every moral, ethical, or religious precept to which he may subscribe on the occasion of his every judgment and action. In short, he can bring differing value judgments into play in accord with the specific roles he may be discharging at any given moment. As Dr. Hamburg pointed out, the scientific stance to which he himself subscribes is one holding that science is but one activity among many others, as of course in their turn other activities are also but partial evidences of the full gamut of man's abilities, functions, and statuses. As for changefulness, one does not presume that the scientific value favors frenetic activity as contrasted with placidity, but rather that the fact of change be recognized and the consequences thereof be anticipated without ingrained negativism.

The holding of these or any other values, however, does not mean that they will guide persons to behavior consistent with them. To use an analogy, desires for gain or achievement in and of themselves cannot guarantee gain or achievement, let alone patterns of social action conducive to any particular ways of gaining and achieving. An "entrepreneurial mentality" will do its holder little good if he has no market in which to exercise his abilities. The values of science, to become effective, must be supported by more general societal values, as well as the public power, institutional structures, and class systems appropriate for the purpose. Again, this summary is not the proper vehicle for spelling out the full range of social systems supportive of scientific endeavor. But we should at least add that any attempts at further specification should include descriptions not only of national society, but also of sub-national organization as well as of the increasingly significant international community.

To have described value systems and institutional orders is still not to have a complete picture, however. Absent is the question of how the interaction of values and the channels for their becoming effective play upon individuals to recruit them either to the scientific endeavor or to a tacit or overt support of that endeavor. In this area, however, the case studies are richly suggestive. Messrs. Rowe, Lockheimer, and Oldham describe in full detail the role of government in the creation or the inhibition of scientific institutions. Mr. Oldham and Mr. Lockheimer go beyond the formal political structure to discuss class and educational factors, as well. Professor DeWitt devotes his chapter on

Africa entirely to the role of education in the creation or inhibition of scientific knowledge and attitudes, while in the chapter on Russia and the Soviet Union he emphasizes government and the institutional structure of science. Mr. Bayne relates the development of science to the national community in Iran, an important way of discussing whether or not individuals are available for recruitment into the role of supportive citizenry as well as of practicing scientist. What the case studies suggest, then, is that the way in which the mobilization and institutional integration of individuals is carried out demonstrates the balance between coercive and voluntaristic practices in given patterns of social behavior. One critical element of any potential model of science development, then, must be the ordering of the coercive, co-opting, consensual, and voluntaristic elements that bear on the recruitment, training, and maintenance of a science establishment.

To this point, we have been discussing how to *think* about the relationship between science and social change. How consciously to *affect* that relationship is an instrumental question that must be recognized as one part of the strategy and tactics of development. And here, we run the risk of straying into the hoary, but still unanswered questions of what development and modernization are, whether westernization and modernization are synonymous, what have been the roles of imperialism and colonialism in past and present relations between the developed and the developing, and so on through the familiar litany.

The specific relationships between science and social change, however, may reveal one particularly significant aspect of the problem of arriving at a general strategy of development. Every author in this book has chosen to see science as only one activity among many others; all have been careful to eschew approbation of the technocratic state or any suggestion that all human actions should be governed by scientific procedures or values. At the same time, all the authors have assumed that scientific advance is a desirable event in any society. The advantage of employing some of the values of a scientific culture is not to reduce all behavior to "scientism," but rather to make differing human activities and values compatible. A "scientific" society, then, is one in which an area of endeavor called scientific can be carved out; it is the relationship between that area and other spheres of human activity that will determine whether the scientific activity can continue unimpeded through long and self-sustaining growth. There is no reason for uncritical acceptance of the idea that the values and procedures which encourage the flowering of science are identical to those that permit societies to flourish. But it would seem that the libertarian, relativistic, pragmatic, and dynamic values of science are as important to modern political organization as to scientific life.

The importance of placing our emphasis on synthesizing differences rather than on reducing all activity to fit a narrow scientific precept, becomes clear if we ask what the conduct of most human institutions would be like if it were pursued under controlled and entirely rationalistic conditions.* Family life would certainly become difficult if all explanation to children were withheld until they were ready to understand scientifically valid reasoning. Religious faith is by definition a-rational, because the deities of religious belief are not susceptible to evidential verification. Aesthetics, and the many other ways of nonscientific learning of nonscientific knowledge would be rejected, along with the many persons who are simply unable to think in other than elementary terms. A completely coherent, scientific society might just as well spell the doom of long-term scientific endeavor as a repressively totalitarian one by putting science at the service of applied politics.

Science attempts to rationalize the hitherto incoherent, and to reduce all data to rational order. The culture of science should attempt to rationalize the hitherto incoherent in social disparity, in order to permit the coexistence of the rational with the nonrational to the benefit of both. The relativism inherent in science is the element common both to the pursuit of science and the general, supportive culture of science. Doing science without the culture of science is a temporally limited possibility, as we have pointed out. But one of the possible consequences of doing without understanding is the destruction of the culture of science, an irrational suicide in the name of shortsighted rationality.

Throughout this study we have assigned a positive value to science and the role it can be made to play in social change conducive to an enlargement of human awareness and choice. Naturally, such an assumption is partly a matter of opinion.

> Science or scholarship can never be more than an affirmation of the things we believe in. These beliefs will, by their very nature, be of a normative character, claiming universal validity; they must also be responsible beliefs, held in due consideration of evidence and of the fallibility of all beliefs; but eventually they are ultimate commitments, issued under the seal of our personal judgment. To all further critical scruples we must at some point finally reply: "For I believe so." †

---

* I did not say "rationalized" conditions. "Rationalistic" refers to a dedication to reason and evidence and scientific method in all undertakings. "Rationalized" refers merely to coherent and logical organization, whether of the rational or the irrational. There is no rational reason that religious faith cannot be rationalized, for example.

† Michael Polanyi, *The Logic of Liberty: Reflections and Rejoinders*, Chicago: The University of Chicago Press, 1951, p. 31.

Ours is a time of the crisis of the institutions and beliefs that produced science and parliaments in the first place. Increasing demands for public freedom and dignity throughout the world are putting to the test of innovation those groups that have been enjoying the freedom that accompanies power. If the privileged free their power to deny the growth and spread of freedom for others, they will probably sacrifice their own measure of innovative and creative liberty. The qualitative content of freedom—what we can do with it—is also changing as new knowledge creates new systems of ideas and thus new choices, ideological as well as material. These pressures for social and ideational change have caused many members of the scientific and academic communities to lose their way. Some, entering into the political realm with their science, have surrendered the freedom to choose their own research, to conduct it as they professionally see most fitting, and to communicate it. Others use half-baked science, especially in social fields, to advocate firm policy positions which are more the product of bias than of conditioned and "responsible beliefs, held in due consideration of evidence and of the fallibility of all beliefs." Professors and university administrators alike sometimes forget the critical importance of university autonomy, a hard-fought right that provides the institutional setting for the doing of science in all its ramifications.

This concluding chapter began by chiding the optimist who expects science to weave an ethically fitting fabric of life. His fallacy is the same as that of the pessimist who trembles that science will dehumanize society: they both believe in the autonomy of science as prime cause. But science is merely another manifestation of that web, in which some of the threads are nationalism, democracy, secularism, and industrialization that we call the modern estate. The good brought with these aspects of modernization is also what has made them possible: the partial liberation of the human mind and temper. The bad that has accompanied them is the ever-present danger of their use to stifle freedom. We are saying, then, that freedom and modernist change are intellectual alchemy—their mingling dissolves the contradiction between ends and means. The pursuit of freedom demands its use; the practice of freedom is its purpose. Scientific change thus is related to social change as both are related to the practice of freedom as instrumentality and as goal. The historical validity of this assertion is this book's major conclusion. Its ethical desirability is not to be debated, "for I believe so."

# INDEX

Academy of Sciences of the USSR, 192–94
Adaptation, education and, 124–25
Africa
educational aspirations and resources in, 139
primary education in, 130–31
scarcity of science graduates in, 136–39
science education in, 125, 127–30
science teachers in, 134–36
secondary education in, 131–34
African Mathematics Program (AMP), 133–34
Agassiz, Louis, 97
ALA (Arabic Language Academy), 71, 73
Alberto, Alvaro, 108, 109
Alencar, Oto de, 99–100
Alexander the Great, 33–35, 40
Alves, Francisco de Paula Rodrigues, 100
American Chiefs of State, Punta del Este meeting of, 91
AMP (African Mathematics Program), 133–34
Applied research, Soviet, 184–88
Arab Scientific Union (ASU), 72
Arabic (modern), development of, 69–75
Arabic Language Academy (ALA), 71, 73
Archimedes, 27, 34
Aristotle, 18, 48
Assimilation, science education and, 125
Astronomical Society (Great Britain), 206
ASU (Arab Scientific Union), 72

Bacon, Sir Francis, 23
Bahasa Indonesia, development of, 80–82
Baldwin, Hanson, 53
Bar-Hillel, Yehoshua, 61
Basalla, George, 95
Basalla model of science diffusion, 95–106
description of, 95
Bates, Henry, 97

Beagle, 97
Bear, K. M., 187
Bergson, Henri, 11
Bernal, J. D., 25
Blanc, Haim, 75–76
Bloch, Ivan S., 51–52
Boyle, Robert, 23–24, 47
Brazil
development of physics in, 106–10
science and politics in, 91–122
Brinton, Crane, 226
Britain, see Great Britain
British Association for the Advancement of Science, 206, 208–9
Bruk, S. I., 186
Bruno, Giordano, 14
Bureaucratization, Soviet science and, 198
Bustani, Butrus, 70

Caesar, Julius, 35
Cambridge University, 205
Campanema, Gustavo, 107
Cassirer, Ernst, 17, 18
Castelo Branco, Humberto, 105, 108, 114, 116, 117
Cavalcanti, Costa, 121
Chagas, Carlos, 100, 101
Change
explanations and appraisals of, 19–21
Japanese government leadership and, 161–66
Japanese receptivity to, 154–69
modern languages and, 65–85
Chaplygin, S. A., 186
Charlemagne, 39
Chebyshev, 186
Chen Tu-shiu, 212
China, impact of science on, 211–15
Chinese Communist Party, 212, 220
Central Committee of, 222
Chinese Cultural Revolution, 214, 222
Churchill, Sir Winston, 209
Civil War, American, 52
CNEN (National Nuclear Energy Commission of Brazil), 92, 121
formation of, 110–14
"Colonial science," 95
in Brazil, 98–100